Soviet Briefing
Gorbachev and the Reform Period

Soviet Briefing

Gorbachev and the Reform Period

Ben Eklof

Indiana University

Westview Press

Boulder, San Francisco, and London

To Nadya, Toma, and Emma

Copyright © 1989 by Westview Press, Inc.

Published in 1989 in the United States of America by Westview Press, Inc., 5500 Central Avenue, Boulder, Colorado 80301, and in the United Kingdom by Westview Press, Inc., 13 Brunswick Centre, London WC1N 1AF, England

Library of Congress Cataloging-in-Publication Data
Eklof, Ben, 1946–
Soviet briefing : Gorbachev and the reform period / by Ben Eklof.
    p. cm.
  Includes index.
  ISBN 0-8133-0791-0. ISBN 0-8133-0792-9 (pbk.).
  1. Soviet Union—Politics and government—1982- . 2. Soviet Union—
Social conditions—1970- . I. Title.
DK288.E35 1989
947.085'4—dc19   88-20575
                                                                                                 CIP

Printed and bound in the United States of America

The paper used in this publication meets the requirements of the American National Standard for Permanence of Paper for Printed Library Materials Z39.48-1984.

10   9   8   7   6   5   4   3   2   1

Contents

Acknowledgments

In writing this book I incurred a number of debts, which I now gratefully acknowledge. During a year at the Kennan Institute for Advanced Russian Studies in the Wilson Center of the Smithsonian Institution, I attended many seminars and discussions on current events. In one way or another the ideas, information, and debates that took place during my stay contributed to my opinions and shaped the direction of my research; unfortunately I cannot list all the names of those from whom I benefited. The Kennan Institute itself provided a stimulating and supportive environment for my work. I am especially thankful to Peter Reddaway and Ted Taranovski for all they have done.

I owe much to the generosity of the staff of the offices of Radio Liberty/Radio Free Europe who opened up their files to my research assistant and allowed use of their facilities in a spirit of intellectual openness. In addition, without the willing assistance of the staff of the Center for National Security, my task of gathering data would have been far more complicated, if not beyond my abilities.

Kate Sly ably served as my research assistant at the Kennan Institute. She undertook to help me update my survey of Soviet events. She put in long hours and demonstrated remarkable resourcefulness and persistence in obtaining information on all the topics covered in this book. Although I am solely responsible for all the opinions and arguments offered below, her help and energy were indispensable.

Others who read and commented upon this work are Janet Rabinowitch, Lisa Freeman, Janet Vaillant, Scott Seregny, Larry Holmes, and the editors of the Carl Beck Papers of the University of Pittsburgh. I am also grateful to the staff at Goucher College, who provided technical assistance during the writing of this book. Finally, my editors at Westview Press have been remarkably efficient, patient, and good-humored, making the process of revising almost a distinct pleasure. I owe much to Martha Leggett, Kathy Streckfus, and Susan L. McEachern.

Ben Eklof

Note on Transliteration

The transliteration of Russian names and words is always problematic. I have used a modified version of the Library of Congress system (without the diacritical mark) but have, rather idiosyncratically, replaced *ii* at the end of proper names with *y*, and otherwise yielded to spellings that I judged have become common in the West.

Abbreviations

The following abbreviations are used in the footnotes:

BS   *Baltimore Sun*
CDSP   *Current Digest of the Soviet Press*
CSM   *Christian Science Monitor*
NYT   *New York Times*
RL   *Radio Liberty Research Bulletin*
WP   *Washington Post*
WSJ   *Wall Street Journal*

I have provided a full citation for each source when it first appears in each chapter, with the exception of a few works cited throughout the text that I believe would have been tedious to reproduce over and over.

Ne réveillez pas le chat qui dort.

—Alexander Herzen

1
Introduction

The year 1987 in Soviet affairs was tumultuous and exciting in a way few could have anticipated. From the January plenum to the Washington summit, from the remarkable Shmelev assault on virtually all the canons of the Stalinist system to the Yeltsin affair, 1987 stands out in its intensity, exceeding even 1982 (the year of Andropov's accession) and 1985 (when Gorbachev came to power) as a year fraught with significance for the course of affairs in the world's largest country.

And 1988 seems to be tumbling along in even more boisterous fashion. Glasnost has unfolded with such rapidity that words spoken or written a year ago that seemed bold and outspoken then have already become tame, common wisdom. The conservative onslaught, culminating in the now infamous Andreyeva letter, and followed (after a distressing, anxiety-ridden period of silence) by a powerful refutation, then gave way to renewed and vastly expanded calls for radical changes in all areas of society and the polity. Events reached an unprecedented state of frenzy as the June Conference approached and the Central Committee presented Theses for the further reconstruction of the Soviet Union. The Conference was so fervently awaited that the May summit meeting between Mikhail S. Gorbachev and Ronald Reagan in Moscow was left in the shadows of public attention.

Gorbachev's policies have coalesced under four headings: *perestroika* (restructuring, transformation); *glasnost* (openness, "telling it like it is"); *demokratizatsiia*; and in foreign policy, *novoe myshlenie* (new political thinking).[1] Not accidently, with the clarification of policy has come not only a consolidation of power, as revealed in the January and June plenums, but also a stiffening of resistance, expressed most forcefully at the October plenum (after which Gorbachev enthusiast Boris Yeltsin resigned under a cloud). In early 1988, as the momentous June Conference approached, Gorbachev seemed to have triumphed over opposition at the top and had positioned himself to push through even more radical measures at the Conference, but he had found no magic formula to overcome bureaucratic footdragging, especially at the local level. Recent events are a reminder that, as Andrei Sakharov noted, "there is a clear distinction between what Gorbachev says and what the Central Committee approves, and a still greater gap between what they approve, and what happens in real life."[2]

In politics and culture, reform has not yet been institutionalized, remaining, in the opinion of some, "atmospheric, cosmetic, and reversible."[3] Changes have been de facto rather than de jure. Nevertheless, just as the sheer scope of glasnost has been breathtaking, so now it is difficult to imagine how any leader could fully restore what was before, under Brezhnev.

After the January and June plenums, the reforms pushed through in June 1987, and the lifting of taboos on virtually all topics, "Gorbachev has passed the point of no return."[4] With the New Economic Mechanism, a plan to introduce cost-accounting and self-financing throughout the Soviet economy (beginning January 1, 1988, and scheduled to be implemented throughhout the country by 1991), an economic transformation of virtually unprecedented scope is under way.[5] No less fascinating or significant is the Soviet attempt "at one and the same time . . . to recover its memory and the capacity to speak with more than one voice; [the Soviet Union] is learning to remember and to debate."[6]

Columnist Joseph Harsch writes that Gorbachev has "reformed, even revolutionized, Soviet foreign policy."[7] *Novoe myshlenie*[8] involves assertions of global interdependence over the class perspective and, despite Gorbachev's emphasis on U.S.-Soviet relations,[9] a simultaneous focus upon "multipolarity" in international relations[10] and a willingness to deal with regional issues on their own merits. Proponents of New Thinking also eschew attempts to export violent revolution[11] and "advocate that local and regional conflicts be more effectively insulated from the East-West rivalry."[12] They condemn the "arrogance of omniscience" in relations with Soviet allies and the "presumption of infallibility" in foreign affairs and put a new emphasis on political approaches and solutions instead of military ones.[13] Militarily, New Thinking has involved renunciation of the view that capitalist powers inevitably tend toward militarism and the ascendancy of a new doctrine calling for "reasonable sufficiency"[14] and "mutual security" rather than parity or supremacy. It accepts asymmetrical cuts[15] in conventional and nuclear forces in the interest of arms treaties. Visiting Czechoslovakia in April 1987, Gorbachev himself "implicitly admitted that the Soviet military buildup had created areas in which the Soviet forces were 'superior' and argued explicitly for eliminating these asymmetries by reducing Soviet forces rather than by permitting an American and NATO buildup."[16]

The Soviet Union has also been refurbishing its image at the United Nations. It has quietly complied with U.S. demands to reduce its staff;[17] in October 1987 it paid off $111 million in current bills[18] and promised to pay back $197 million more in peacekeeping debts dating back over 30 years. In 1988 the Soviet Union has also begun to pick up the slack left by the U.S. withdrawal of funding from UN family-planning programs. It has made an eleven-point proposal to strengthen the effectiveness of the United Nations and the powers of the Security Council. In *Pravda* (September 17, 1987) Gorbachev called for new efforts by the UN to reduce Third World debt, improve world health, and tackle environmental problems. The Kremlin has urged new functions for the UN, including investigating acts of international terrorism, verifying arms control agreements, and monitoring human rights across the globe. Gorbachev has called for new means to make UN resolutions "binding." Moscow may well "want a stronger United Nations to help extricate it from numerous third world conflicts with a minimum loss of face."[19] Finally, the Kremlin has proposed cooperation with several Western governments in combating international terrorism, including negotiating extradition treaties for the return of terrorists.[20]

Previously unthinkable, too, was the idea of a party secretary rejecting the notion of infallibility in relations with Eastern Europe, reconsidering the invasion of Czechoslovakia in 1968,[21] even of learning from these countries (especially the Hungarian economy). If initially Gorbachev adopted a stern line and was primarily interested in the stabilization of conditions in Eastern Europe, in the past year he has clearly been trying to enlist the leaders of Eastern Europe in his reform program, even to prod them on. (His speeches have been censored, especially in Romania, and circulate among the population in semi-clandestine manner.) The most plausible explanation for this shift in approach is that during his first year Gorbachev was engrossed in consolidating his authority, at a time when stability was highly desirable in Eastern Europe. Now that he has turned to actively promoting a reform agenda, a major component of his economic renewal will be the improvement of the quality of goods coming from Eastern Europe and a general activization of trade, which will best be served by parallel economic and political reforms.[22]

Skeptics point out that glasnost has not extended to foreign policy discussion in the press and that "there has been no overt repudiation of Brezhnevism in foreign relations." Is the New Thinking merely "tactical and deceptive . . . the latest example of the strategy of *reculer pour mieux sauter*?" As Peter Reddaway argues, such an argument may well be used internally as a justification for reform made within higher circles in Moscow: "But it seems . . . wiser to regard the USSR, for the time being at least, as a great power pursuing great power interests, i.e., to take Gorbachev's claim at its face value."[23]

The Sources and Their Limitations

Frankly, we are all too breathless from these events to fully trust our own judgment at this time. But nothing much would be ventured in asserting that events of the past eighteen months have irreversibly altered the face (and perhaps the soul) of the Soviet Union. What happens in the Soviet Union, however we interpret it, will weigh heavily in the course of world affairs. Although historians prefer to wait until time ripens a new perspective and are rightly wary of premature analysis, the task of sifting evidence and integrating events should not be left exclusively to those concerned primarily with the present. This book represents an attempt to chronicle the events of a period that will, I am sure, ultimately rank with others perhaps less monumental than the revolutionary year of 1917 (itself the most significant conjuncture of the twentieth century) but nevertheless marking real turning points in Russian and Soviet—and perhaps global—history. I have in mind 1929 (the year in which Stalin's collectivization drive was launched); 1956 (the beginning of de-Stalinization); and, reaching back, 1861 (the Emancipation and Great Reforms of Alexander II). With perhaps only a small degree of wishful thinking, Nikolai Shmelev observed in June: "In terms of the hopes that they have aroused and in terms of their depth, frankness and boldness, the past two years' discussions of our problems have constituted a genuine rebirth of our public thought and national self-awareness. The 27th Party Congress (January 1986) marked the beginning of revolutionary changes in our society."[24]

This work began as a personal endeavor to sort things out, to comprehend what is happening in what is surely the most interesting country in the world right now. I aim for a measure of clarity and accuracy rather than originality—though I do assert my own opinions. I build upon the research and observations of others, including journalists and specialists here and in the Soviet Union. I also base my own observations upon nearly five years spent in the USSR, three of them working for a Soviet publishing firm, and upon the ongoing research I carry out for a course on contemporary Soviet society taught at Indiana University. Undoubtedly, some of what I say here will come unraveled in the near future, but I believe the situation I depict reflects both immediate events and some of the deeper forces at work.

Why not begin with the 27th Party Congress, or with Gorbachev's coming to power on March 10, 1985, or with Yuri Andropov, or with the death of Brezhnev? The reader will detect a note of inconsistency in my approach, for one of the themes elaborated below is that the new periodization imposed on recent history by proponents of perestroika—contrasting the time of *zastoi*, or stagnation, with the new era of *uskorenie*, or acceleration—is self-serving and inaccurate. Put simply, this perspective ignores the beginnings of the reform process in education, agriculture, industry, and even culture that reach back well into the 1970s. Moreover, it improperly frames events by overlooking evolutionary processes independent of the political structure. Specifically it overlooks the emergence of a "civil society," which has recently been identified by Robert Tucker, S. Frederick Starr, and others.

My reasons for beginning in 1987 are opportunistic: There is simply no way both to keep abreast of events and to reach back far into the quickly receding past. Others have provided brilliant analyses of the "sea changes" taking place in the past generation (Moshe Lewin, Robert Tucker) and have offered cogent interpretations of the events of the first two years of Gorbachev's rule (Jerry Hough, Thane Gustafson, Seweryn Bialer, Archie Brown, Tim Colton, Peter Reddaway). Still others are interpreting developments in individual sectors: for instance, Murray Feshbach's studies of the health-care system; Louise Shelley's works on crime; Beatrice Szekely's and John Dunstan's analyses of education—to name but a few. The pages of *Current History* (annually, the October issue), *Soviet Economy, Soviet Studies*, the *Harriman Institute Forum*, and *Problems of Communism* are rich with contemporary analysis. But the published works of leading scholars lag, generally, a year or so behind events, while synopses of recent events make no attempt at interpretation.

This endeavor represents an uneasy compromise between the mission of the journalist to report and the task of the historian and social analyst to ponder, reflect, and place in perspective. I have relied heavily upon the vast, and largely reliable, Western corps of analysts who pore over the Soviet press and produce summaries, translations, and surveys in *Current Digest of the Soviet Press*, Foreign Broadcast Information Service, *Radio Liberty Research Bulletin* and on the pages of the *New York Times, Le Monde, The Washington Post, Christian Science Monitor*, and other periodicals.

I read Russian fluently and follow closely several Soviet publications. But, as Soviet analyst and guru Murray Feshbach has pointed out, the project of studying the Soviet Union has changed fundamentally in three short years. Instead of poring through unremittingly boring, repetitious publications looking for occasional and rare nuggets of information from which more general conclusions about the quality of Soviet life can be extrapolated, we now have a torrent of revelations on virtually every aspect of Soviet society, making it impossible for any single scholar to keep fully informed.

As a result, it will take years to fully absorb the riches now available, not to mention comprehend the complicated processes at work.[25] My strategy has been to rely, in the first instance, upon available translations, abstracts, and analyses of the Soviet press. When I found an abstract or translation interesting, I went back to the original. In this way I learned of the works of Vasily Seliunin, Andrei Nuikin, Shmelev, and others cited often below.

This strategy is the only way to keep abreast of events. Unfortunately, it also allows the biases of the Western intelligence community, Sovietologists (many American specialists are not aware that this word in Russian—*sovetolog*—has a strongly pejorative flavor), and journalists to affect the initial sorting and selection of material to be analyzed. For example, Radio Liberty gives a disproportionate amount of attention to human rights, religious issues, and problems in Soviet society and the economy. At times, it takes a positive delight in highlighting the ills besetting the USSR.[26]

The inundation of Western academia with intellectuals from the Third Wave of Soviet emigration in the 1970s has also been a mixed blessing with a marked impact on Soviet studies. Many of these emigrés, personally seared by political repression, the humiliations of the process of emigration, and anti-Semitism in the USSR, have adopted an unremittingly hostile, even Manichean view of their former homeland. As Jerry Hough also pointed out, the Soviet education process itself, by instilling the viewpoint that "you are either with us or against us," that there is only one Marxist perspective and one socialism, inadvertently encourages the kind of uncompromising rejection of all aspects of Soviet Marxist ideology that one often encounters among these emigrés. The virtual absence in Soviet education of any discussion of "middle-level" theories in social analysis, of sociological thought in the Weberian or Durkheimian traditions, leaves many emigrés without coherent intellectual strategies or vocabulary (except a curiously inverted Marxism-Leninism) to deal with the complex issues they must often address as "experts" on their own country. Thus, Gail Lapidus writes of the "poverty of socio-political thought" in the USSR, "a poverty which extends even to the Soviet emigration."[27] The most salient impact of this Third Wave has been to substantially augment conservative, hard-line approaches to Soviet politics.

My approach also leaves me dependent upon Western correspondents serving in Moscow. Few American journalists arrive in the Soviet Union with an adequate command of Russian (or other Soviet languages) and most have but a superficial knowledge of the cultures, histories, and societies involved. To their credit, most do a credible, and some do a very good, job, but more in-depth prior training would certainly enhance their reporting. Even when correspondents speak the language, the difficulties Western journalists have obtaining information or access to sources are daunting.

This situation may finally be changing. Newspaper editors, academics, and others are now far more willing to talk to journalists, and unofficial sources no longer fear to meet with journalists. The Soviet press, according to returning *Washington Post* correspondent Celestine Bohlen, is "a far greater asset to Western reporters than ever before." And Western reporters are "inching toward a situation where they are being required to be reporters in the old-fashioned sense of the word."[28] Yet, Bohlen continues, there is still little "openness" about high-level political battles, and Western journalists are "still hampered by the hysteria of the Moscow intelligentsia." Western journalists still cannot travel freely about the country, and the foreign press were excluded from the proceedings of the momentous June Party Conference.

Glasnost notwithstanding, then, the proceedings of the core institutions of the system—the Politburo, the Secretariat, and the Central Committee, to name the most important—remain wrapped in secrecy. To mention but one example, the Yeltsin affair remains clouded in mystery. The events of the key Central Committee meeting of October 1987 are still unpublished, and the various versions of Yeltsin's speech floating about (and even read out loud at street gatherings in Moscow in June 1988) remain unauthenticated. It is undoubtedly true that the range of public discussion and disagreement among the leadership is much greater now than it was only a few years ago (though the scope of policy options discussed within channels has always been at least as great as that offered in our own two-party system). But the veil of obscurity clouding the political process—narrowly understood as power relations and policy disputes in the party and bureaucracy—has not been lifted here as it has over the workings of society. Another recent example: *Pravda*'s summary of the supremely important Politburo meeting occurring two days after the June Party Conference merely listed the committees set up to implement the Conference resolutions and concluded with the laconic comment that "at the session, certain other questions concerning party affairs and public matters were discussed."[29] For this reason, and given the uniquely vertical nature of communications, the centralization of institutions and resources, and the enormous weight of the Soviet state, the real limitations to glasnost pose a major obstacle. The reader should understand that unsubstantiated rumor and rather brazen speculation continue to play a major role in the analysis of *kto-kogo*, or power relations in the Kremlin.

In short, there are real limitations to the sources I have employed. There will be a temptation to focus upon events and personalities rather than upon deeper structures (in particular, in the political arena), to consider religious and human rights issues out of proportion to their real significance in Soviet life today. There is, unfortunately, an inevitable focus on Moscow to the exclusion of the provinces. The concerns of the intelligentsia (glasnost, pluralism, and professional dignity) remain at center stage. Anxiety about the fate of perestroika comes through, both because of this "Moscow hysteria" and because of Western skepticism about the possibilities of mixed economic systems. The remnants of a built-in corrosive skepticism about motivations (nobody but time-serving hacks could possibly serve in such a system) can also be detected. But the task of finding out what is going on is by no means hopeless, and it is infinitely interesting.

Perspectives

I am trained as a historian, of the Imperial period at that. In an informal talk given at the Kennan Institute for Advanced Russian Studies in mid-1988, Robert Tucker rued the lack of historical perspective in Soviet studies and, in particular, the widespread insensitivity to the prerevolutionary history of the Russian Empire. This informal comment I use, quite shamelessly, to rummage about in affairs of the present.

A genuine understanding of contemporary events in the Soviet Union must incorporate both density of detail and a historical perspective; it must include cultural, political, economic, but also societal spheres. I assume, as a social historian, that to understand the forces at work in the Soviet Union today we must look beyond the power struggles at the top and understand that change in the USSR has always been a process of negotiation between leaders and basic social groups. Although the unique centralization of the Soviet system cannot be overlooked, Western historians have, in the past generation, been critical of approaches to Russian history that treat the state as prime mover and ignore the interplay between politics and evolutionary social change. History written "from below" has insights to add to the study of the contemporary Soviet Union.

As a historian I assume, too, that domestic and foreign events are interconnected. Most historians of foreign policy have rejected the value of investigating diplomacy in isolation from the internal life of a country, and in the case of Russia, the impact of foreign affairs upon domestic concerns has been powerful. The interplay of defeat in war and internal reform is a theme in Russian history reaching back at least to the time of Peter the Great. Fear that Russia's great power status was eroding led to the Great Reforms of the 1860s, and dread that Russia would slip back to the status of "an India or China" prompted another spurt of internal reforms at the turn of the century. The belief that a pluralistic, decentralized Russia would be incapable of keeping up with its rivals was a powerful ideological weapon in the struggle of the tsars to enlist support against the imposition of limitations upon autocracy. Discouraged by the failure of reform at home, Russian tsars often turned to the foreign arena in an attempt to leave their mark upon history. And Russia's cultural and political history has been deeply colored by its relations with the West.

Because events far outpaced my ability to keep abreast, I reluctantly decided to omit discussion of foreign policy issues. Future editions of *Soviet Briefing* will remedy this shortcoming. Unfortunately, this means passing over in silence an area in which Gorbachev has made extraordinary initiatives (toward Europe, the United States, and China), some notable gains, while simultaneously enhancing his own prestige at home. We must overlook Eastern Europe, an area extremely sensitive to the currents of change within the Soviet Union and posing significant dangers for Gorbachev,[30] but where we also see the extraordinary spectacle of a "Soviet leader with a genuine popular following among some segments of the East European public." One might well argue that discussion of Eastern Europe should be included with ethnic issues in a larger chapter on minorities in the last colonial empire—the issues are that interwoven.[31]

A Distinctiveness Not Warranted By the Facts

The most powerful message of Hedrick Smith's *The Russians*, published in the early 1970s and selling more copies than all academic works on the Soviet Union since World War II combined, was that Soviet society and polity are but variants of the prerevolutionary political culture. We must be aware of Russia's distinct historical tradition and unique geopolitical legacy; of its role in the world economy and culture as a "perpetual latecomer"; of the distinct imprint made by its semicolonial and dependent status at the turn of the century (and the burden imposed to catch up militarily in order to regain the status of a great power).

At the same time, we cannot overlook the fact that the processes of modernization have created patterns with marked resemblances to those obtaining in much of the developed world. Although I believe that history has left a deep imprint on popular culture and contemporary institutions in the Soviet Union, much of what we ascribe to "Russian tradition" is merely the residue of a vanishing peasant culture, which itself had much in common with peasant culture throughout the globe. This peasant culture, still vital and intact after 1917, was both undermined and preserved (in warped fashion) during Stalin's forced and brutal transformation of the country, and we can detect its imprint in attitudes toward work, authority, and even self in the culture today. But the transformation wrought by urbanization, industrialization, and universal secondary education is today etched far more deeply in Soviet society than are these increasingly faint residues of the past.

This perspective, long argued by Cyril Black, has recently been vigorously asserted by distinguished scholars such as Frederick Starr, Robert Tucker, and Moshe Lewin, who have emphasized the gradual emergence of a "civil society" in the Soviet Union and the pressure this society is now exerting upon the polity to adapt. Soviet nationalities expert Ralph Clem argues that "Western scholars have attributed a uniqueness to Soviet society on the assumption that a 'totalitarian' state is capable of decisively controlling basic social processes," an assumption now regarded with great skepticism. He insists: "We in the West have tended to impute to Soviet society a distinctiveness that is not usually warranted by the facts."[32] While conceding that the concept of civil society most forcefully described in the writings of John Locke, John Stuart Mill, and Alexander de Tocqueville (grounded in ideals of freedom of speech, the press, assembly, and religion, and holding that society is distinct from government) has little precedent in Russian political culture, Starr believes that "civil society in the Soviet Union will be shaped by Russian traditions, just as those in Great Britain and France bear the very different mark of their national heritages." But, he adds, "Starkly different structures can fulfill similar functions. To acknowledge the differentness of Russia's political heritage does not disqualify it from experiencing evolutionary change."[33]

I assume, too, that despite the fundamentally different ways the societies are ordered, Soviet politicians (and the public at large) function with roughly the same mixture of self-interest, opportunism, and ideals as we see around us in the West. It is a measure of the depth of our animosity to that country that such a pedestrian statement need be made. To believe otherwise, however, is, as George F. Kennan Jr. has repeatedly pointed out, to make the most radical and implausible assumptions about human nature. People, as we know, like to operate in their own self-interest while continuing to believe that they are acting in the interests of their country, whatever the real correspondence between the two. People in the West are perfectly capable, as well, of holding mutually incompatible beliefs and whistling their way through life without ever troubling to notice the lack of fit.

It is true that censorship, official lies, and the peculiar nature of Soviet ideology, with its monolithic claims to truth, omniscience, and infallibility, have imposed extraordinary strains on the credulity of the Soviet citizen and politician. It is also the case that in the USSR political life is more imperious and invasive of the civil sphere. But I believe that, at root, even among those who detect something terribly wrong in the system, and *can conceive of an alternative*, most believe it can and must be changed from within. The alternative is so troubling that, for most people, psychological mechanisms simply keep it from view. Fortunately for the Soviet people, and for us in the West as well, it is now possible to conceive of substantive change for the better without contemplating the anarchy and violence which has been so much a part of a tragic history. No small measure of credit for the altered vistas belongs to one individual, Mikhail Sergeyevich Gorbachev, for recognizing the changes taking place in his society, for responding to the mounting crisis in that society, and for growing in office enough to produce a sweeping program of change as significant—though far more humane in vision—as that introduced in the Stalinist 1930s.

Notes

1. For a brief discussion of the new vocabulary, see William H. Luers, "A Glossary of Russia's Third Revolution," NYT, July 7, 1987.

2. Cited in NYT, November 1, 1987.

3. Comments culled from remarks of speakers at the Conference on Gorbachev Initiatives, Meridian House, Washington, D.C., November 1–3, 1987.

4. Philip Taubman, "Gorbachev's Gamble," *New York Times Magazine*, July 19, 1987: 43.

5. The best summary and analysis of the economic reform to date is by Gertrude E. Schroeder, "Anatomy of Gorbachev's Economic Reform," *Soviet Economy*, Vol. 3, No. 3 (July-September, 1987): 219-241.

6. Daniel Singer in *The Nation*, December 12, 1987: 716.

7. CSM, July 15, 1988.

8. Key advisers to Gorbachev in foreign affairs are Anatoly Cherniaev, his foreign policy aide; Anatoly Dobrynin, ambassador to Washington, 1962-1986; and Alexander Iakovlev, head of the Central Committee's propaganda department (CSM, March 11, 1987). In a talk at the Kennan Institute in the autumn of 1987, Vernon Aspaturian argued that foreign policy formulation has shifted from the Foreign Ministry to the Communist Party Central Committee Secretariat, and notably the international department.

9. See, on U.S.-Soviet relations: *Gorbachev's Russia and American Foreign Policy*, ed. by Seweryn Bialer and Michael Mandelbaum (Boulder, Co., 1988).

10. Timothy Colton, *The Dilemma of Reform in the Soviet Union* (New York: Council on Foreign Relations, 1986): 186. According to this doctrine, elaborated by Alexander Iakovlev, there are three major capitalist centers: the United States, Western Europe, and Japan.

11. For a survey of Soviet literature on the new foreign policy, see RL 292/87 (July 29): 1-6. A brief interview with a major proponent of the new views, Evgeny Primakov, director of the Institute of World Economics (IMEMO) is in CSM, March 11, 1987.

12. Timothy Colton, *Dilemma*: 184; WP, December 3, 1987: A25. See also, on Soviet policy toward the Third World: Robert S. Litwak and S. Neil Macfarlane, "Soviet Activism in the Third World," *Survival* (January–February, 1987): 21-39; and Galia Golan, "Gorbachev's Middle East Strategy," *Foreign Affairs*, Vol. 66, No. 1 (Fall, 1987): 41-57.

13. CSM, March 11, 1987.

14. According to Primakov, "maintenance at minimal cost" of a "situation where neither side can avoid a destructive retaliatory strike" (CSM, July 16, 1987). On the new Soviet military doctrine, see (in addition to the entries below) the following short comments: CSM, May 1, 1987: B5; September 3, 1987: 13; November 17, 1987: 18-19; December 2, 1987: 6; WP, November 30, 1987.

15. Lawrence T. Caldwell, "United States-Soviet Relations and Arms Control," *Current History*, Vol. 86, No. 522 (October, 1987): 306-308, 344-347.

16. CSM, July 16, 1987; Matthew Evangelista, "The New Soviet Approach to Security," *World Policy Journal*, Vol. 3, No. 4 (Fall, 1986): 561-599; idem, "Exploiting the Soviet 'Threat' to Europe," *Bulletin of the Atomic Scientists*, (January-February, 1987): 14-18; Michael McGwire, *Military Objectives in Soviet Foreign Policy* (Washington, D.C., 1987); idem, "Soviet Military Objectives," *World Policy Journal*, Vol. 3, No. 4 (Fall, 1986): 667-695; Gerhard Wettig, "Sufficiency in Defense—A New Guideline for the Soviet Military Posture?" RL 372/87 (September 23): 1-5; David R. Jones, "The Two Faces of Soviet Military Power," *Current History*, Vol. 86, No. 522 (October, 1987): 313-316, 336-337, 344, 346-347; Richard F. Staar, "The Warsaw Treaty Organization," *Current History*, Vol. 86, No. 523 (November, 1987): 357-360, 387-389.

17. WP, March 31, 1987.

18. Ibid.

19. NYT, October 18, 1987; WP, October 19, 1987 and November 14, 1987.

20. NYT, April 1, 1987: A3; CSM, March 20, 1987.

21. The suggestion of Georgy Smirnov, director of the Institute of Marxism Leninism, at a press conference (WP, November 5, 1987: A35). One Soviet academic reportedly responded, when asked if all this meant an end to the Brezhnev doctrine: "That kind of thinking would not be possible now. . . . If we keep on with our reforms, Czechoslovakia will probably invade us" (CSM, March 11, 1987). However, the Brezhnev doctrine has not been explicitly repudiated, and most East Europeans believe Soviet troops would be used in the last resort to keep the bloc together.

22. Colton, *Dilemma*: 209-213. For a brief analysis of Gorbachev's

difficulties in devising a policy for Eastern Europe, see CSM, April 27, 1987, 16, and WP, April 13, 1987. For a recent survey of Eastern Europe, see F. Stephen Larrabee, "Eastern Europe: A Generational Change," *Foreign Policy*, No. 70 (Spring, 1988): 42-64. See also: Michael Kraus, "Soviet Policy Toward East Europe," *Current History*, Vol. 86, No. 523 (November 1987): 354, and idem, "The USSR, Eastern Europe and Glasnost," *Freedom at Issue*, No. 7 (January-February, 1988): 7-10.

23. "Gorbachev the Bold," *New York Review of Books*, May 28, 1987: 22.

24. Nikolai Shmelev, "Avansy i dolgi," *Novyi mir*, No. 6 (June 1987): 142. This article is discussed at greater length below. See also the summary in Joint Economic Committee, *Gorbachev's Economic Plans* (Washington, D.C., 1987), Vol 1: Herbert S. Levine, "The Agenda of Economic Change: Overview," 1-9; and an abstract of the article in CDSP, Vol. 39, No. 38 (October 21, 1987): 1-7.

25. Among the recent works analyzing Soviet society under Gorbachev, the following are quite useful: Michael Paul Sacks and Jerry G. Pankhurst, eds., *Understanding Soviet Society* (Boston, 1988); James Cracraft, ed., *Contemporary Soviet Society* (2nd Edition: Chicago, 1988); Seweryn Bialer and Michael Mandelbaum, eds., *Gorbachev's Russia and American Foreign Policy* (Boulder, Co., 1988); Moshe Lewin, *The Gorbachev Phenomenon* (Berkeley, Ca., 1988).

26. See also *Survey*, especially the August 1987 issue (Vol. 29, No. 4) dedicated to the topic "How Good is the Soviet Record: A Documentary Review of Housing, Health Care, Employment, Social Security." The material offered in translation is excellent, but the tone of the work is virulently anti-Soviet.

27. Gail Lapidus, "Gorbachev's Reforms: Redefining the Relationship of State and Society." Paper prepared for the American-German conference on the Gorbachev Reform Program at The Kennan Institute, Washington, D.C. (March 20-22, 1988): 33.

28. "Meeting Report," Kennan Institute for Advanced Russian Studies (May 9, 1988).

29. *Pravda*, July 5, 1988.

30. Gorbachev's new (March 1988) adviser on relations with other Soviet countries is Georgy Shakhnazarov, a well-known and respected advocate of political reform. Party secretary for relations with Eastern Europe is Vadim Medvedev, an economist and protégé of Iakovlev.

31. For my summary of Soviet foreign policy in 1987, see *World Topics Yearbook*, ed. by Marilyn Robb Trier (Tangley Oaks, Ill., 1988).

32. Clem argues: "In the West . . . comparative research in the social sciences has long been hampered by an unscientific tradition which holds that societal traits are unique to time and place, and not amenable to broad generalizations because of cultural conditioning and human unpredictability. (Ralph Clem, "Ethnicity," in *The Soviet Union Today: An Interpretive Guide* (Chicago, 1983): 285.

33. S. Frederick Starr, "Soviet Union: A Civil Society," *Foreign Policy*, No. 70 (Spring, 1988): 35-36.

2
The Politics of Reform

In three years as general secretary, Gorbachev has brought about a "unique power inversion," overturning the traditional rules of the game by which Soviet leaders have come to power—by first building a following among provincial leaders, then at party congresses, the Central Committee, and finally at the very top. In this process, prospective leaders have followed "centrist positions" and used "policy issues as tactical pawns." But the new leader has gone a different route: "Since the 27th CPSU Congress (January 1986) he has advanced a policy program that has grown more radical by the day—before he has fully consolidated his power at the top and middle levels of the system."[1]

In a nutshell, this program began as one of "acceleration" (*uskorenie*), highlighted in Gorbachev's first major speech in April 1985, and to be achieved by tightening discipline and halting corruption. It has evolved to more systematic, affirmative measures aiming to institutionalize change; since 1987 these measures have been labeled as "radical reform," even "revolution." Stephen Cohen has identified five categories of reform in the Gorbachev program: (1) glasnost; (2) decentralization in state economic management; (3) economic privatization; (4) economic marketization; and (5) democratization.[2] In its more radical versions, economic reform seeks to establish a mixed economy with starkly reduced state planning, a robust, private sector, and integration with the global market—all in due haste.[3]

As the June Conference approached, strikingly radical political theses were aired, among them a call by prominent sociologist Tatiana Zaslavskaia for alternative political groupings, a "popular front" like the one established in Estonia in April. Such an organization could nominate political candidates, propose legislation, and bring forth issues for national referendum; it would fall short of being a formal political opposition but might mark the first step toward a multi-party system.[4]

Uncorking Change

Reform efforts have been a regular feature of the political landscape in the USSR since the time of Joseph Stalin, and most of the measures now proposed have a lineage reaching back several years, if not decades. What is unique about the Gorbachev period is the systematic nature of the reforms, the comprehensive and interlocking aspects of the program, and the decision both to carry out reform under public scrutiny and to actively recruit genuine popular input into both formulation and implementation. At no time before Gorbachev had any Soviet leader sought to reform economic, cultural, and political spheres simultaneously, and at no point before 1987 was the very validity of the Stalinist variant of socialism—the system as well as the odious individual—publicly questioned.

Prominent political scientist Seweryn Bialer believes that "the key question is not primarily how much further Gorbachev will go with his iconoclastic ideas, but rather how deeply the process that he has initiated will penetrate Soviet society."[5] Historians have a different perspective: As S. Frederick Starr aptly put it, "Gorbachev is not creating change so much as uncorking it. . . . Fundamental shifts in Soviet society are going forward, and these increasingly define the national agenda."[6] The shift from a policy of tightening up the existing system to overhauling it that took place between 1985 and 1987 represented a recognition that "the rise of corruption must be laid directly to the regime's failure to open legitimate channels for the new energies rather than to some cancerous venality that had entered the body politic."[7] Starr criticized an excessively narrow concern with Kremlin politics at the expense of understanding the underlying and evolving social reality. Likewise, Moshe Lewin has concluded that "observations that confined themselves to the top of the [political] hierarchy could not yield insights into the regime's trajectory."[8]

Of course, the most distinctive feature of the post-Brezhnev period has been the vast generational transition under way in the country's local and national leadership, in fortuitous combination with the succession (following several mini-successions) in the very top post. To dismiss this transition as the stuff of mere Kremlinology would be fatuous; it is real, it is important and it must be summarized here. But Starr and Lewin's comments should serve as a timely caution against fixating attention on the Ligachev-Gorbachev struggle (if such it is) at the expense of understanding the pressing national agenda weighing upon whomever retains the leadership reins.

Seweryn Bialer concurs that "major reforms . . . grow out of major crises," and emphasizes that the new leaders who have taken the reins of power in the 1980s recognize that they have "inherited a country and a system in a state of material and spiritual crisis." By the time Leonid I. Brezhnev died in 1982 this crisis, long in incubation, constituted a genuine national emergency.[9]

Still, if Kremlinology took the policy out of politics (leaving naked power struggles by opportunistic careerists), there is no need to remove the issue of power from policy disputes. In fact, as Zaslavskaia noted, "the principle of the radical redistribution of power is 'built into' the very scheme of restructuring . . . there can be no revolution without resolving the question of power."[10] And so it is appropriate to begin with the old question of *kto-kogo*, of personal turnover and power alignments.

Housecleaning

Gorbachev's housecleaning began before he assumed the post of general secretary, for Andropov had placed him in charge of personnel with a mission to begin replacing the leadership at the level of district and regional party secretaries. Thane Gustafson estimated that "throughout the country perhaps one-fifth of all officials" in local party organizations (PPO) had been removed by mid 1986, "and the number of government officials transferred or dismissed may reach into the tens of thousands." In Uzbekistan, Kazakhstan, Georgia, Moscow Oblast, and the southern cities of Krasnodar and Rostov-on-the-Don,[11] major "cold" purges installed new leadership at all levels. Turnover was so great that the police even recruited 55,000 Young Communist League and Party members to replace dismissed corrupt officials. As of early 1986, in the Council of Ministers 39 of the 101 members of March 1985 had departed, and 14 of 23 Central Committee heads of departments had been replaced.

At the 27th Party Congress (January 1986), a new CPSU Central Committee was elected with 307 full and 170 candidate (non-voting) members. The turnover in both categories amounted to 41 percent. The number of Politburo members, down to eleven after the February 18 ouster of Moscow city boss Victor Grishin, was brought back to twelve with the elevation of Lev Zaikov, who bypassed candidate status. Zaikov has been a member of the powerful Secretariat since July 1985. Previously in charge of defense industries, he now supervises the entire economy. Only two other individuals (Gorbachev and Egor Ligachev) simultaneously hold Politburo and Secretariat posts. The Secretariat itself was enlarged to eleven members from eight (two departures, five additions). Notable additions were Anatoly Dobrynin, ambassador to the United States for twenty-four years, who now has responsibility for supervising foreign affairs, and Alexandra Biriukova, age 58, in charge of overseeing the quality and distribution of goods, and the first woman in the top leadership in twenty-five years.

In 1986, other major personnel changes included the following: Victor Fedorchuk—transferred from his post as minister of the interior and replaced by A. Vlasov, an official with no police or legal experience; D. Kunayev—removed as first secretary of Kazakhstan and replaced December 16 by a Russian, G. Kolbin, who gained a reputation as an able leader while party chief of Ulianovsk province; Oleg Troianovsky—resigned as Moscow's chief delegate to the UN (since 1976) and appointed ambassador to China. In addition, Iuri Dubinin, age

55, replaced Troianovsky, but shortly thereafter was appointed ambassador to the United States. Dubinin formerly served in Paris and Spain, and was head of the European department of the Soviet foreign ministry (1971-1978). A. Belonogov, 55, formerly ambassador to Egypt, then succeeded Dubinin at the UN. Andrei Agentov retired after serving as foreign policy adviser to four Soviet leaders and was replaced by Anatoly Cherniaev, an official of the CC international department, and Admiral of the Fleet S. Gorshkov retired as commander in chief of the Soviet navy (since 1956). He is credited with building the Soviet navy from a coastal to a global force. Gorshkov, who died in 1988, was succeeded by Vladimir Chernavin, 57, a staff officer and naval commander of distinction with extensive submarine experience.

The year 1987 began with the appointment of Alexander Iakovlev, nonvoting member of the Polituro; Belorussian party leader Nikolai Sliunkov, 58; and CC department head Anatoly Lukianov, 56, to the CC Secretariat, bringing the total number of national secretaries to twelve. All CC secretaries except V. Dolgikh are recent appointments. Gorbachev's consolidation of power was then significantly furthered at the June plenum of the CPSU Central Committee, which elevated three men to full, and one to nonvoting membership in the Politburo, and by the Rust affair (involving a young West German who flew a private plane through Soviet defenses in May and landed on Red Square), which allowed him to shakeup the military, replacing Defense Minister Sergei Sokolov with a supporter, Dmitri Yazov.[12] The three new voting Politburo members are Aleksandr Yakovlev, 64 (a key Gorbachev protégé); Nikolai Sliunkov (the party's senior economic adviser); and Viktor Nikonov, 58 (responsible for agriculture). The new candidate member is Yazov.[13] In February 1988 Nikolai V. Talyzin, who had only recently been appointed head of Gosplan and was in charge of a key government commission studying economic reform, found himself out of a job only a month after the new enterprise law went into effect.[14]

Another signal change was the retirement of Geidar Aliyev in 1987.[15] The 64-year-old deputy prime minister and Politburo member had risen in the secret police under Stalin, served as KGB chief (1967-1969), then party head (1969-1982) in Azerbaijan republic, and had built himself a reputation for fighting corruption. He was brought to Moscow by Andropov. But Aliyev had been accused of neglecting health, housing, and other social issues, while personally indulging extravagant tastes (he allowed a bronze bust of himself to be built in his home town), and was publicly blamed for the failures of the consumer industry, his main responsibility on the Politburo. He was also known for his lavish praise of Brezhnev, and as "Brezhnev-bashing" has become popular, Aliyev has become a favorite target. In June 1988 Soviet news (Vremya) showed an enormous marble palace Aliyev had built for Brezhnev's visit to Azerbaijan: "We don't know if Brezhnev was satisfied with the accommodations," the news commentator reportedly said, "but he only stayed there three days." Aliyev apparently gave Brezhnev a $20,000 ring to commemorate the visit.[16]

Gorbachev's push to win control of the Ukraine, and to replace Vladimir Shcherbitsky, the only remaining Brezhnev holdover on the Politburo, resulted in the exposure of corruption and abuses of power in the Voroshilovgrad region in Donets basin, the dismissal of several regional party leaders, and accusations (made by Ligachev in January 1987) that the Ukraine was "intolerably slow to restructure the management of the agroindustrial complex in accordance with the party's requirements" and had turned from a breadbasket into a net grain consumer. But Shcherbitsky remains on the Politburo and is still entrenched in the Ukraine.[17]

All in all, the personnel turnover has been impressive, even revolutionary. In May 1988 the *Washington Post* (citing an unnamed Reagan administration official) listed the following changes under Gorbachev: At least 40 percent of the Central Committee members and three-quarters of Central Committee department heads; 90 of 157 regional first secretaries and 8 of 15 first secretaries of Soviet republics; 72 of 101 ministers and 11 of 13 deputy ministers on the state council administering the economy; 10 of 12 members of the CP Secretariat; and 8 of 14 members of the Politburo.[18] In some local towns and districts, the position of first secretary had changed hands three or more times by early 1987.[19]

In the arts and media, as Timothy Colton rightly points out, retirements and replacements have been a key weapon in the "thaw."[20] Most of these changes took place in 1986. On February 24 of that year Mikhail Nenashev, previously editor of the reformist newspaper, *Sovetskaia Rossiia*, replaced B. Pastukhov as chairman of the State Committee of Publishing, Printing and Book Sales. On June 18, the conservative Petr Demichev, minister of culture, resigned after twelve years, to be replaced later in the year by Vasilii Zakharov, 52, former chief ideologist of the Leningrad Party and deputy to Yeltsin in Moscow. The Academy of Sciences elected a new President, Guri Marchuk, 61, a math and science administrator. On June 28 Vladimir Karpov, 64, editor-in-chief of *Novyi mir* who was once jailed for criticizing Stalin, was elected secretary of the powerful Writers' Union (but has since turned out to be an unenthusiastic reformer). Karpov was succeeded at *Novyi mir* by Sergei Zalygin, a founder of "village prose" (a major literary movement with political implications) as well as an outstanding writer and critic of Stalinism, but not a Communist party member. Ivan Frolov, an unorthodox thinker and former editor of the academic journal *Voprosy filosofii*, was named chief editor of *Kommunist*, the Central Committee journal, and became a close consultant of Gorbachev's.

The most remarkable turnover occurred in the film industry. Elem Klimov, 41, was elected head of the Union of Film Workers at its Fifth Congress in May 1986. Klimov, who had been politically censored on a number of occasions, replaced Lev Kulidzhanov, who had been criticized for toadyism by Gorbachev at the 27th Party Congress (but who was nevertheless elected to candidate status in the Central Committee). Several prominent film directors of an orthodox hue, including Sergei Bondarchuk, were not reelected as delegates to the Fifth Congress (and Bondarchuk has become a prominent opponent of glasnost), and the union secretariat old guard was replaced by directors and screenwriters of less orthodox persuasion (Panfilov, Abdrashidov, Shakeev, Bykov, Norshstein).

A key event in 1987 was the retirement of conservative CC Secretary Mikhail Zimianin at the January plenum. Zimianin had survived the 27th Party Congress and had maintained a conservative line in history and philosophy. With his removal and Iakovlev's assumption of control over the Science and Education Department, glasnost and personnel changes swept the social sciences.[21]

Specialists have noticed a decline in the rate of turnover after the spring of 1986. This may be a sign of the inevitable slowdown ensuing once a general housecleaning had been conducted,and the old "Dnepropetrovsk mafia" swept out. But as Colton argues, Gorbachev may well have his eye on past attempts at reform and may be trying to avoid antagonizing his own men, as Nikita Khrushchev did, by holding them in constant fear of dismissal and disgrace. Colton notes: "Gorbachev may take pleasure from battering the bureaucracy, but this alone has not solved his problems."[22] The transition from exclusive use of appointments from above as the major instrument of reform to structural reform will require coalition building as well as personnel turnover.

Leaders, For and Against

Who are the Gorbachevites? A number of fellow graduates of Gorbachev's alma mater (Moscow State University) have advanced to prominent positions. Among them are Ivan Frolov (editor of *Kommunist*), aide for ideological affairs; Valery Boldin, head of the Central Committee's General Department (responsible for handling all documents passing through the Politburo); Anatoly Lukianov (formerly holding Boldin's position), now in charge of the legal reforms; Valentin Chikin, editor of *Sovetskaia Rossiia* (but no friend, it turns out, of perestroika); and Lev Spiridonov, deputy editor of *Pravda*.[23] The Gorbachev coterie, according to Jerry Hough, has drawn not only from Moscow State University, but also from the Stavropol region (and contiguous territory), the Caucasus, and the Komsomol (Young Communist League) apparatus from the late 1950s and early 1960s.[24]

In broader terms, the new leadership is younger and better educated than the old guard and according to Colton, have fewer involvements with the organizations in their control; they have been transferred in, or have been promoted several rungs at one time. Geographically, Gorbachev has reversed Brezhnev's policy of recruiting from within the locality and instead has rechanneled potential leaders through Moscow and then back into the provinces as "carpetbaggers" sent out to fight graft, local featherbedding, and nepotism.[25] Bialer found the new leadership less ideological, more concerned with efficiency, more likely to believe in partial reform and stepped-up discipline to exploit the immense hidden resources of the system, but firmly committed to its fundamental principles. More recently, however, Bialer has modified his group portrait, concluding that this generation is less homogeneous than he thought and that it contains an important stratum radically critical of Soviet structures and prepared for deep reform.[26] Bialer, Colton, and others take for granted that this leadership remains predominately urban, male, Slavic, and white-collar (by origin as well as occupation).

Jerry Hough argues that "any assessment of Gorbachev's consolidation of power hinges upon his relationship . . . to Ligachev, Ryzhkov, and Chebrikov." All three rose precipitously under Andropov, but Hough argues that from the start they have been clearly subordinate in status to Gorbachev and were part of "a network of people with whom he had developed a special trust in the past."[27] Hough fervently contends that talk of dissension at the top or throughout the system is disinformation designed to give Gorbachev and his reforms "a precarious appearance," to politicize normal footdragging (thereby making it dangerous) and to rally radical reformers to the center.[28]

Most specialists believe, however, that allegiance to Gorbachev among the top leadership is fragile, that it is based upon his performance and upon a congruence of belief on individual issues rather than upon long-standing patronage relations or groupings. Several observers have noticed that he has drawn heavily from two provincial organizations—western Siberia and the Urals—for his recruits, but most theorize that these politicians must be seen as relatively independent rather than as cronies. One current interpretation puts a troika in power, with Gorbachev at the top, Iakovlev second in command, and Ligachev now a distinct third.

Only two Politburo members (Iakovlev and Eduard Shevardnadze) can be definitely called allies by conviction, as can candidate member Georgy Razumovsky.[29] Ligachev is an enigmatic figure, but he clearly has his differences with Gorbachev, as does Viktor Chebrikov. Shcherbitsky is no friend, and Vitaly Vorotnikov as well as Mikhail Solomentsev (chief of the Party Control Commission) belong, perhaps, to a "middle ground, neither strongly opposing nor supporting Gorbachev."[30] The leanings of Sliunkov[31] and Nikonov (widely regarded as an incompetent) are unclear, as are the opinions of Gromyko.

Premier Nikolai Ryzhkov and, one must assume, his apparent protégé Sliunkov "share many of Gorbachev's assumptions and policy goals" but may be "reluctant to countenance [so] radical an economic reform" as Gorbachev desires. Yet Ryzhkov reportedly joined Gorbachev in attacking Ligachev at an April 1988 Politburo meeting—perhaps this event signals closer ties than previously assumed?[32]

Yeltsin's replacment as Moscow party boss is Zaikov, 64, who made his career in the defense industry and as party leader in Leningrad. There he was known as a "determined advocate of industrial modernization," but where he stands otherwise is still unclear. Everyone agreed that the choice of a replacement for Yeltsin in this crucial position would be fateful for Gorbachev (and would provide a test of his clout). But where does Zaikov stand? And who chose him? Philip Taubman of the the *New York Times* Moscow bureau wrote in July 1987 that Gorbachev was giving Zaikov more authority in party personnel affairs as a counterweight to Ligachev.[33] Likewise, Anders Aslund of the Kennan Institute finds Zaikov keeping a distance from Ligachev, despite his connections with the Leningrad group. At this point, however, few specialists are ready to label him a firm supporter of Gorbachev. Thus, on many issues, Gorbachev may find himself in the minority in the Politburo.[34] Still, at least one Western analyst claims to have detected a "drift toward greater radicalism" among others in the top leadership, which, of course, would mean augmented support for Gorbachev.[35]

Because Gorbachev's support in the Politburo may be tenuous, some analysts earlier believed that he was trying to shift decision-making power to the Secretariat.[36] Six of the twelve secretaries are now voting members of the Politburo, and a seventh is a candidate member. But in 1988 analysts were inclined to believe instead that Gorbachev intended to reduce the power of the Secretariat. According to some accounts, the Secretariat no longer meets weekly (instead, two or three times a month) and is "beginning to devolve some issues to other parts of the party and government hierarchy."[37] Gorbachev's proposals for a presidential system proposed at the June Conference, as well as the general reform thrust aimed at lessening party control over the economy and society, would, of course, ultimately reduce the role of the Secretariat.

Where the military and the KGB line up is a vexing question. Among specialists, a debate has long raged about military-party relations. One side perceives an intrinsic conflict between the interests of the two and a marked military resentment of the party. The other side either sees a convergence of interests and an overlap of personnel so extensive as to make the boundaries between the two indistinct or, alternatively, sees the party as being firmly in control. With this debate unresolved, there is little chance of finding a consensus on military reaction to Gorbachev.

In 1986, a clean-up campaign began, targeting corruption in the military. Some analysts believe that the political profile of the Soviet military rose markedly in late 1987. Television appearances and other publicized meetings with the press appeared to place Yazov and other leaders "in the camp of Ligachev and Chebrikov," according to one reporter.[38] Admittedly, Gorbachev has no strong ties with the military, and he has made it clear that the armed forces must make do with less in order to make resources available in the early stages of perestroika. But the military may not be unhappy with this restriction, at least in the short run, and may well even anticipate some gains from perestroika (see Chapter 5). As of yet, it is unclear how the military feels about the new doctrine of reasonable sufficiency or about proposals for reductions in conventional forces.

If Chebrikov is an opponent of glasnost (and perhaps of perestroika),[39] it does not necessarily follow that the entire KGB appparatus stands behind him. It will simply not do to think of the KGB as monolithic or as uniformly opposed to reform. *New York Times* correspondent Taubman is correct in pointing out that many high-ranking figures connected with the agency have long advocated reform. In provincial cities, the KGB is often regarded as the only relatively uncorrupted institution. With access to the "unvarnished" truth, the KGB is also aware of the dimensions of the problems facing the country.[40] Moreover, Andropov's campaign against corruption during the 1970s must logically have brought to prominence many KGB operatives committed to his goal of cleaning up the country. It also follows—since we lack any evidence of a major purge within the KGB—that there must now be a strong anti-corruption contingent on hand.

Of course, few would portray the KGB as an enthusiastic supporter of all of the ramifications of glasnost. Peter Reddaway is quite right in stressing that both the military and the KGB (not to mention the party) are by training and temperament averse to the kind of "anarcho-syndicalism" that Gorbachev's program of glasnost and worker self-democracy may represent. They cannot be unaware of the implications of this program for the relationship between the state and the individual (elaborated on elsewhere in this text). They can be little comforted by Gorbachev's argument that "democracy is not the opposite of order. . . . It is order of a higher degree."

In a recent analysis of the domestic role of the KGB, Amy W. Knight[41] argues that because the Soviet image is improving in the West, and because expanding scientific contacts facilitate espionage activities, the KGB is happy. But the three primary internal functions of the KGB—coercion and punishment; deterring deviant behavior; and providing the leadership with information about popular sentiments—have all been adversely affected by perestroika. According to Gail Lapidus, glasnost has also subjected the KGB to unprecedented public criticism for abuse of power,[42] while legal reforms now under consideration imperil its traditional freedom of action.

If there is debate over how enthusiastic the police and military are about perestroika, there is near consensus (Jerry Hough being the noteworthy exception) that Gorbachev has a real problem at the center with the Central Committee. Here, by most accounts, he has the allegiance of only a minority; the new members added since the 27th Party Congress are not necessarily in Gorbachev's camp. One curious problem Gorbachev faces is that of "dead souls"; that is, every major official he replaces who also has a seat on the CC retains that seat and is likely to work to obstruct Gorbachev's progress. Analysts have concluded that "dead souls" make up 19 percent of the CC full membership. So, it may be that his original purpose in convening the June 1988 Party Conference was to "reduce the number of opponents and pave the way for the election of more staunch supporters of the reformist course at the 28th Party Congress in 1991."[43]

However, a month before the Conference, official sources made it clear that no such housecleaning was scheduled (and none, in fact, took place).[44] Some in the West saw this as a major defeat for Gorbachev; one Hudson Institute specialist claimed on the eve of the Conference that "if the career apparatchiki can prevent a large turnover of the Central Committee membership, Gorbachev's ability to restore momentum to his reform program will be in doubt."[45] Others argued that Gorbachev now felt that further turnover was unnecessary and could even be politically counterproductive: "Gorbachev is now strong enough," one Soviet official told a Western journalist. "He doesn't want a civil war."[46] The entire issue was further clouded by an obscure dispute between specialists over just which party rules applied to conferences and whether membership could be renewed at such meetings.[47]

Developments at the June Conference suggest we are in fact witnessing a transition from the politics of "personnel bashing" to coalition building and structural reform (as Colton and others argue). This argument gains force if we conclude that the radical agenda, which some felt was the next step (at the 1991 Party Congress) after the sought-after personnel turnover, was in fact on the agenda at the Conference itself. Nevertheless, most analysts continue to see the absence of turnover on the Central Committee as a failure rather than a deliberate tactic on Gorbachev's part.[48]

They Will Stop at Nothing

Gorbachev has encountered widespread opposition in the bureaucracy and in local party cells, a resistance amply documented in the Soviet press and especially evident in the delegate selection process for the June Conference, where several of Gorbachev's most prominent supporters were denied seats. It is not coincidental that the locus of resistance at the center—the Central Committee—has a powerful contingent of provincial party leaders who reportedly make up a strong opposition bloc. Obstructionism at the middle levels of the bureaucracy was identified in the famous *Novosibirsk Report* of 1983 as the chief obstacle to all reform efforts in the Soviet Union. Since then, the provincial apparatus has been the target of unrelenting attacks by radical reformers such as Shmelev, Nuikin, and Zaslavskaia. Shmelev, in particular, portrays an officialdom who believe that "Moscow is far away" and blithely continue to act as if the many new laws and decrees of perestroika were irrelevant. These local officials fiercely hound attempts to set up cooperatives, resist the contract system in agriculture, and continue to control every detail of farm life with petty regulations on what to plant, when, and how. Shmelev believes that the population has concluded that "the local (power structure) is more powerful than Moscow."[49] Over time, outright resistance to perestroika can probably be squelched; the problem, many point out, is that rather than coalescing into organized opposition, local bureaucrats are more likely to seek to "absorb rather than repel reform."[50]

The theme of provincial resistance to Moscow (or St. Petersburg) is a familiar one to historians. The reform efforts of Peter the Great and Catherine the Great encountered a provincial morass, "nests" of officials colluding to protect privileges and conceal rampant corruption. Nicholas I vainly created a superministry to get around the bureaucracy (at the time so grotesquely depicted by Nikolai Gogol and Alexander Herzen). Russia's greatest satirist, Mikhail Saltykov-Shchedrin, launched his career with his "Provincial Sketches," containing many vignettes that reformers find applicable even today. At the turn of the century, Tsarist Russia's most energetic reformer, Peter Stolypin, believed that a massive overhaul of local government was vital to the survival of the autocracy, but he saw his proposals go down in defeat. And at the root of the collapse of the Provisional Government (which succeeded the autocracy in March 1917, but was overturned by the Bolsheviks in November the same year) was what historians have labeled "the failure of local government": the inability of national leaderships to set roots in the provinces.[51] Of course, the Tsarist (and early Soviet) problem was primarily one of "undergovernment," the combination of centralized rule without linkages to the countryside. *Zemstvos*, after all, were created in 1864 to fill a "vacuum" in local government created by the dissolution of the bonds between serfs and nobles. Gorbachev, in contrast, confronts a swollen bureaucracy that envelops all levels and all sectors of the economy, polity, and society and that has a vested interest in suppressing the individual and group initiative he seeks to encourage as the dynamo of perestroika. But the analogy between Tsarist and Soviet Russia, in terms of corrupt local power elites capable of suppressing reforms, is strong enough to draw the attention of reform advocates today and to make classic prerevolutionary critics of the bureaucracy favorite sources for quotation. In June 1988, Zaslavskaia vividly depicted the situation today:

> The deeply embedded nests of organized crime in the country are being uprooted. These nests brought together corrupt personnel in the trade sector, wheeler-dealers in the shadow economy, venal officials and even law enforcement agents. These large criminal networks established a reign of lawlessness in their "satrapies." Some of the mafias have been exposed and prosecuted, but others remain well concealed. They cannot afford to passively wait out the situation—for them perestroika means losing everything. And they will stop at nothing.[52]

Should Gorbachev fail, the defeat is likely to originate not in the center, or only there, but in the provinces, where he is encountering local power elites bent on defending "not ideals, but selfish interests."[53]

Ideals or Interests?

Andrei Nuikin, in a much-read article, wanted to know what was behind the resistance to Gorbachev. To this point, the discussion has focused upon institutional loci of support or opposition at the center and in the provinces, and on the mind-set, or platform, of reformers. In the broadsides of the advocates of reform, opponents are portrayed as defending interests rather than ideals and as being deeply implicated in corruption. But Ligachev, the villain of glasnost, was himself "exiled" to Tomsk under Brezhnev for his outspoken criticism of venality and was reportedly the only major provincial party secretary in the 1970s not on the take.[54] Suslov, the "kingmaker" of the post-Stalin era, combined a rigid Stalinist orthodoxy (he had been an enthusiastic participant in the purges) with an ascetic, incorruptible life-style. It may well be that Gorbachev's provincial opposition is based exclusively on the defense of local power and privilege; leaders in the provinces do not have to set long-term national policy or deal with the bigger issues. But it is patently unfair to dismiss the beliefs of those leaders known to have reservations about perestroika or glasnost as mere fig leafs concealing gross personal interests. That being said, what do they want?

Ligachev and probable ally Chebrikov of the KGB have been called "traditional" or "Andropov-type" reformers: personally incorruptible,[55] they agree that the Soviet Union has mounting problems, but they attribute these problems to people rather than institutions, and see the solution in a moral regeneration of society brought about by stepped-up discipline, as well as in technocratic modernization. They are especially uncomfortable with the free-flowing criticism of party history that epitomizes glasnost. And with good reason, as William Pfaff has pointed out:

> It is difficult to see how Gorbachev and his colleagues can come to grips with their nation's terrible past without destroying their own positions. . . . If Gorbachev successfully compels his nation to confront its past, he may simply provoke a crisis in the system, ending with its rejection of him [and a] subsequent reactionary restoration. . . . The alternative to that seems to be a crisis in which the Party's own legitimacy, its right to rule the country, would be challenged.[56]

Conservatives have long resisted a reexamination of the past, not the least because they personally had much to conceal about their roles in the purges, deportations, and other sorry pages of Stalin's time. Ligachev and Chebrikov continue to resist, but for different reasons: a genuine apprehension about the fate of the party and anxiety about popular demoralization. Ligachev pointed out at the June Conference that his own relatives had been victims of Stalin.

The policy of democratization, interpreted in different ways by the top leaders, is extremely controversial, and Gorbachev failed to win acceptance for his election platform at the January plenum. Democratization involves the election (either openly or from lists drawn up by higher authorities) of delegates to local soviets, of factory directors, and even of local party secretaries. Gorbachev failed to win acceptance for secret multicandidate elections within the party, but received grudging acceptance for other elections, at least on an experimental basis in some areas. On June 21, 1987, elections took place for 2.2 million delegates to the local soviets as well as for "people's judges" on local courts, and in some places, for the first time, the voters were offered multiple-candidate ballots.

Democratization involves not only the selection of candidates (and limitations upon terms of office for all, including the general secretary, according to resolutions approved at the June Conference), but also the revitalization of soviets at all levels, freeing them from the pervasive control of the parallel party hierarchy. It has included, as mentioned elsewhere in this text, proposals for formal political organizations, which would lessen the political monopoly of the Communist party in Soviet life. Gorbachev has no interest in a multiparty system, as he noted in his December interview with NBC television, and proposals of this type (widely discussed in May and June) received a firm rebuff at the Conference.

Thane Gustafson asserts that Gorbachev has no intention whatsoever of dividing power; "on the contrary . . . his main aim is to regain the real control that his predecessors were losing."[57] Determining Gorbachev's genuine beliefs is, as Gustafson himself has elsewhere astutely noted, difficult; one measure of the leader's political brilliance has been his ability to disarm potential opposition by concealing his real aims, revealing them only as the situation unfolds.[58] But a belief in the emancipatory power of democratization would not, in any case, fit well with the needs of the moment; should Gorbachev refrain from using traditional strong-arm tactics, he will "find that others . . . local Party leaders, in particular . . . will do so in his place. . . . Control not exercised at the top will tend to be recaptured at middle levels."[59]

This paradox is one potential reformers have faced throughout Russian history. Local government has been notoriously corrupt and arbitrary, as we have seen; yet autonomous self-governing organizations, societies, or corporate bodies have never been allowed to develop. So, in seeking to improve the well-being of the country, reformers have tried to improve and streamline central agencies and to augment their power to implement change; the alternative was not self-government but the local tyranny of entrenched privilege and patronage. In the process, reformers have sought to stimulate popular initiative, but only in order to apply pressure to foot-dragging local institutions and in directions defined from above.

The same ambiguity seems to exist today. The continuing push for intraparty democracy (involving open discussion, multiple candidates, limited terms, and secret ballots) led one analyst to conclude that "this policy called demokratizatsiia is aimed squarely at the middle of the Party apparatus."[60] In the month preceding the June Conference, Gorbachev seemed to line up squarely with those calling for turning over day-to-day management of the economy and society to the soviets, leaving the party in charge only of ideology and setting the overall direction of the country. This move would, of course, virtually eliminate the need for the powerful, suffocating provincial party apparatus.[61] Gorbachev's proposals for a new presidency also seemed designed to bypass the party structure.

How will Gorbachev reconcile the need for a strong hand at the center, at least during the period of transition (and the exigency of maintaining order in the increasingly restless border regions), with the calls for democracy from below? As one analyst pointed out, the solution thus far adopted is not reassuring: "To make the same man the General Secretary and president in the one-party Soviet system is hardly a prescription for true political pluralism."[62] So far, no plausible formula has been offered. On the one hand, *demokratizatsiia* directly threatens the privileges and prerogatives of those at the middle levels of power and will meet fierce resistance. On the other hand, the accompanying proposal approved at the Conference to make party secretaries the leading candidates to run the "revitalized" soviets provoked general dismay among reformers, and seems entirely inconsistent with Gorbachev's goals. After all, putting the local "boss" in charge of the new democratic institutions does not seem an ideal way to get away from the old command methods of behavior (or to encourage the separation of party and government).

Gorbachev also supports the notion of democracy at the workplace, that is, election of plant directors. According to Vladimir Maslov, a Central Committee economist, economic reforms would require "a total democratization of administration" and the elimination of the *nomenklatura* system (under which posts in government or the economic administration are filled by party appointees; there are estimated to be 750,000 nomenklatura positions). Maslov called for election of economic managers up to the general-director level and the institution of a system of elections by which three candidates (one nonparty) would compete for all management jobs.[63] Ligachev and others have clearly distanced themselves from such proposals, arguing that democratization should mean giving local *party* organizations more leeway in decision making but that firm central control should be maintained over appointments of management in industry.

Workers' control, or economic democracy, was at the heart of the radical vision in Russia in the early twentieth century. Its full suppression after the

Civil War (1921) led to a major movement of opposition with the Communist party and to disillusionment among many of the Bolshevik's most ardent supporters. Gorbachev's talk of democracy at the worksite restores this tradition and is bound to appeal to those who still believe Marxism can be revitalized in the USSR.

We should not summarily dismiss, as many of my Western colleagues do, talk of democracy at the workplace. It is true that democratic relations in the factory run entirely counter to the Western experience and to "the vertical line of organizational authority, the line-staff division, the need for technological division . . . the authoritarian nature of the modernization of economic institutions characteristic of all advanced societies." If an "iron law of oligarchy" has been discovered to apply to trade unions, cooperative movements, and religious organizations in the West, what hope is there for local democracy in a country with such deep-seated and pervasive authoritarian traditions?[64] But recent Western studies of authority at the worksite in the age of advanced computers suggests that increased input from below may well be a prerequisite of future gains in productivity. According to Shoshana Zuboff,[65] in order for the potential of new information technology to be realized, a more egalitarian and democratic organization of work is necessary. Effective performance in the workplace will now require a "sense of initiative and commitment, an eagerness for inquiry . . . the consideration of options, and active participation in a collective process of discussion and problem-solving." My own contact with Soviet analysts in the West convinced me that no other single proposal provoked as much skepticism, even ridicule, as Gorbachev's argument for workplace democracy—perhaps because we have so little of it. But worker input was, by all accounts, a key part of the modern Swedish "miracle," and if Zuboff's arguments prove to have merit, the call for restructuring the workplace may well be timely and farsighted.

There Is No Going Back

A brief narrative of events from early 1987 to mid-1988 strongly suggests that as Gorbachev's program became both more articulated and more radical, opposition gained steam.[66] This opposition coalesced in the autumn of 1987 and forced Gorbachev to step back (the Yeltsin affair). But when in the early spring the opposition overplayed its hand (in the infamous lengthy complaint aired as a letter in *Sovetskaia Rossiia*), Gorbachev then brilliantly counterattacked, giving the radical reformers the upper hand on the eve of the June Conference; the conservatives were muted, if by no means in full retreat. Throughout this period, Gorbachev's brilliance as a political strategist was a key element. A brief narrative of these events follows; the related topic of support and opposition among the various social strata receives consideration in Chapter 6.

At the 27th Party Congress in 1986 Gorbachev ran into concerted resistance to his as yet only partially formulated proposals for democratic reform.[67] In retrospect, too, the January (1987) plenum, postponed three times because of opposition, was only a qualified advance for Gorbachev, as his proposals for democratization met with lukewarm support. The reinterpretation of Soviet history was challenged from the start, both within the profession and among the leadership.[68] The June 1987 plenum marked a real departure, confirming a sweeping set of economic reform measures; but during Gorbachev's prolonged vacation (fifty-two days, August 7- September 27), Ligachev and others uttered distinctively conservative grumblings. On September 1 a ban was imposed on demonstrations in Moscow, and on September 10 Chebrikov gave a major speech linking criticism and subversion, lambasting the "demagogy and nihilism" of some writers and artists.[69]

Escalating minority discontent in the Baltic region (demonstrations to commemorate Stalin's victims, protests against industrial projects bringing in Russian workers and against despoliation of the environment, and proposals for making Estonia economically independent, with separate citizenship for its people); demonstrations by Crimean Tatars (wanting to return to their homeland); and the increasingly shrill debate over social issues as well as the Soviet past all reportedly led to a "marathon session" of the Politburo on September 27 (the day of Gorbachev's return) in which a majority apparently concluded that "matters had gotten out of hand."[70]

In November it was revealed that Moscow Party Chief and fervid advocate of reform Boris Yeltsin had been dismissed from his post after a heated Central Committee meeting (October 22) at which he blasted opponents of perestroika (perhaps in response to the September Politburo session). The most widely accepted explanation of events is that Yeltsin, in a fit of frustration, vented his fury at the slow pace of reform and criticized Ligachev in person. The events were then leaked in order to discredit Yeltsin and, indirectly, Gorbachev (as well as glasnost in its most fervid opponent). Rumors had it that the KGB initially leaked a version which has Yeltsin blowing up at Gorbachev.[71]

But one respected Western analyst made a strong case that Yeltsin's dismissal had less to do with the struggle over "grand strategy" than with Yeltsin's own abrasive personality and his abusive practices as Moscow boss (using information from anonymous letters, frequent resort to unreasonable deadlines, looking for scapegoats, and treating subordinates in Stalinist ways). According to this argument, Yeltsin was a transition figure with an ambiguous attitude toward glasnost, limited capacity for challenging fundamental assumptions and structures, and conventional approaches—in short, far less than the epitome of perestroika many in the West believe him to be.[72]

However events are interpreted, the Yeltsin affair represented a significant setback to reformers. Gorbachev's failure to defend Yeltsin in the ensuing uproar, combined with his tepid attack on Stalinism November 2, are generally seen as indicators of the leader's weakened position and precursors to what has been called the "first major domestic political crisis of the Gorbachev era."[73]

In the following weeks, Glavlit, the censorship organ, began to flex its muscles after a long sleep, reportedly cutting several articles from reform-oriented journals. In December, while Gorbachev was in Washington, Ligachev reportedly took advantage of the absence to set aside plans for the formal rehabilitation of Nikolai Bukharin (planned for early 1988). Sometime early in 1988, the Politburo apparently surprised Gorbachev by voting down the proposed law on cooperatives (see Chapter 5) that would legalize various forms of private initiative. Upon returning from Washington, Gorbachev had the vote reversed.[74]

With growing resistance visible at the end of 1987, the upcoming party Conference was increasingly seen as decisive for Gorbachev's future.[75] Reports in December described resistance at local plenums to personnel changes sought by Gorbachev in preparation for the Conference and even the removal of some Gorbachev supporters. Early in 1988 reports surfaced of plots to turn the June Conference from a purge of conservatives to a coup against Gorbachev himself.

According to one interpretation, conservatives were so emboldened by Gorbachev's retreat in November that by January they were ready for open defiance and chose the occasion of the release of Mikhail Shatrov's play *Onward...Onward* to launch their broadsides. At a meeting between Gorbachev and media leaders on January 8, *Pravda* editor Viktor Afanasiev bitterly attacked the play. Two days later *Pravda* printed a critique of Shatrov which was followed by a barrage of letters from a group of conservative historians. Others rallied to Shatrov's defense,[76] and on February 29 *Pravda* printed a letter by eight leading figures in the theatre who called the attack on Shatrov Stalinist in tone and intent. According to this interpretation, the Shatrov episode represented a major victory for perestroika because it was fought largely on openly anti-Stalinist grounds (the play premiered in Tomsk in March).

This victory by the Gorbachevites led the conservative opposition to redouble its efforts, leading in turn to "a landmark in current political developments," the Andreyeva letter in *Sovetskaia Rossiia* on March 13, 1988. The letter ("I Cannot Betray My Principles") was at least nominally written by a Leningrad chemistry teacher, but it was unquestionably altered by the newspaper editor and "Stalinist adventurer" Valentin Chikin into a manifesto of the opposition (approved, perhaps by Ligachev).[77] Dev Murarka calls it a "collective effort" by those in "a great hurry" to undermine Gorbachev and perestroika, a way of rallying support to roll back the reform agenda before the 19th Party Conference.[78]

Packed with anti-Semitism, patriotic xenophobia, and nostalgia for Stalinism, the Andreyeva letter was a bombshell. Many intellectuals were convinced that it could only have been published with authorization by the

Politburo and felt it meant that the leadership had abruptly dropped perestroika. For the next three weeks reformists huddled in cowed silence:

> Those twenty days of silence—during which dozens of party organizations met to applaud the "change of course," while Ligachev himself, addressing a group of newspaper editors, described the [letter] as "an example to follow," and photocopies of the text were distributed among the staffs of numerous papers so that they could study it better—saw the development of a battle of decisive importance for the fate of the democratization of Soviet society.[79]

According to Robert Kaiser, the Ligachev meeting with editors (on March 14) was "an electrifying event"; some editors told their staffs that they had to let their consciences dictate how to proceed but warned that the consequences could be dire if they stuck with perestroika; the news agency Tass sent out instructions to the provinces to reprint the Andreyeva letter in local newspapers (in Tambov, of all places, meeting a refusal). Party lecturers criticized Gorbachev and economic adviser Abel Aganbegyan by name.

At the same time, Gorbachev and Iakovlev were abroad, visiting Yugoslavia. When they returned on March 18, they had some difficulty finding out exactly what had happened and who was behind events (apparently they couldn't rely upon the KGB for information). When Ligachev himself left to visit Vologda, Gorbachev brought newspaper editors together again to reassert the reformist line and apparently called Ligachev an "impediment to reform." In the next few days a stormy Politburo meeting took place; Gorbachev may have left the membership alone to debate the issue while he returned to his dacha to await the outcome. Initially divided, the leadership finally agreed to support Gorbachev.[80]

On April 5, Gorbachev (working, many feel, through the pen of Iakovlev) struck back in *Pravda* with a harsh refutation of the Andreyeva letter. Conceding that under glasnost *Sovetskaia Rossiia* had the right to its opinions ("there are no forbidden topics today"), the *Pravda* article nevertheless declared: "We are all learning to live under conditions of broadening democracy and glasnost and undergoing a great learning process. It is no easy learning process. It has proved harder than we presumed to rid ourselves of old thoughts and actions, but . . . there is no going back."

According to press accounts, "the whole intellectual, moral and political climate in the Soviet Union changed dramatically. . . . It was as if a heavy fog had lifted."[81] In the following weeks, attacks on Andreyeva and the foes of perestroika were prominent in the press and on television. Ligachev apparently received a reprimand at an unannounced Politburo meeting, was forced to take a vacation from his activities, and undoubtedly suffered a serious reversal.[82]

But it should not be assumed that the conservatives have been decisively defeated. *Pravda* reported that in the aftermath of the Andreyeva exchange at least a quarter of its letter writers expressed support for the basic positions put forth in the conservative manifesto. And on May 5, leaning on the argument that glasnost was "a principle, not a tool," the editors of *Sovetskaia Rossiia* printed an oblique defense of its position.

And what is Ligachev's position today? Early in 1987 it was rumored that Gorbachev follower Iakovlev, often called the architect of perestroika, was elbowing Ligachev out of his position as overseer of ideology,[83] but an open fight was brewing between the two by December. Ligachev more than held his own, while Iakovlev temporarily dropped out of sight, reportedly ill, only to appear again in the early spring.[84] Ligachev has publicly boasted that he, not Gorbachev, chairs meetings of the Secretariat, and he has refused to adopt much of the language of perestroika (and particularly reference to market forces). After becoming embroiled in the controversy over the Andreyeva letter he was forced to take a vacation and to reiterate his support for perestroika, and it was rumored that he had finally lost control of the media to Iakovlev. Still, his bearing at the June Conference did not bespeak a man humiliated, beaten, or even on the defensive.

In mid-August 1988, as Gorbachev was once again vacationing, Ligachev appeared on television to warn of the dangers of a market-oriented restructuring, to complain about workers' strikes, and to lash out at improved relations with capitalist countries as "only confusing the minds of the Soviet people and our friends abroad." Five days later Iakovlev, speaking to party workers in the Baltic, "issued a virtual point by point rebuttal of Mr. Ligachev's speech."[85] One diplomat concluded that "Ligachev is clearly being smoked out," but we can only conclude at this date that the rivalry between the two remains unresolved, and that each represents a powerful constituency.

Conservative strength was also revealed in the delegate selection process for the June Conference. Although Gorbachev was actively stumping in April and May, cajoling local party secretaries in special meetings to ensure that only perestroika supporters be invited to serve as delegates to the convention, reports were widespread that reformers were having difficulty winning election (or endorsement by local party electoral committees). The elections themselves, scheduled to begin in April, were at least a month late, held up by wrangling over procedures and credentials. Late in May, Andrei Sakharov and others, disturbed by evidence of election difficulties and fearful that the Conference could turn into a conservative coup, urged Gorbachev to postpone it until the autumn, when secret elections could be conducted and reformist candidates be ensured success. Widely read pronouncements by playwright Alexander Gelman and Nikolai Shmelev spoke with great alarm at the strength of ongoing bureaucratic resistance and lackluster support within the party apparatus. And at a meeting with editors of Soviet newspapers on May 7, Gorbachev struck a conciliatory note, holding out an olive branch to his opponents and admitting that radical reform proposals had caused "panic" among the population.[86]

In May it appeared that Gorbachev had won a significant victory in wrangling over selection of Conference delegates, for his insistence that the only criterion for choice of delegates be their commitment to perestroika won acceptance, at least in principle.[87] As the date of the Conference grew nearer, radical reformers put forth genuinely far-reaching proposals for political change.[88] And on May 26 the leadership published an 8,000-word document representing a draft program, or "Theses," for discussion at the Conference.

The Theses, officially approved by the Central Committee, call for limitations on tenure in elected office to two five-year terms (with exceptions, by secret ballot, if an official is endorsed by 75 percent of his electors); measures to enhance the legislative power of the parliamentary system of soviets; full rehabilitation of Stalin's victims and an extension of glasnost to all problems, past and present; and new legal guarantees for freedom of the press, speech, conscience, assembly, and the inviolability of privacy. In the words of the Theses: "everything is permissible unless prohibited by law."

If the proposals, accepted at the Conference, are fully implemented, the procedures for election to office will be ineffably changed to include "genuine competition, wide discussion of candidates, and voting by secret ballot."[89] How far the country has progressed is indicated by Zaslavskaia's comment that "three years ago the very publication of such theses would have produced massive shock."[90]

Instead of shock, the Theses have merely added fuel to the fire following the denouement of the *Sovetskaia Rossiia—Pravda* dispute. On June 7 *Komsomolskaia pravda* summarized some of the proposals circulating among the public on the eve of the Conference: curbing the powers of the KGB; abolishing internal passports; printing transcripts of Politburo meetings; making public the budget of the Communist party; eliminating the privileges of the nomenklatura; limiting party authority to control of its own membership and essentially decoupling party and government; and giving official authority to an umbrella organization to represent the multitude of existing informal groups as well as to nominate candidates and propose legislation. The editors of *Komsomolskaia pravda* dryly commented: "It is possible that some of the positions put forth . . . may seem controversial to some of our readers." After about seventy years of fostering less than sparkling debate, these paragons of the Socratic method told Soviet readers that "discussion cannot just consist of noncontroversial opinions."[91]

But early in June, Soviet press coverage revealed that many pro-Gorbachev candidates had not, in fact, been selected as Conference delegates and that others had been added only at the last moment after intervention by the top leadership. According to these reports, nominations by the rank-and-file party membership at 4,900 party meetings had often been squelched by officials at the local level. In the words of *Izvestiia* correspondent Alexander Bovin, "The party apparatus has taken the preparation for the Conference in its . . . hands, and, with minor exceptions, it smashed the young seedlings of party democracy. As earlier, the lists of candidates went from top down."[92]

Nobody Has a Monopoly on the Truth

In this overheated environment, the Party Conference met from June 28 to July 1. The long-awaited gathering was a momentous event in Soviet history, if only for the spectacle, replayed in every home with a television, of a free-wheeling debate over issues of substance and between identifiable personalities (the Ligachev-Yeltsin feud stands out). The message conveyed by the process itself was captured in one laconic phrase buried in the resolutions of the Conference that almost casually reversed fifty years of dogma: "Nobody has a monopoly on the truth."

A full analysis of the significance and impact of the Conference is premature. The Politburo has promised full publication of the stenographic report of the Conference proceedings. A detailed comparison must be made between the Theses approved by the Central Committee and the resolutions passed at the Conference itself. In time, hopefully, we will learn what went on behind closed doors in the days and months preceding the Conference and how the issues were hammered out in the meetings of the committees entrusted with drawing up the resolutions. According to Tass, six resolutions were passed at a concluding session that was "unusually long and stormy," and by less than unanimous votes. Some resolutions reported out of committee were not approved. All of this is very heady stuff, and only first-hand accounts in sufficient number to allow cross-verification will provide the evidence for a real history of the June Conference.

My own first, tentative impression of the Conference (unadulterated by the views of professional analysts, which have not yet reached me) is that it was a brilliantly averted near-disaster for Gorbachev, similar to, but on a far greater scale than, the Rust affair, the Yeltsin affair, and the Andreyeva letter. He calmly assessed a situation developing in a dangerous direction, and then deftly responded. At least a month before the Conference began, his advisers announced that there would be no turnover of the Central Committee, for such changes could take place only at party congresses (no mention was made of the debate in party circles about which rules applied to conferences and the argument made by reformists that the 1939 rules—allowing such turnover—had been defeated). In this manner he avoided ignominious defeat at the session itself.

The delegate selection process itself served as a trial run in the electoral process, giving all involved experience and insight into the flaws and possibilities of the process, firmly identifying supporters and opponents of perestroika, and establishing the rudiments of local coalitions for political action in the future. But the results of the elections were catastrophic, producing an assembly of delegates whose interests and privileges Gorbachev was threatening to take away and a public whose expectations had been elevated beyond all reasonable measure by the Great Debate leading up to the Conference (as well as enraged, in places as far apart as Estonia and Sakhalin, by the strong-armed tactics of the local party organizations).

So, at the Conference Gorbachev acted as he has in the past (consider the Yeltsin affair) by allowing his more radical supporters to speak (in this case, Leonid Abalkin) and then loudly and decisively rejecting their positions. Bowing to the center, Gorbachev gratified those functionaries fearful of losing all, and as debate and criticism threatened to spill out of control, he brought the meetings to a close (53 of 274 delegates who had requested the podium had been able to speak). At this point, as I see it, the delegates gratefully voted through the six resolutions, which, in fact, mark a ringing endorsement—a consolidation if not a furthering—of the basic proposals of glasnost, perestroika, and democratization.

For example, the resolutions affirmed the inalienable rights to freedom of information, privacy, self-expression, and the dignity of the individual and asserted that there could be no perestroika without glasnost (which should be guaranteed by new laws). The resolutions insisted on the need to deepen democratization, beginning with the party, by opening up discussions, establishing firm control by the "elected organs" over the bureaucratic apparatus, and reducing the size of that apparatus. Gorbachev won approval of measures calling for multiple-delegate slates in all elections, for a fixed term of service (ten years), and for revitalization of the soviets "from top to bottom." Embodied in the resolutions was also his plan to separate governmental and party institutions (thereby ending the notorious *podmena*), to establish a bicameral legislative Supreme Soviet (including delegates from cooperatives and unofficial public organizations), which would be in virtually permanent session (at present the legislative organs meet for one week every year to rubber stamp proposals) and would be invested with genuine legislative, executive, and "control" functions. This Soviet will elect a president by secret ballot. The resolutions mandate an end to the system of nomenklatura appointments and declare that "the Conference regards as an important aspect of reform of the political system the decentralization of administration, and a redistribution of functions and authority that will guarantee maximum local initiative and independence." (Other resolutions dealing with minority relations, the economy, and legality are discussed below.)[93]

At the same time, the disturbing "ambiguity" of much of the phrasing of the original Theses, pointed out by Tatiana Zaslavskaia,[94] persists in the Conference resolutions. In her opinion, this ambiguity was deliberate and reflects the need for political compromise. But, while answering the question of what the country needs, the resolutions leave largely unsettled *how* to get there. As the participants in the Second Novosibirsk Seminar concluded this spring:

We have clearly defined what has been—a command-based economy, bureaucratic management, and hypercentralism. We have defined what will be—a fundamental transformation of all social relationships, structures, and institutions. We have an idea, finally, of what would put the heart at rest— responsible democracy, socialist pluralism, and a competitive economy geared to the consumer. But how this can be achieved, what the mechanism of transformation is, which social forces will promote these changes and which will hinder them and why—these questions have not been well answered.[95]

A follow-up meeting of the Politburo on July 4 established special commissions entrusted with pursuing the fulfillment of the Conference resolutions. A special Central Committee plenum met in late July; at this plenum Gorbachev spoke about translating the lofty resolutions of the Conference into reality, the stuff of politics: "Time is pressing on us, comrades, and this should be stated bluntly," he reportedly told the assembled delegates. Gorbachev wants competitive election procedures in the selection of party officials to be in place by fall 1988 and the codification of new election procedures for the soviets to be finished by November. His timetable calls for the election of a new national legislature by March and the first assembly of this legislature, the Congress of People's Deputies, to meet a month later. The Central Committee approved a proposal to establish a commission to oversee implementation of the resolutions approved at the June Conference, and named Gorbachev as its head. In addition, it approved three resolutions (not yet published) dealing with reorganization of the party apparatus, party election procedures, and overall implementation of the resolutions of the June Conference.[96] But only time will tell how the Soviet leadership will resolve the many ambiguities embodied in the resolutions: how the right to self-expression will be combined with laws "protecting socialism and the state interests"; how freedom of speech and the written word can exist when the media are owned and operated by the state; how the rights of individuals to press charges against the bureaucracy can be protected; how party and government can be separated in practice; how decentralization can take place without anarchy and in the face of powerful institutions and traditions; and how the security organs (as well as the party) can be forced to obey the law.

Life-or-Death Battle?

One reporter claimed, early in the year, that the power struggle had turned into "a life-or-death battle" and that "the whole Soviet political spectrum [has] polarized into conservative and leftist factions," leaving Gorbachev clinging to an "eroding" center.[97] There can be no denying the strength of resistance to Gorbachev, but is this resistance organized and is it even internally coherent? As

Moscow insiders reported: "Gorbachev supporters take heart from the fact that [during the crisis over the Andreyeva letter] Ligachev and his allies had no coherent plan for forcing a change in the party line or the removal of Gorbachev during the dark March days."[98]

This observation brings us back to the question of the "national agenda," and to the belief, widespread among Western analysts, that a broad consensus exists among the new leadership that the Soviet Union is undergoing a systemic crisis of major dimensions. We must also keep in mind that, as George Kennan argues, it is one thing to grumble and "murmur behind his back" or to sit on one's hands until it becomes clear how things will turn out. But, he continues:

> It would be another thing to overthrow him and face the question of who should succeed him. The other members of the senior bodies of the party . . . find themselves extensively and formally committed to his program by the decisions they have already taken. And there could be no turning back. No one wants to revive . . . the regime of Brezhnev. . . . A successor would find himself in a position in which he could neither advance nor retreat. Nothing could be more dangerous.[99]

But if the opposition does not threaten to topple Gorbachev, what are his chances of pushing through his agenda for reform? He faces a dilemma familiar to Russian rulers: how to mobilize public participation in the implementation of goals set by the center. Thane Gustafson observes that, "Gorbachev is like the puppet-maker who dreams of giving life to his carvings: what will he do when they start to move on their own?"[100] To his credit, the Soviet leader seems genuinely to have accepted the fact that tapping popular energy will of necessity involve a measure of disorder and the airing of the distasteful opinions of others, to the point that some Western correspondents felt that Gorbachev seemed to genuinely relish the banter and give-and-take at the June Conference.

Notes

1. Thane Gustafson and Dawn Mann, "Gorbachev's Next Gamble," *Problems of Communism*, Vol. 36, No. 4 (July-August, 1987): 1.

2. Stephen Cohen, "The Friends and Foes of Change," round-table discussion ("Soviet Change Under Gorbachev: How Significant") at the 19th National Convention of the AAASS, Boston, November, 1987.

3. Timothy Colton, "Gorbachev and the Politics of System Renewal," in Seweryn Bialer and Michael Mandelbaum, eds., *Gorbachev's Russia and American Foreign Policy* (Boulder, Co., 1988): 163.

4. NYT, May 25, 1988.

5. "Gorbachev's Program of Change," in Seweryn Bialer and Michael Mandelbaum, eds., *Gorbachev's Russia and American Foreign Policy* (Boulder, Co., 1988): 232.

6. "Soviet Union: A Civil Society," *Foreign Policy*, No. 70 (Spring, 1988): 27.

7. Ibid., 27.

8. Moshe Lewin, *The Gorbachev Phenomenon* (Berkeley, Ca., 1988): 102.

9. Bialer, "Gorbachev's Program of Change": 233, 249. Bialer makes the intriguing argument that the "Chernenko incident," i.e., the decision to allow an ailing mediocrity to succeed Andropov in this atmosphere of crisis, provoked "anger, disgust and shame" among much of the leadership and the educated public and significantly weakened the position of the Old Guard (Ibid., 245).

10. *Izvestiia*, June 4, 1988.

11. In a recent article in *Argumenty i fakty*, these very areas were listed as predisposed, by socioeconomic conditions, to high levels of property crime: No. 12 (March 19, 1988).

12. For a biographical sketch of Yazov, see Dale R. Herspring, "On Perestroika: Gorbachev, Yazov, and the Military," *Problems of Communism*, Vol. 36, No. 4 (July-August, 1987): 103-106. Yazov is from a Siberian peasant family, was wounded in combat on the Leningrad front in World War II, graduated from Frunze Military Academy (1956) and Voroshilov General Staff Academy (1967), and headed the Central Group of Forces (Czechoslovakia, 1969), the Central Asian Military District (1980), and the Far East Military District (1984). At the time of his appointment he was deputy minister of defense in charge of personnel, his area of special interest.

Herspring calls Yazov a "natural ally" of Gorbachev, but Peter Reddaway and Anders Aslund of the Kennan Institute doubt such an assertion.

13. The ability to name four new members at one sitting was, according to Gustafson and Mann, an "impressive display of his strength" ("Gorbachev's Next Gamble": 3). Others are not convinced that these appointees are Gorbachev loyalists.

14. Timothy Colton, "Gorbachev and the Politics of System Renewal": 163-165.

15. His retirement followed the expulsion in January from the Politburo of D. Kunayev (who may face criminal charges).

16. WP, June 25, 1988.

17. NYT, March 22, 1987. On power politics in the Ukraine, see Mann and Gustafson, "Gorbachev's Next Gamble": 16-18.

18. WP, May 18, 1988.

19. This according to Colton, "Gorbachev and the Politics of System Renewal," in Bialer, *Gorbachev's Russia*: 161.

20. Colton, "Gorbachev and the Politics of System Renewal": 166.

21. Jerry Hough, "Gorbachev Consolidating Power," *Problems of Communism*, Vol. 36, No. 4 (May-June, 1987): 34.

22. Colton, "The Politics of System Renewal": 161-162.

23. CSM, May 29, 1987.

24. Jerry Hough, "Gorbachev Consolidating Power": 30.

25. Colton, "Politics of System Renewal": 161.

26. "Gorbachev's Program of Change": 247.

27. "Gorbachev Consolidating Power": 29-30.

28. Ibid.: 45.

29. Comments by Archie Brown at a Conference on Gorbachev, Meridian House, Washington, D.C., November 1, 1987.

30. This was the opinion of Marc Zlotnik of the CIA as of April 1987 ("Meeting Report," Kennan Institute for Advanced Russian Studies). Dusko Doder notes, however, that Solomentsev and Vorotnikov were brought in by Andropov, and that the former had seen his career blocked by Brezhnev. Dusko Doder, *Shadows and Whispers: Power Politics Inside the Kremlin from Brezhnev to Gorbachev* (New York, 1986) : 201.

31. Sliunkov is a protégé of Premier N. Ryzhkov and an expert in the machine-building industry. Hough argues that he is a "more serious economic reformer than Ryzhkov," and that he played a major role in pushing a radical version of reform at the June plenum ("Gorbachev Consolidating Power": 35).

32. Brown, "Soviet Political Developments and Prospects," *World Policy Journal*, Vol. 4, No. 1 (Winter 1986/1987): 63.

33. "Gorbachev's Gamble," *New York Times Magazine*, July 19, 1987: 41.

34. RL 233/87.

35. Colton, "The Politics of System Renewal": 177.

36. Gustafson and Mann suggest that his greatest strength resides in the Secretariat: "Gorbachev's Next Gamble": 3, 6-10.

37. This, according to Paul Quinn-Judge in the CSM, July 1, 1988.

38. Bill Keller in NYT, January 21, 1988. John Dunlop and Henry S. Rowen also place Yazov and Chief of Staff Sergei Akhromeyev in close alliance with Ligachev: *The National Interest* (Spring, 1988): 23.

39. An argument vigorously argued by Amy Knight writing for Radio Liberty Research Bulletin: "Viktor Chebrikov and the Politics of Perestroika," RL 252/88 (June 22): 1-6.

40. "Gorbachev's Gamble": 41. Dusko Doder also makes a case for revising our image of the role of the KGB in internal politics (*Shadows and Whispers*: 84-90).

41. *Police and Politics in the Soviet Union* (Winchester, Ma., 1988), and the review by Gail Lapidus (*New York Times Book Review*, May 29, 1988).

42. On this, see also RL 198/88 (May 11), "The KGB under Glasnost: Creating a New Image."

43. RL 238/88 (June 5): 2.

44. For a summary, see RL 233/88 (June 1).

45. Robert Clough in the CSM, June 28, 1988.

46. WP, May 17, 1988.

47. Comments by Archie Brown at Meridian House, Washington, D.C., November 1, 1987. See also RL 233/87 (June 26). A discussion of resistance in the Central Committee, of its role in the political process today, and of the Conference, is in Gustafson and Mann, "Gorbachev's Next Gamble": 5-6. On the likelihood that the Conference would be appropriated by conservatives, see BS, January 24, 1988. A very different view on Gorbachev's position in the CC is offered by Hough, "Gorbachev Consolidating Power": 32-33.

48. For comment, see RL 238/88 (June 5); RL 237/88 (June 8); WP, June 29, 1988.

49. Nikolai Shmelev, "Novye trevogi," *Novyi mir*, No. 4 (April, 1988): 161, 163, 165. Other examples of the local power structure hindering perestroika can be found below in Chapters 4 and 5.

50. Colton, "The Politics of System Renewal": 178. See also Zaslavskaia's comments in *Izvestiia*, June 4, 1988, and the intriguing article in *Nedelia*, April 25, 1988: 10-11, arguing that an informal alliance of managers and engineers existed to thwart the reforms at the production site.

51. For a brief discussion, see Marc Raeff, *Understanding Imperial Russia: State and Society in the Old Regime* (New York, 1984).

52. Interview in *Izvestiia*, June 4, 1988.

53. Andrei Nuikin,"Idealy ili interesy?" *Novyi mir*, Nos. 1-2 (January-February, 1988): 190-211; 205-228.

54. This, according to Robert Kaiser (WP, June 12, 1988).

55. On Ligachev's reputation for honesty during his lengthy tenure as party chief in Tomsk, see Doder, *Shadows and Whispers*: 201.

56. "Remembering," *New Yorker*, December 7, 1987: 146-147. For a brief summary of criticism of the "excesses" of glasnost by Ligachev and Chebrikov, especially in the area of literature, see WP, September 29, 1987, and, more recently (by Chebrikov), RL 252/88.

57. Thane Gustafson, "The Crisis of the Soviet System of Power and Mikhail Gorbachev's Political Stratgegy," in Bialer, ed., *Gorbachev's Russia*: 217.

58. Jerry Hough, *Opening Up the Soviet Economy* (Washington, D.C., 1988): 39.

59. Gustafson, "Crisis of the Soviet System of Power": 217.

60. Robert Clough, CSM, June 28, 1988.

61. For a summary of discussion of the role of the party on the eve of the Conference, see WP, June 19, 1988.

62. Dmitri Simes in NYT, July 8, 1988.

63. BS, May 24, 1987.

64. Bialer, "Gorbachev's Program of Change": 257.

65. *In the Age of the Smart Machine: The Future of Work and Power* (New York, 1988).

66. For an earlier argument that resistance to Gorbachev was strong, see CIA specialist Mark Zlotnik's comments in a talk to the Kennan Institute on April 29, 1987 ("Meeting Report," Kennan Institute for Advanced Studies).

67. For a good discussion of the 27th Party Congress, see Robert Tucker, *Political Culture and Leadership in Soviet Russia* (New York, 1987): 151-160; and Vladimir Shlapentokh, "The XXVII Congress—A Case Study of the Shaping of a new Party Ideology," *Soviet Studies*, Vol. 40, No. 1 (January, 1988): 1-20.

68. On this, see Chapter 3 and Dev Murarka, in *The Nation*, October 24 and 31, 1987.

69. WP, September 29, 1987; CSM, September 14, 1987. In the CSM article Paul Quinn-Judge argues unconvincingly that Chebrikov's apparent lack of enthusiasm for perestroika damages the theory that the KGB has been behind economic reform ever since Andropov began to push for change. Quite simply, he identifies the person with the institution.

70. BS, January 24, 1988; CSM, September 28, 1987.

71. On the Yeltsin affair see: WP, Nov 22, 23, 1987; NYT, Nov 23, 1987; and the various articles abstracted in CDSP, Vol. 39, No. 45 (December 9, 1987): 1-4 and No. 46 (December 16, 1987): 7-12.

72. See Timothy Colton, "Moscow Politics and the Yeltsin Affair," *The Harriman Institute Forum*, Vol. 1, No. 6 (June, 1988): 1-8.

73. Seweryn Bialer, *US News and World Report*, March 28, 1988: 30.

74. This, according to Robert Kaiser, in an important article, "How Gorbachev Outfoxed his Rivals," WP, June 12, 1988.

75. Marc Zlotnik of the CIA identifies five overlapping groups in opposition to Gorbachev: those fearful of being exposed for corrupt practices; older members resisting mandatory retirement clauses pushed by Gorbachev; regional party leaders jealous of their patronage; a prodefense faction; and ideological conservatives (Taubman, "Gorbachev's Gamble": 40. Taubman mentions six groups, but lists only five).

76. *Moscow News*, January 10, and *Sovetskaia kultura*, February 4.

77. The most recent discussions of the origins of the Andreyeva letter (or letters—there may have been three of them) are: Giuletto Chiesa, "Secret History of the Anti-Gorbachev Manifesto," *l'Unita*, May 23, 1988; RL 215/88 (May 23) and RL 243/88 (June 5); *Sovetskaia kultura*, May 26, 1988.

78. Dev Murarka, "The Foes of Perestroika Sound Off," *The Nation*, May 23, 1988: 715.

79. "Secret History of the Anti-Gorbachev Manifesto," cited in RL 215/88 (May 23): 2. At the June Conference, Dmitri Ulianov, head of the Theater Union, bitterly recalled this period: "Our hearts ached, but people were rooted to the spot. . . . They knew that it was wrong, and yet they waited, shaking, but patiently and obediently as if doomed."

80. This is the interpretation of Kaiser, "How Gorbachev Outfoxed his Rivals."

81. Dev Murarka, "The Foes of Perestroika Sound Off," *The Nation*, May 23, 1988: 715.

82. Although at least one close observer doubts he had a hand in the Andreyeva letter: "It is hard to believe that Ligachev, a highly intelligent conservative reformer, would be a party to such a crude maneuver" (Murarka, "The Foes of Perestroika Sound Off": 717).

83. As "senior secretary" (full member of the Politburo and member of the Secretariat), Iakovlev was by now equal to Ligachev; in effect, by mid-1987 there were two "chief ideologists." RL 233/87 (June 26).

84. This, according to Antero Pietila (BS, January 24, 1988).

85. CSM, August 15, 1988.

86. Elizabeth Teague and Viktor Yasmann, "Gorbachev Strikes a Conciliatory Note," RL 202/88 (May 11). Teague feels that Gorbachev may recognize that the party is evenly split between opponents and supporters and that a victory over Ligachev at this time would be hollow, since he would take with him half of the party into opposition.

87. According to one interpretation, in a Politburo meeting of April 28 "organizational matters" were discussed, transferring responsibility for preparations for the Conference from Ligachev to close Gorbachev ally

Razumovsky (see Elizabeth Teague, "Conference Preparations Run Into Trouble," RL 194/88 (May 7). This article also contains a brief discussion of the confusion over procedures for selecting delegates.

88. See, for example, CDSP, Vol. 40, No. 23 (July 6, 1988): 7-9 (translation of an article in *Komsomolskaia pravda* [June 7, 1988]: 1).

89. WP, May 27, 1988. The Theses were published in *Pravda*, May 27: 1-3 and *Izvestiia*, May 27: 1-2. The full text in translation is in CDSP, Vol. 40, No. 21 (June 22): 1-10.

90. Zaslavskaia, interviewed by *Izvestiia*, June 4, 1988; NYT, June 8, 1988.

91. Cited in NYT, June 8, 1988; for another summary, see WP, the same day.

92. *Izvestiia*, June 5, 1988, as reported in the NYT, June 9, 1988.

93. This summary is drawn from *Pravda*, July 5, 1988.

94. *Izvestiia*, June 4, 1988.

95. *Nedelia*, No. 18, 1988.

96. This summary of the July plenum follows closely the report in NYT, July 30, 1988.

97. Antero Pietila, BS, January 24, 1988.

98. Kaiser, "How Gorbachev Outfoxed His Rivals," WP, June 12, 1988.

99. "The Gorbachev Prospect," *New York Review of Books* (January 21, 1988): 7.

100. "Crisis of the Soviet System of Power": 217.

3
Glasnost

Society Has Learned to Talk to Itself

Returning to the Soviet Union this year, emigré Alex Goldfarb observed: "Remarkably, most of the people I met in Moscow were not afraid to speak their minds in terms unthinkable 12 years ago."[1] But, he added, glasnost has "created more problems than it has resolved," and "the consensus about glasnost was angst rather than optimism." In the first half of 1988, criticism of virtually all aspects of Soviet society became even more strident and taboos were lifted on more and more subjects, leaving only a handful of topics out of bounds.

Glasnost has moved in overlapping phases and has dealt with a range of issues: from attacking shortcomings in society and defusing rumors to a reexamination of history ("restoring some of history's ambiguity," as one journalist put it) and a limited competition of ideas; from criticism of the past to "a political debate over the future of the Soviet system." The cultural program of the reformists includes "encouragement of a broad spectrum of opinions, a defense of the individual's rights to express these opinions and a willingness to address a wider array of social problems" than previously tolerated.[2]

At the same time, by most accounts, movement has not been uninterrupted, nor has it been unilinear. Some analysts see a period of steep reformism or "heady liberalism" from roughly May 1986 to September 1987; a conservative backlash between October 1987 and April 1988; and a renewed reformist offensive from April 1988 to the present (the signposts for these changes are each discussed individually elsewhere in this text). On the eve of the June Conference, an unprecedented "freewheeling referendum on the future of the country" was under way, producing a "cornucopia of heresies"[3] and a furious, virtually uncensored debate unimaginable two years ago and tumultuous even by the standards of the era of glasnost.

A vexing issue, already on the agenda, is "the debate over who will control the debate."[4] A new press law, being drafted by the Supreme Soviet and initially scheduled to be published in 1986, is still under consideration. The objective of the law is to set guidelines on such topics as the right to receive and spread information, censorship, and procedures governing publication of critical material, distribution of foreign periodicals, and the status of journalists and foreign correspondents.[5] The long delay in the appearance of this law suggests the real difficulties the authorities are having formulating principles that would allow society to communicate with itself while simultaneously allowing the party to retain ultimate control.

According to most recent reports, a draft of a new law on glasnost will be readied for public discussion late in 1988. Apparently three variants of a law had been proposed by Moscow think tanks: (1) no specific law on glasnost, but amendments of existing legislation to ensure openness in public life; (2) a law defining and delineating glasnost; or (3) a law on secrecy. Many thought the third version was the most democratic: "We would only have to list what was forbidden, and everything else would be allowed." But the second variant prevailed, according to legal expert Iuri Baturin, "because we bore in mind the lack of a sense of legality among the people, and because of the necessity of overcoming resistance to glasnost mounted by those who dislike it and who see it as a threat to their positions."[6]

William Pfaff has asserted, "Behind all the practical issues which concern Mr. Gorbachev . . . there lies the fundamental question of the individual's relationship to the Soviet state. . . . What Mikhail Gorbachev has done is to raise the possibility of a national life that does not rest upon lies and cynicism."[7] Gorbachev clearly realizes that economic difficulties are inseparable from political issues, from what Colton has called the "crisis of coherence" in the system. Others, including Ligachev, see a deep moral crisis, the erosion of an ethical basis for principled public behavior.[8] In his celebrated article, Shmelev went one step further, decrying:

> rampant apathy, indifference, theft and lack of respect for honest work.
> . . . There are signs of an almost physical degradation of the Soviet people
> as a result of drunkenness and sloth. And finally, there is distrust of
> announced goals and intentions, and skepticism about the possibility of
> organizing economic and social life in a more sensible fashion.[9]

If Shmelev exposed the ills besetting Soviet society, a long letter, prominently featured in *Pravda* on May 2, 1988, elaborated even further upon these ills and pointed the finger squarely at the Communist party and its leadership. The letter's author, V. Selivanov, rued the degeneration of Soviet society in terms of moral values and work ethic and argued that corruption, alienation, and dishonesty were so widespread that honesty or conscientiousness actually invited hostility and retribution from others. At the heart of the problem is the overcentralized and authoritarian Soviet political and economic system that emerged in the late 1920s. The Communist party, in charge of this system, has been overrun by time-servers, self-promoters, and cynical riffraff, while honest and dedicated people have steered clear of it. The party has encouraged the proliferation of administrative supervisory posts at the expense of truly productive occupations. Lack of democracy has brought the country to the brink of ruin; not only Stalin, but Khrushchev and Brezhnev as well share the blame for the suppression of democracy.[10] This criticism of the party (rather than of individual members only), itself a milestone, received what appears to be an endorsement in *Pravda* June 7.[11]

Gorbachev seems to be reaching for a form of pluralism that would retain the one-party state but stimulate genuine civic participation. This goal is not necessarily a contradiction in terms, but it will, as Robert Tucker has pointed out, require "a necessary and useful disjunction between, on the one hand, loyalty to the state and, on the other hand, agreement with the policies of a particular government in power or acceptance of that government as a desirable one for the nation."[12] It means an end to the "double morality," "divided consciousness" or "cross-talk" so characteristic of Soviet political culture, of what Reddaway calls "traditional communist triumphalism."[13]

Straight talk is not only a matter of political morality; it is at the heart of restoring coherence in communications. On the one hand, people must begin to believe what they are told; on the other hand, the rulers need unimpeded responses from below. Noise has drowned out information or meaning: "The crux of the matter is the impoverishment and segmentation of communication by means of secrecy, compartmentalization, oversimplification, and sometimes [often!] lies."[14] Or, in the vivid words of one Soviet writer, "Soviet life is entangled in a web of magical silences and uncodified taboos more nettling than those in any primitive society."[15]

Behind all of the concern for openness lies the simple fact that the public had instituted its own version of glasnost before Gorbachev came to power. In the 1970s the leadership vigorously suppressed such "horizontal technologies" as the intercity telegraph, private telephones, xerox machines, and personal computers—all at substantial cost to the advancement of science. But despite extensive controls over the dissemination of information and labored attempts to maintain "top-down vertical systems of communications," the Soviet public learned to "routinely evade" such controls through cassette-tape recorders, videocassette recorders, and other devices of "techtronic glasnost." To paraphrase one specialist, society has learned to talk to itself.[16] Because of the "greater porousness of Soviet frontiers to information from the global environment," the Soviet leaders really have no viable choice but to devise a form of communication and political interaction that will allow multiple voices to be heard, however this network is institutionalized. This is what glasnost is all about: The Soviet leadership is bowing to reality and has realized the preposterous nature of attempts both to suppress information and to make scientific and technological progress the cornerstone of economic progress.

We Need Only One Glasnost

At the end of August 1987, a number of unofficial organizations held a conference in Moscow, bringing together more than 300 representatives of forty-seven clubs and societies to discuss social questions.[17] Soviet newspapers have admitted that such groups appeared as many as twenty years ago and that they now number in the thousands and "are growing as fast as mushrooms in the rain." Not all are political: Amateur musical ensembles, numbering more than 100,000, are the most widespread, but there are also punks, vigilantes, pacifists, environmentalists, and computer clubs, all demonstrating various levels of organization and structure and degrees of sophistication.[18] In October, representatives of seventeen unofficial publications met in Leningrad to try to form cooperatives recognized by the state. They hoped to gain access to printshops and to publish a journal of journals that would include selections from the various publications.[19]

Unofficial (called "informal") groups are now being studied by a special commission of the Central Committee.[20] Perhaps the most troublesome informal organization has been Pamiat (Memory), composed of Russian nationalists advocating protection of the environment and of historical monuments; they have also been accused of extreme Russian nationalism, and anti-Semitism. The group poses a problem for reformers, who find Pamiat's views repugnant and dangerous but believe in promoting freedom of expression. In May Pamiat staged two demonstrations in Moscow and met with then city boss Yeltsin.

In November the Communist Youth League (Komsomol) drafted a proposal to gain control over independent groups by bringing them into the Komsomol network and "eliminating ugly phenomena . . . alien to the Socialist way of life." The official youth organization has been sharply criticized in the press and by an internal report for being "overly bureaucratic, self-important, and intolerant of unorthodox opinions" and has been involved in ugly clashes with independent groups.[21] In early February 1988, *Komsomolskaia pravda* printed an attack on several organizers of independent groups. The article, representing the views of the Komsomol central committee, could serve as a signal to local authorities to begin cracking down on independent groups. But some members of independent groups are also Komsomol members and express the opinion that the youth league is not uniformly reactionary and that a cooperative relationship could provide a legal shield and offer access to printing presses. The Komsomol is now internally riven by disagreement and plagued by declining enrollments (down to 38 million, a decline of about 4 million since 1985: The proportion of all youth ages 14-15 choosing to join has dropped by a quarter), indifference, and even hostility among youth. That the new head of the Komsomol, Viktor Mironenko, is apparently having difficulty convincing his own son Dima to join is not an encouraging sign to party leaders.[22] In the future the role of the Komsomol will be crucial in determining just how the linkage between society and party takes shape. It might be argued that how the Komsomol goes, so will go glasnost.[23]

At any rate, the response to the establishment of unofficial journals[24] shows that pluralistic notions will meet strong opposition. One writer argued in a Moscow newspaper that once glasnost was perfected, there would be no need for an unofficial press; everything anyone needed to know would be printed, and "we need only one glasnost."[25] In addition, as events gathered steam and groups became increasingly vociferous in articulating grievances and demands, the police began to crack down; they prevented a public gathering against anti-Semitism, dispersing a much publicized demonstration by Latvians in Riga in commemoration of freedom day, and harassed an independent seminar on human rights in Moscow. In the early summer of 1988, a group declaring itself a new political party ran into stiff repression from the police. In May 1988, Soviet police confiscated printing equipment and destroyed the files of the independent magazine *Glasnost*, then arrested its editor, Sergei Grigoriants (he was held for seven days on charges of "malicious disobedience to a police officer").[26] Analysts of Soviet culture Nancy Condee and V. Padunov believe that since late 1987 a powerful movement has been under way to absorb (through legitimation or through expulsion) the major thrusts of cultural glasnost into existing or newly created institutions.[27]

Without Glasnost There Can Be No Perestroika

The June Conference reaffirmed the centrality of glasnost to the goals of perestroika. The following is a paraphrase of key passages in the resolution on glasnost.

The first three years, the resolution asserts, have convincingly demonstrated that glasnost in party, soviet, and public organizations has promoted a better understanding of both past and present, shed light on the "braking factors" of perestroika, and awakened powerful patriotic forces, activism, and purposeful striving for the good of the country and socialism.

Glasnost is an evolving process, and a consistent expansion of glasnost is a necessary condition of the democratic essence of a socialist order. Glasnost is vital to ensure the "irreversibility" of perestroika.

Much information still remains inaccessible to the public, and here and there can be found attempts to restrict glasnost in party, soviet, and public activities by the construction of bureaucratic barriers. Resistance to attempts to reveal shortcomings, abuses, bureaucratism, and examples of heavy-handed behavior by communists (*komchvanstvo*) persists. The number of letters complaining about such activities is not diminishing. Even now, there are instances of persecution and reprisals for criticism. . . . Glasnost sometimes gives way, too, to slander and personal libel.

The party and people need to know the full, objective truth in order to make informed judgments and decisions. The party must wholeheartedly support the basic principle of glasnost, that there is "an inalienable right of every citizen to receive full and reliable information on any subject of public life not falling under the category of a state or military secret . . . the right to open and full discussion of any socially significant issue." The party should itself be a model of glasnost in its own proceedings. . . . Its existing regulations should be modified accordingly.

Glasnost should also govern the activities of enterprise managers, kolkhoz chairmen, leaders of cooperatives, the Komsomol, trade unions. . . . Workers should be informed of the decision-making processes on issues pertaining to work and public life.

Glasnost applies to the law enforcement agencies and to crime statistics. Unjustified limitations upon access to statistical information on socioeconomic, environmental, and political issues should be lifted, as upon access to all library collections.

Glasnost does not permit restraints upon critical forays by the press, but does not include publication of unobjective information "impinging upon the honor or dignity of the individual." Glasnost predicates the social, legal, and moral responsibility of the media in its conduct . . . and does not allow the appearance of demogogy, national, regional, or corporate egoism or of insidious groupings (*gruppovshchina*). All sides in an argument must be fairly reflected, without distortions. Nobody has a monopoly on the truth (and there should be no monopoly over glasnost).

Legal guarantees should be provided, including the constitutional right to access to information . . . precisely defining the limits of necessary secrecy and providing penalties both for illegal publication of secret data and for withholding data (not officially categorized secrets).

Glasnost cannot be used in manners detrimental to the Soviet state, society, individual rights, or to propagate war, violence, racism, religious or national intolerance, to propagate sadism or pornography, or to "manipulate" glasnost itself.

Without glasnost, there can be no perestroika.

Everyone Wants Less Boring TV

A process of literary relaxation has been under way for some time now. Julian Graffy has identified four areas of liberalization: (1) bold new Soviet writing; (2) works by living Soviet writers previously unpublishable at home; (3) works by great Soviet writers of the early twentieth century never previously published in the USSR; and (4) works by living emigrés.[28] The year 1987 was labeled "the richest in the entire history of Russian literature,"[29] partly because of the outpouring of works resulting from the lifting of a sixty-year ban and publication of many works already completed before the Gorbachev period. According to Paul Quinn-Judge of the *Christian Science Monitor*, Gorbachev's "[term] in power has produced one lasting achievement: a literary and cultural revival that many Soviet observers feel has no precedent in the last 60 years of Soviet rule."[30]

The leading force in this revival has been the major literary journals and, among them, *Novyi mir, Znamia, Ogonek, Druzhba narodov*, and *Iunost*, which have published long-suppressed works by Mikhail Bulgakov, Andrei Platonov, Anna Akhmatova, Marina Tsvetaeva, and Nikolai Gumilev. The public has seen praise of, publication, or exhibition of the works of emigrés such as Marc Chagall, Joseph Brodsky, and Vladimir Nabokov. Probably the greatest sensation was caused by the release of Anatoly Rybakov's *Children of the Arbat*. And in 1988 Evgeny Zamiatin's classic (1921) anti-utopian novel, *We*, appeared for the first time in the Soviet Union, as did George Orwell's *Animal Farm* and *1984*, Franz Kafka's *The Castle*, and Arthur Koestler's *Darkness at Noon* (which has already influenced discussion this year of Stalin's purges). Readers also were treated to Boris Pasternak's *Dr. Zhivago*, in serial form, and Vasily Grossman's novel on World War II, *Life and Fate*, which graphically portrays life in the camps and draws explicit comparisons between Nazism and Stalinism.[31] Zalygin reported at a press conference in mid-1988 that he was negotiating with Alexander Solzhenitsyn (who, amazingly, has been invited to visit the USSR) to publish *Cancer Ward* or *First Circle*. Helsinki Watch, a human rights group, calculates that its list of writers jailed, exiled, or forbidden to publish in the USSR had been reduced by two-thirds in 1987, and surely more by now.[32] One disturbing aspect of literary output in the past three years, however, has been the sparseness of new names; no major new talents have yet emerged.[33] The literature of glasnost has been dominated by publication of long-suppressed Tolstoyan blockbusters, and has witnessed the revitalization of a venerated genre, now called *novaia publitsistika*, or the new publististic prose). Soviet writers have returned to the hallowed question: What is to be done, with little concern how to say it.[34]

The Soviet press publishes some 80,000 titles each year, but "availability of books is generally in inverse proportion to demand," for the state has been more concerned with spreading ideology and education (including technology) than with publishing popular novels. The result has been "an extremely critical book famine from Moscow to the farthest ends of the country," namely, extreme shortages and a brisk black market in the classics of Russian literature, less favored Soviet writers, and even potboilers meant to entertain.[35] But public tastes should now be taken into account; on January 1, 1988, Goskomizdat (the state publishing and printing agency) was scheduled to go on self-financing and to be responsible for up to 50 percent of its losses.[36]

Television has already made changes:[37] As Archie Brown dryly commented, "Resistance to glasnost may be fierce, but everybody wants less boring TV." Viewers now watch documentaries on sensitive topics; reporting of disasters; excellent, formerly suppressed movies; and more American and European programs.[38] Television coverage of the United States, though still distorted, now includes more positive references to life in America.[39] For the Soviet audience, television has become a major source of information and insight on public concerns as well as on official views. Condee and Padunov identify television as the ideal medium for "cautious, graduated reform" in the "liberal spirit" of Gorbachev's approach (diversity of opinion, individual expression of opinion, breadth of permissible topics). It has no emigré tradition, provides maximum access to the consumer or viewer but highly controlled access from the would-be producer, and has "sophisticated editing and censoring capabilities inaccessible to the amateur." Thus, "it is paradoxically the most tightly controlled arena of culture—television—that remains the most active in broaching controversial topics and lobbying for liberal reform."[40]

In May 1988, Tass quietly announced that henceforth Soviet citizens would be able to buy a number of Western publications at their local kiosks.[41] If these publications, including the *International Herald Tribune, Newsweek, The Economist*, and *The (London) Times*, do actually become widely available, this will mark a decisive step in the Soviet Union's entry into the international community. It will increase the already considerable pressure upon Soviet editors to render their newspapers more lively and pertinent or suffer declining subscriptions (as has *Pravda* recently). This step will be both emblematic and supportive of the growing pluralism of Soviet culture (if not politics).

As for foreign broadcasts, jamming (a practice used since 1948) has, since 1980, been restricted to transmissions into Eastern Europe of Radio Liberty and Radio Free Europe, leaving BBC, Voice of America, and Deutsche Welle transmissions virtually unimpeded. But there is no indication that the Soviet Union has dismantled its technical capacity to jam, and earlier "reprieves" followed by renewed jamming should make us cautious about Soviet intentions in the long-run. To this date, the official Soviet position distinguishes between "propaganda" and information and reserves the right to interfere with the former. Moreover, since the Reykjavik summit, the Soviets have complained that they are in an "unequal situation," surrounded by transmitters broadcasting into the USSR but with no opportunity to institute medium-wave transmissions into the United States. Until "reciprocity" and "equity" are established, this argument runs, interference with Western broadcasts are fully justified.[42]

In a Thaw Even the Dung Melts

Gorbachev retains the firm support of most Soviet intellectuals. Prominent supporters from this group are the *shestidesiatniki*, or "men of the sixties," who were active during the Khrushchev thaw.[43] A listing of the most prominent and active proponents of reform would include Iakovlev; editors Ivan Frolov, Vitaly Korotich, and Sergei Zalygin; journalist Fedor Burlatsky; economists Nikolai Shmelev, Leonid Abalkin, Abel Aganbegyan, Gavril Popov, and Oleg Bogomolov; sociologist Tatiana Zaslavskaia;[44] and historian Iuri Afanasiev.[45]

But some conservative writers, including Valentin Rasputin, probably Russia's most popular author today, have expressed doubts about perestroika, and many within the hierarchy of the Writers' Union and other institutions clearly feel threatened by glasnost.[46] One conservative, writing in *Pravda*, called posthumous publication of the works of persecuted or neglected Soviet writers "necrophilia."[47] Although cinematography and theater have won major battles against censorship, "in literature . . . attempts at restructuring are facing stubborn and organized opposition both in the higher academic echelons and among the leadership of the USSR Union of Writers."[48]

Peter Reddaway describes a remarkable article by Iuri Bondarev, who has been targeted as a symbol of the stifling mediocrity of the "period of *zastoi*." In this article, Bondarev attacked the "false democrats of literature" who had "laid siege" to Russian literature and, like the Nazi invaders of 1941 (!!) forced it to retreat to avoid total destruction. He called for an end to the retreat, a new Stalingrad, to save the nation's values.[49] But at the turbulent 1986 Eighth Congress of the USSR Writers' Union, Bondarev made an eloquent plea for environmental protection and blasted Stalinist "bearers of bureaucratic culture."[50] Bondarev's Stalingrad metaphor is striking because it supports polls cited concerning the continuing influence of the age group 60-75 on Soviet thinking and highlights the military cast of mind of this group. Bondarev's views are also noteworthy because they remind us that supporters of one issue (conservation) are not necessarily advocates of reform on all counts (say, pluralism). Finally, the political disadvantage of a full-scale assault on a period (the *zastoi* of Brezhnevism) is that by necessity it turns *all* who prospered in that period into opponents of reform.

Condee and Padunov claim that we in the West have erred in equating "turbulence along the entire cultural front" as necessarily implying gains for perestroika, in "seeing . . . rapid developments *ipso facto* as radical reforms." They believe that Westerners have underestimated the force of "conflicting strains of cultural perestroika" that run counter to, or are unconcerned with, the basic cultural platform of the Gorbachevtsy. Among these conflicting cultural strains are the exploding youth culture, avant-garde art, and the "much larger group" of *russisty*, or russophiles.

Taken aback by the emergence of virulently nativistic currents, Moscow wits comfort themselves with the folk saying: "In a thaw, even the dung melts."

Russophilism includes, but is not limited to, the Pamiat movement, and involves "a broad base celebration of all things Russian . . . a categorical rejection of both Western and Soviet multinational cultures, along with modernism in general." According to Condee and Padunov, the russophiles offer the only cohesive philosophical and political alternative to the Gorbachevtsy, and the *russisty* are now engaged in a major struggle with the supporters of Gorbachev for control of key editorial boards, artistic unions, and research centers. Condee and Padunov believe that a number of major journals remain "strongholds of conservative values" and even that the conservatives are "consolidating their control over the cultural process."

At the same time, they see that the "centripetal nature" of cultural reform since the 27th Party Congress is now "weakening"; that jockeying for position within the cultural establishment is now usurping the energy of the reform movement; that a new "artistic mafia" is now becoming entrenched in the bureaucratic apparatus; and that since late 1987 (beginning with the decision of the Council of Ministers on October 23 to prohibit individual or cooperative independent publishing ventures), a broader tendency has emerged "to redirect cultural reform away from private initiatives . . . and back into existing cultural institutions" (whether the initiatives be in publishing, politics, rock music, or religion, and whether the existing institutions be connected with the Writers' Union, the Komsomol, or the new RSFSR Council on Religious Affairs).

This analysis adds nuance to our often simplistic understanding of the process of Soviet culture and points to ominous aspects of this process. It remains to be seen, however, whether their suggestion that the major trend today is a conservative one (if only because the *russisty* are more united in belief than their more disparate opponents) will prove accurate. In reality, as the authors themselves have noted, while correctly stressing the diversity of the "liberal" camp, they may have overstated the degree of cohesion among those in the conservative movement. But their description of the cultural field as a contested one is surely correct.

Acts of Lawlessness, Enormous and Unforgivable

The past itself has become a major battleground, for a major issue of glasnost has been a truthful retelling of history. A disproportionate number of recent literary works have addressed this concern. As one observer put it: "Usually nations wrestle with their present for the sake of the future. . . . [Here] the struggle is between the past and the future."[51] The hunger for historical truth in general is evident in the sight of people sitting in the aisles to watch the film *Repentance* (an uncompromising attack on Stalin) at local theaters. In addition, early in January the editors of the humdrum magazine *Moskva*[52] announced they could accept no more subscriptions in 1988; they had been inundated with requests after announcing they would serialize the entire corpus of the Tsarist historian Nikolai Karamzin's famous *History of the Russian State*. (In October 1987, a publishing house also announced plans to publish the twelve-volume work.)

Karamzin is not the only Tsarist historian to retain popularity. Russia's two greatest historians, Sergei Soloviev and Vasily Kliuchevsky, have long been *defitsitnye*, that is, their collected works have sold for huge prices on the black market. Last year the State Publishing Committee announced that the collected works of these two authors would be reissued, in print runs of 100,000 (Soloviev's history runs to twenty-nine volumes). A flood of letters to the newspapers forced the publisher to promise another 100,000 to 150,000 copies. Plans for the publication of Karamzin's work have also been altered to increase the print run from 490,000 to over 600,000 copies. Letters to the editor cite Tsarist historians for providing a genuine canvas of the historical past, free of omissions and distortion.

William Pfaff writes that "the vital element of . . . glasnost . . . is an attempt to bring the underground knowledge that Soviet society possesses of its past into public view and . . . by recognizing the validity of individual memories . . . reinforce the government of Mikhail Gorbachev.[53] Pfaff claims that popular memories of collectivization are still vivid ("any peasant will show you the graves"), and that unpublished works have nevertheless found their way to readers, proving that earlier beliefs in the effectiveness of Soviet totalitarianism in erasing the historical memory are invalid.

I too recall visiting friends in the Ukrainian countryside, and they showed me the sites of peasant cottages destroyed during collectivization. In the Baltic, the memories are even more precise and vivid. But Pfaff is probably too optimistic about Soviet memory as a whole. In September 1985 Iuri Afanasiev wrote an article in *Kommunist* ("The Past and Ourselves") lamenting the pervasive amnesia that was destroying both the "individual personality" and a social consciousness. Dev Murarka argues that:

> One peculiar and highly negative effect produced by official historiography has been that the younger generation does not even know who the truly evil men were in Soviet history, and why they are so regarded. Many young people were unmoved by Tengiz Abuladze's anti-Stalin film *Repentance*, for example, because they did not know anything about Lavrenti Beria or his even more infamous predecessor as head of what became the KGB, Nikolai Yezhov."[54]

Still, the new fascination with history is not entirely new. In 1983 Katerina Clark pointed to "an overriding concern with memory" in Soviet literature, both in autobiographical excursions and as "a means for exploring the traditions and national identity of the author's own people." Clark observed that "such writers have often included historical material that Soviet historians have not been able to touch. And of course the theme of memory has been used by many as an occasion for a new look at the evils of Stalinism."[55] But the role played by literature (rather than academic history) in this process bears noting; as critic Natalia Ivanova wrote: "Today literature is shaping the history of society at its own risk, running ahead of the scholars. It is emancipating the mythological consciousness."[56]

A few Soviet historians have become very popular, even achieving something approaching celebrity status. One is Valentin Pikul, whose work *Favorit* on the lovers of Catherine the Great is extraordinarily popular.[57] This suggests that the popular interest in Soloviev and Kliuchevsky is not only a matter of historical honesty and hints at why the public turns to literature to recover its past. Soviet history textbooks rigidly ignore discussions of the role of the individual in history (except, of course, Lenin); thus, biography, easily the most popular genre of historical writing in the West, is studiously avoided. In addition, the prose style of Soviet historical writing is generally atrocious, while Kliuchevsky was a superb writer.

If the interest in the past is not entirely new, what is new is that "Gorbachev and the Politburo seem to have accepted . . . that the Soviet system must recover its memory as one important aid to reckoning with its problems."[58] The interpretation of the Soviet past, and particularly of Stalin, remains the single most vociferously debated issue; how it is resolved will help determine how people feel about the Communist party, about the institutions around them, about how they organize their lives (and, in the case of the elderly, about how they spent their lives).[59]

William Pfaff argues provocatively that Americans, who treat history as "bunk," have difficulty understanding the recent Soviet preoccupation with their past. He believes that, paradoxically, we share with the USSR a belief in "inevitability" and a conviction of a special Providence, but that we differ in that "at least we do not claim infallibility." According to Pfaff, this has made the issue of historical truth one of enormous consequence for Gorbachev (and, he might have added, for the party):

> Public policy in the Soviet Union has suppressed the truth about decisive episodes of Soviet history. The nation continues to be governed by people who find no alternative to resting their claims to legitimacy upon their continuity with this past, about which everyone has for years lied, yet about which everyone knows the truth—or a part of the truth, or enough of the truth to recognize the extent to which the present rests upon a construction of deliberate and desperate lies about the past. . . . An honest account not only of the colossal injustices and crimes of Soviet history but of the unforgivable inefficiency and waste with which Soviet affairs have been conducted since 1917 inevitably poses a question about the Revolution itself.

Pfaff argues that on the eve of World War I Russia was an evolving, dynamic society experiencing movement toward reform and that "without the World War (and Revolution) it is at least imaginable that Russia today might possess political institutions more or less resembling those of modern Europe. . . . It might have arrived late, but . . . it would have arrived. . . . The Soviet record since 1917 has in crucial respects been one of regression . . . but if this is so, what justifies the ordeal that Communist authority has put the country through?" He concludes:

> [Gorbachev's] society, like any other, needs to connect with its past in order to deal with its present: to make moral sense of the past in order to possess moral confidence in itself and in its future. What is now going on in the Soviet Union is an affair of consequence because it is happening in a nation that more than any other has committed itself to the future, justifying everything by what it is supposed to become, and by what it triumphantly claims to have left behind. The discovery that nothing is left behind until the truth about it has been told is a radically unsettling fact, implying, as it does, that the truth about the future remains unknown.[60]

In the light of my comments about Soviet historical writing, I am abashed to cite at length someone who is not a professional historian to summarize the significance of the concern for history of both party and people! That Russia, undisturbed by revolution, would have evolved in the direction taken by modern Europe (only a few steps behind) is debatable, as is the "dynamism" of the Tsarist order. But Pfaff has aptly and vividly touched upon the issues of concern to all: the legitimacy of the party, the justification for the enormous sufferings imposed upon the people, the teleology of the Revolution, and the still untouchable issue of "regression" (from the conditions of pre-1917). The brief summary below does scant justice to the topic, for the veritable explosion of revelations in 1988 has made it impossible to keep up.[61]

Before 1987 Gorbachev generally treated historical topics gingerly, probably because he believed that they were peripheral to the matters at hand, that is, "reboosting" an essentially sound system, but also out of a fear that reexamining the past could deflect vital energies and engender unnecessary divisions. But as Gorbachev has come to view politics and economics, perestroika and glasnost, as inseparable, so has he turned to the Soviet past.[62]

On March 13, 1987, a top ideological adviser, Georgy Smirnov, argued in *Pravda* that the current malfunctioning of the system had roots in the October 1964 plenum, which removed Khrushchev and ended the modest democratization and decentralization initiated at the 20th Party Congress (1956).[63] Stalin's competence as a war leader again surfaced as a major issue and in April, a debate occurred on the pages of *Literaturnaia Gazeta* over the interpretation of collectivization.[64]

As Dev Murarka argues, "the leadership was moving toward a new and deeper phase of de-Stalinization," encompassing the economic and the spiritual as well as the political. Although the 20th Party Congress initiated the denunciation of the Stalinist personality cult, "a selective denunciation of his misdeeds was no longer enough," and a rewriting of the basic script of Soviet history was under way. According to this revised script, not only did the Brezhnev period suffer from general stagnation (compared sometimes to the reign of Nicholas I, 1825-1855, with the country slipping far behind the West in military and industrial might, but the entire system created by Stalin from 1929 has also come under critical scrutiny. Stalin's leadership in World War II has once again become an issue, especially in the recurring demand that Soviet casualties be more carefully studied in order to understand why so many people died. Even more dangerous has been the call for publication and open discussion of the secret clauses to the Nazi-Soviet Pact of 1939 (by which Poland was divided and the Baltic states annexed). Thus, from criticizing the man and some of his policies, anti-Stalinism has come recently to signify an attack on the entire order he created as antisocialist, degenerate, and even a coup against the Revolution of 1917.

The resurrection of NEP (New Economic Policy, 1921-1929), championed, among others, by Fedor Burlatsky, Andrei Nuikin, and Vasily Seliunin,[65] represents an attempt to legitimate antibureaucratic, proconsumer, and promarket policies and to restore the notion of a party encouraging political and cultural pluralism (if not a multiparty state). It is, at core, a frontal attack against the Stalinist model.[66] As Stephen Cohen commented: "Anti-Stalinism is an essential part of Gorbachev's program. Perestroika is an effort to dismantle the system created in the thirties. Bukharin was the real defender of NEP. That's why Bukharin keeps forcing himself back onto the historical and political agenda." The full rehabilitation of Bukharin, the symbol of pluralism and tolerance, occurred in February, and in the spring of 1988 he was reinstated in the party.[67]

The reemergence of a neosocialist opposition within the reformist camp is a phenomenon worthy of note. Some two decades ago Roy Medvedev published his *On Socialist Democracy*, laying out the critique of the Soviet system from a "Leninist position"—a Leninism informed by the currents of European Marxism. But few Western analysts felt that neo-Marxism had much support, either in the party or among intellectuals. The current critique of the Stalinist system draws heavily upon notions of "alienation," a core concept of a humanist socialism that turns to the writings of the young Marx rather than to his later, more deterministic works. (In 1988 Medvedev began to appear at press conferences, on television, and in *Moscow News*—notably in a debate over the roots of Stalinism—and he has reportedly signed a contract to publish his authoritative *Let History Judge* in the Soviet Union.)

A long-standing justification of Stalinism is in the old adage: "you can't make an omelette without breaking eggs"—that is, no matter which way industrialization and modernization has been pursued, it has resulted in casualties. But in the case of Soviet Russia, just how many casualties? In his autobiography, the poet Evgeny Yevtushenko recalled sitting around a campfire with college students in the 1960s, where he heard estimates of the number of Stalin's victims ranging no higher than a few thousand. Even relatively recent official references to the purges admitted only "thousands" repressed. But Shmelev has now reported that 17 million people passed through Stalin's camps and that 5 million peasants were deported during collectivization.[68] In a startling revelation, one historian has disclosed that the number who perished in Stalin's purges of the 1930s remained unknown but that the 20 million lives lost in World War II does not fully account for the 27.1 million drop in the country's population between 1940 and 1945.[69] In 1988, even higher figures slipped out on the purges, and for the first time writers talked in terms of "millions" of victims in the famine of 1932-1933 and collectivization (one estimate of the number who suffered in the latter runs as high as 19 million).[70]

Historical themes prevail in literary works recently published: Boris Pasternak's *Doctor Zhivago* deals with the fate of the individual in revolutionary times; Vasily Grossman's *Life and Fate* draws parallels between Nazism and Stalinism; Anatoly Rybakov's *Children of the Arbat* looks at Stalin's destruction of the party and intelligentsia; and Michael Shatrov's play on (the treaty of) *Brest-Litovsk*, among other things, calmly and objectively discusses Leon Trotsky.[71] Tengiz Abuladze's film *Repentance* has played to overflowing audiences throughout the country and won the Lenin Prize for 1988. Libraries report waiting lists several months long for copies of magazines carrying novels on life in the country in the 1930s and 1950s.[72]

The press has extensively discussed proposals to honor Soviet POWs and MIAs from World War II in the same way as other veterans.[73] The names of many prominent party victims of Stalin's purges now receive favorable mention in the press (in addition to Bukharin, the most notable Bolsheviks recently rehabilitated are G. Zinoviev, L. Kamenev, and A. Rykov). Prominent economists and, notably, agricultural specialists in favor of gradualism and a mixed economy have also been rehabilitated.[74] Leaders of liberal and radical political parties under tsarism who opposed the Bolsheviks have also been resurrected.[75] The history of foreign policy has also been, ever so gingerly, touched upon.[76]

In his speech on November 2, 1987, on the eve of the seventieth anniversary of the Revolution, Gorbachev praised Bukharin and Khrushchev and, for the first time, publicly criticized Stalin by name,[77] referring to his "many thousands of victims."[78] He added: "The guilt of Stalin and his immediate entourage before the party and the people for the wholesale repressive measures and acts of lawlessness is enormous and unforgivable." But Gorbachev clung to a defense of the basic contours of Soviet history and of the system created by Stalin and continued the old-style vilification of Trotsky and others. In this speech Gorbachev announced the formation of a commission to review the issue of rehabilitation of Stalin's victims. At the same time he defended collectivization and the Nazi-Soviet Pact and omitted Stalin's failings during the war.

Given the radical arguments put forth in 1987, Gorbachev's speech "shocked many of his supporters"[79] and disappointed those who had expected him to go much further in laying out Stalin's crimes.[80] Coming in the midst of the Yeltsin affair, it led to arguments that the Soviet leader was backing down from radical reform. In fact, the speech corresponded more closely with what Ligachev, who often puts forward his own views on Soviet history, has been saying this year; namely, that the system was fine but that Stalin had abused it (and that Stalin, too, was not all bad).[81] A panel of Soviet historians lauded the speech but complained that restricted access to archives impeded open research and that many archives opened in the 1950s and 1960s have since been resealed.[82]

In December 1987, the journal *Glasnost* carried an article by an employee of the Supreme Court, Dmitry Yurasov, stating that officials were burning archives containing information about people falsely accused during the Stalin era at a rate of 5,000 case files per month.[83] The heightened attack on the radical director of the Historical-Archival Institute, Iuri Afanasiev, seemed to lend further credence to the picture of retreat.[84]

But only a month later another historical play by Mikhail Shatrov, *Onward...Onward* renewed the attack on Stalin in even more polemical, unforgiving tones.[85] And historian Afanasiev was back on the attack, criticizing the "barriers" being thrown up against new historical research. He also attacked the documentary *More Light*, a highly praised and reasonably open film dealing with the entire sweep of Soviet history, for looking for a "false balance," when in reality times (under Stalin and Brezhnev) were simply bad.[86]

In the first six months of 1988 the torrent of historical revelation increased; vivid descriptions of the abuses of the Stalin era fundamentally shook the confidence of many Soviet citizens. In mid-May, a special documentary film on Soviet television showed purge scenes and included personal testimony from surviving victims,[87] and in June 1988 another forty prominent party leaders repressed by Stalin were fully exonerated.

In public statements in 1988 Gorbachev himself moved briskly toward even more candid criticism of the past. And Valentin Falin, head of the Soviet press agency Novosti, told Western reporters in May that Gorbachev was planning to give a major speech, perhaps at the party Conference, dealing far more directly and candidly with the crimes of the Stalin era (he didn't). Falin claimed that in recent months, as a result of a special historical commission reviewing Soviet archives, Gorbachev "had learned a lot that is new to him."

Changes have been so drastic that in 1987 and 1988, high school teachers have found themselves without approved textbooks on the Soviet period of history.[88] And in June 1988 Soviet educational authorities made the unprecedented step of canceling final exams in history for secondary students.

Many pupils were coming to class asking their teachers about issues and events skirted by textbooks and the official curriculum but extensively discussed in the press, on television, and in newly published novels. Even more embarrassing, what their leaders were saying directly contradicted what was written in their textbooks.

Moreover, to this date it remains unclear whether the revision of Soviet history will be a reshuffling, with some heroes becoming villains and some villains resurrected as heroes, or will entail a fundamental restructuring of the way history is approached, with tolerance for far more ambiguity, irresolution, and complexity (especially at the popular and textbook level). On the one hand, the efforts to reperiodize Soviet history fall into the first category: The good period of real socialism is now the revolutionary and Civil War stretches as well as NEP (1917-1929), which went astray under Stalin's evil guidance (1929-1953). Lenin has become the "cultural totem" of the Gorbachevtsy[89] and the entire decade from 1917 to 1929 labeled as "Leninist" (although Lenin died in 1924). Thus, perestroika becomes a "return to the pure revolutionary consciousness" that fashioned the policies of the NEP, a logical outgrowth of Leninism. Khrushchev (1953-1964), though not without warts, was fundamentally good, but his successor, Brezhnev (1964-1982), created the infamous period of *zastoi* and corruption (in contrast to which, of course, the Gorbachev era is a radiant one).

Here the case of Leon Trotsky will serve as a bellwether of historical glasnost. To people brought up in the Soviet system, Trotsky is the arch-villain, the veritable bogeyman of the culture. Yet, unlike Bukharin, the politics he advocated, including forced-draft industrialization, harsh treatment of the peasantry, and virtual militarization of the labor force, find little favor among Gorbachevtsy today. Trotsky was the enemy of NEP, and his militant stances, his role in crushing the Kronstadt rebellion in 1921, and other aspects of his biography place him in bad odor with "democratic socialists" trying to recover a kernel of sustenance in the disastrous policies of the postrevolutionary period.

As a result, nobody has any interest in restoring Trotsky to his rightful place as a charismatic, brilliant, and forceful leader who was the architect of the October Revolution, the founder of the Red Army, and a close ally of Lenin's. Shatrov and others have dealt with Trotsky somewhat more calmly, but their treatment falls far short of restoring him to his rightful place, and elsewhere his name continues to be vilified with outrageous smears, anti-Semitic in tone, that would do service to the worst of Stalinist historiography. Should he be rehabilitated, it would be in the service of truth, and that alone, for restoration of his name would not simultaneously add luster (or historical lineage) to policies now advocated.[90]

Yet the very scope of debate today is unprecedented, and the lifting of taboos has gone far indeed. The publication of a lengthy letter on the front page of *Pravda* on May 2, 1988, may represent a landmark in the rewriting of the Soviet past, for in this letter the Communist party leadership, past and present, is directly taken to task for the woes of the Soviet system. And the proposals approved by the Central Committee for discussion and ratification at the June Conference include a harshly worded denunciation of the Soviet past, tracing present problems back to the suppression of inner-party democracy after the death of Lenin. Yet another divide was crossed with criticism of both Lenin (albeit obliquely) and the first leader of the Cheka (Soviet secret police), Felix Dzerzhinsky, for suppression of opponents within and without the party.[91]

Several facts stand out about the ongoing revision of history. First, until recently most rewriting took place in literature and journalism as part of the new civic awareness embodied in the *novaia publitsistika*. The historical profession itself was deeply divided and in great turmoil in 1987,[92] and conservative figures continued to hold important positions in the profession. On many topics the archives remained closed to domestic as well as foreign historians, and Western works on Soviet history continued to be held in *spetskhrany* (closed repositories), meaning that special clearance is required before Soviet historians can look at them. There were hopeful signs in early 1988, including appointment of a new editorial board for the journal *Voprosy istorii* and declaration of a new policy for that journal. A special commission is reviewing the contents of *spetskhrany* in order to return the majority to open stacks.[93] But the doors of the archives are hardly likely to open wide soon.[94] Western analysts point to remaining "blank spots" in the Soviet historical canvas, both in domestic history and in foreign relations.[95]

But the pace of change can be breathtaking. In March, Moscow police used snowplows to end a demonstration on the thirty-fifth anniversary of Stalin's death. The demonstrators, protesting the revival of Stalinism in the country, called for erection of a monument to his victims. The snowplows were put away for the summer, and in July the Politburo announced plans to erect a monument in Moscow . . . to Stalin's victims.[96]

Notes

1. "Testing Glasnost: An Exile Visits His Homeland," *New York Times Book Review*, December 6, 1987: 49. The very fact that Goldfarb was allowed to return is testimony to the impact of glasnost.

2. Nancy Condee and Vladimir Padunov, "The Frontiers of Soviet Culture: Reaching the Limits?" *The Harriman Institute Forum*, Vol. 1, No. 5 (May, 1988): 1-8.

3. On this debate, see the NYT, June 9, 1988.

4. Above from NYT, August 13, 1987.

5. See RL 14/87 (January 8) and 208/87 (June 1) for an informative discussion. In addition, the Soviet Union has stopped jamming most foreign radio broadcasts, including the Voice of America.

6. The above is from RL 151/88 (April 13): 1-5.

7. BS, December 6, 1987: 7K.

8. On the perception of moral decline and a crisis in values, see the lively discussion by Robert Tucker in *Political Culture and Leadership in Soviet Russia* (New York, 1987): 132-133, 173.

9. Nikolai Shmelev, "Avansy i dolgi," *Novyi mir*, No. 6 (June, 1987): 145. The translation is from CDSP, Vol. 39, No. 38 (October 21, 1987).

10. *Pravda*, May 2, 1988, cited in RL 207/88 (May 17): 1-5.

11. This appeared in an article discussing readers' critical responses ("so it's the same old song") to less than candid treatment of the dismissal of party leaders in Armenia and Azerbaijan for "ill health" (*Pravda*, June 7, 1988).

12. Tucker concludes that the notion of "open political pluralism, even if within the framework of single-party rule . . . [is] a transcending of the Bolshevik Revolution's legacy [but is] not part of the program for cultural renovation that Gorbachev has enunciated": "Gorbachev and the Fight for Soviet Reform," *World Policy Journal* (Spring, 1987).

13. Peter Reddaway, "Gorbachev the Bold," *New York Review of Books*, May 28, 1987: 22.

14. Colton, "Gorbachev and the Politics of System Renewal": 7 and 8-11. (This is a first draft of the paper for the East-West Forum published under the same name and cited often in this text. These lines were not included in the final version.)

15. Cited in ibid.: 8 (the writer is Yefim Etkind).

16. S. Frederick Starr, "Soviet Union: A Civil Society," *Foreign Policy*, No. 70 (Spring, 1988): 31-33.

17. RL 374/87 (September 18) citing *Moscow News* and *Ogonek* (September 13). See also RL 220/87 (June 11) and 380/87 (September 23): 1-5, and CDSP, Vol. 39, No. 39 (October 28): 1-7, for Soviet press coverage.

18. A good discussion is in RL 220/87 (June 11): 1-8.

19. WP, October 28, 1987. At present unofficial journals must rely upon copies of typed manuscripts, keeping circulation to fewer than 100.

20. The commission was instigated by the leading economic reformer, Tatiana Zaslavskaia, and is headed by Vadim Churbanov. On this commission, and on the Perestroika Club, as well as on the goals and programs of various unofficial groups, see NYT, October 18, 1987.

21. See NYT, November 8, 1987, for discussion and examples of such clashes, and NYT, February 8, 1988, for a follow-up, including a brief sketch of the new leader, Viktor Mironenko.

22. As reported to Bill Keller in the NYT, February 6, 1988.

23. *Komsomolskaia pravda* carried an article December 22, 1987, calling for a revised history of the Young Communist League, filling in blank spots and eliminating the distortions. Of course, glasnost within the Komsomol is imperative if it is to serve a constructive rather than repressive and controlling function.

24. *Glasnost* in Moscow and *Mercury* in Leningrad, as well as *Bulletin of Christian Opinion* and unofficial publications in half a dozen Soviet cities, including Odessa and Novosibirsk.

25. NYT, August 13, 1987.

26. NYT, May 19 and May 20, 1988.

27. "The Frontiers of Soviet Culture": 1-8.

28. "The periodicals: *Novyi mir*," *Times Literary Supplement*, December 4-10, 1987: 1350.

29. RL 387/87 (September 30): 1; see also the comments by renowned Soviet literary scholar Iuri Kariakin in *Znamia*, No. 9, 1987: 210, cited in RL 377/87 (September 28): 1.

30. CSM, December 4, 1987.

31. For a fuller list, and more knowledgeable discussion of the works published, see Condee and Padunov, "The Frontiers of Culture": esp. 4-5.

32. NYT, September 13, 1987.

33. See Natalia Ivanova, "Zhurnaly v fokuse mnenii," *Literaturnaia obozrenie*, No. 4, 1988: 100. The article (97-101) is a useful critical survey of the output and leanings of the major journals.

34. Condee and Padunov, "Frontiers of Soviet Literature": 3. The same point is made by Natalia Ivanova in "Zhurnaly v fokuse mnenii": 97-101.

35. *Izvestiia*, July 15, 1987: 3, cited in CDSP, Vol. 39, No. 28 (August 12, 1987): 23. The author blames, among other things, the growing proportion of books being published devoted to collected and selected works: 800 authors will be so honored during this five-year plan, a doubling from ten years ago. Many of these "authors" are officials and their "writings" are their public speeches, seldom memorable. The point is that such collections have become artifacts, badges of rank.

36. NYT, September 13, 1987.

37. Conference on Gorbachev Initiatives, Meridian House, Washington, D.C., November 1, 1987.

38. NYT, October 4, 1987.

39. See RL 126/87 (April 6) and NYT, February 22, 1987. For a general discussion of Soviet television, see Ellen Mickiewicz and Gregory Haley, "Soviet and American News: Week of Intensive Interaction," *Slavic Review*, Vol. 46, No. 2 (Summer, 1987): 214-228; as well as Ellen Mickiewicz, "The Mass Media," in *The Soviet Union Today* (Chicago, 1988): 293-302.

40. Condee and Padunov, "The Frontiers of Soviet Culture": 7-8.

41. Cited in RL 213/88 (May 20): 11.

42. For a cogent history and evaluation of the issue, see RL Supplement 8/87 (September 23): 1-17.

43. RL 211/87 (June 5):3. One of that generation, Andrei Vosnesensky, has noted that the present period is far freer than the 1960s (Ibid.: 4).

44. For a biographical portrait of Aganbegyan, and briefer sketches of Zaslavskaia, Bogomolov, and Abalkin, see NYT, July 10, 1987: (D1). Anders Aslund identifies Abalkin, Aganbegyan, Bogomolov, and Zaslavskaia as Gorbachev's brain trust in economic matters but notes that none of this group has been given a political slot (in the CC, or even as a deputy to the Supreme Soviet); in his view, despite Gorbachev's effort to place them, "they lack political status and weight" ("Gorbachev's Economic Advisors," *Soviet Economy*, Vol. 3, No. 3 [July-September, 1987]: 259-266).

45. The twenty most prominent activists within the Gorbachev circle were all born between 1927 and 1935 (CSM, June 26, 1987).

46. See Voinovich in RL 88/87 (March 5).

47. All the above from P. Quinn-Judge, CSM, December 4, 1987. Conservatives were heartened by Ligachev's visit to the offices of *Sovetskaia kultura* in July 1987, when he called for greater state control over culture, criticized recent reforms of the Theater Workers' Union in the direction of self-determination, protested the infusion of Western elements into Russian culture, and lamented "certain negative tendencies" in Soviet literature (RL 273/87: July 14). On the Theater Workers' Union, see RL 9/87 (December 23, 1986).

48. RL 143/87 (April 15): 1.

49. Cited in "Gorbachev the Bold," *New York Review of Books*, May 28, 1987: 24.

50. See the vivid description in Tucker, *Political Leadership and Culture in Soviet Russia*: 167-170.

51. Dev Murarka, "The Foes of Perestroika Sound Off," *The Nation*, May 23, 1988: 717.

52. To be sure, it was *Moskva* that in earlier days (1966-1967) first published Bulgakov's *Master and Margarita*, arguably the best novel ever produced in the Soviet Union.

53. *New Yorker*, December 7, 1987: 142-143.

54. *The Nation*, October 24, 1987: 447.

55. Katerina Clark, "New Trends in Literature," *The Soviet Union Today*, ed. by James Cracraft (Chicago: Bulletin of the Atomic Scientists, 1983): 264.

56. "Fear and Risk," *Moscow News*, No. 19, 1988: 3. This article includes a fascinating discussion of "everyday Stalinism."

57. Another is Natan Edelman, who has become prominently involved in debates with supporters of Pamiat.

58. Colton, "Gorbachev and the Politics of System Renewal," Paper prepared for East-West Forum, New York, April 24, 1987: 6.

59. A listing of articles directly or indirectly discussing Stalin or Stalinism in the past year alone would fill several pages. For a comment on the significance of this debate, see William Pfaff, "The Questions Not Asked," *New Yorker*, August 1, 1988: 60-65.

60. *New Yorker*, December 7, 1987: 140-150.

61. For a collection of recent articles on this subject, see the special issue of *Soviet Studies in History* entitled "Glasnost and the Historians," ed. by William Husband: Vol. 27, No. 1 (Summer, 1988).

62. A concise summary of Gorbachev's early statements on Soviet history can be found in Colton, "Gorbachev's Reforms and the Soviet Historical Context," Paper prepared for the American-German Conference on the Gorbachev Reform Program: Kennan Institute for Advanced Russian Studies (Washington, D.C., 1988).

63. Smirnov is the new director of the formerly conservative Institute of Marxism-Leninism. These comments, and the following comments on the historical profession, come from Dev Murarka, "Recovering the Buried Stalin Years," and "A New Revolution in Consciousness," in *The Nation*, October 24 and October 31, 1987.

64. RL 169/88 (April 29): 1-5.64. RL 169/88 (April 29): 1-5.

65. See, besides the articles by Shmelev, Burlatsky, and Nuikin referred to here, the recent, important historical essay by Vasily Seliunin, "Istoki," in *Novyi mir*, No. 5, May 1988: 162-189—encompassing the entire sweep of Soviet history, and especially the origins of the Soviet state. See also the excellent discussion of the significance of the debate on NEP in Tucker, *Political Culture and Leadership in Soviet Russia*: 73-74, 85-87.

66. NYT, January 19, 1988.

67. CSM, February 6, 1988. After Gorbachev's favorable reference to Bukharin in the November speech, *Ogonek* published (in the first week in December) an article on his widow. This article was followed by a long article in *Nedelia*, the weekly supplement to *Izvestiia* (late December).

In January, Cohen (whose work has been translated into Russian, but which is confiscated at the borders when foreigners try to bring it in) was invited by Afanasiev to give a lecture on Bukharin at the Moscow State Historical-Archive Institute. Cohen reported it was a "mob scene" and added: "Afanasiev thought it was the first time, at least since the twenties, that any Westerner had been invited to speak in public on such a controversial subject" (NYT, January 19, 1988). And then, in June 1988, Cohen reportedly signed a contract with Progress Publishers in Moscow to make available in the Soviet Union a Russian translation of the work (still being confiscated at the borders)! See also RL 53/88 (February 5) and WP, July 10, 1988 (Bukharin's posthumous readmission to the Communist party).

68. In a talk behind closed doors at a research institute attached to the CPSU CC; reported in CSM, June 16, 1987. The magazine *Znamia* has published graphic descriptions of collectivization.

69. The population dropped from 194.1 to 167 million; from a conversation between orthodox party critic Feliks Kuznetsov and historian Iuri Poliakov in *Literaturnaia gazeta* (September 30, 1987), cited in RL 391/87 (October 2): 2.

70. For related stories, see WP, April 5, 1988 (citing an unspecified article in *Argumenty i fakty* that placed the number of farmers who suffered under Stalin at 10,000,000); *Sobesednik*, No. 22, 1988 (Dmitry Yurasov on material in Soviet archives on those who suffered in the purges); WP, May 17, 1988 on popular views on Stalin and Stalinism; *Izvestiia*, April 12, 1988 (historian V. Dashichev estimates "millions" of intellectuals suffered under Stalin); and RL 167/88 (survey of recent material). See also RL 387/87 (September 30):2-6; RL 205/88 (May 17), for a summary of a two-hour television documentary on Stalin (May 16); RL 4/88 (December 21, 1987), for materials in the Soviet press defending Stalin; and Vera Tolz, "Blank Spots in Soviet History," RL 119/88 (March 21):1-12.

71. For a recent plea for legal vindication of Trotsky, see the comments by economist Otto Latsis, cited in NYT, June 29, 1988 (from *Komsomolskaia pravda*, June 28, 1988).

72. *Izvestiia*, August 8, 1987; CDSP, Vol. 39, No. 32 (September 9): 9. For further discussion, see Colton, "Gorbachev and the Politics of System Renewal": 43-46.

73. Their names are currently omitted from local war memorials. See the discussion in CDSP, Vol. 39, No. 35 (September 30).

74. Namely, Alexander Chaianov and Nikolai Kondratiev. Chaianov's works,

well known in the West, will be published for the first time [since the 1920s] in the Soviet Union.

75. See, for a summary, RL 96/87 (March 5); 373/87 (September 17); 385/87 (September 28); 43/87 (January 29); 169/87 (April 29); 21/87 (January 14) for related discussions of history and historical figures.

76. On November 4, 1987, *Moscow News* published an article by Andrei Sakharov pressing for full disclosure of the events surrounding the Cuban missile crisis (in response to the airing of the film *Risk,* which portrayed Khrushchev positively but failed to mention that the crisis began when the Soviet Union began to place missiles on the island. In October, a Soviet delegation to a conference assembled at Harvard University to reexamine the Cuban missile crisis surprised the Americans with their candor and willingness to accept a share of the blame for the crisis (CSM, December 1, 1987: 14). In November, Smirnov called for a review of the events of the Prague Spring (WP, November 5, 1987). Historian Afanasiev has also called for a more truthful airing of the history of Soviet-Polish relations, including the Katyn massacre (RL 391/87 [October 2]: 10).

77. Cited in NYT, November 8, 1987. At the same time, he ignored Trotsky's role in the Revolution and Civil War and spoke disparagingly of his role in the debates of the 1920s. On Trotsky see also *Sovetskaia Rossiia,* September 27, 1987.

78. Gorbachev noted that "once and for all [we have] overcome the attempts at trifling with history when, at times, we believed what we wanted to believe rather than what was." For the speech see CDSP, Vol. 39, No. 44 (December 2). The full text in Russian was in *Izvestiia,* November 3. For brief analyses, see William Taubman's comments in NYT, November 5, 1987; Daniel Singer, *The Nation,* December 12, 1987: 716-717.

79. BS, January 24, 1988.

80. See NYT, November 8, 1987 for detail; and WP, November 4, 1987.

81. For a brief discussion of Ligachev's views on history, see WP, September 29, 1987. His most detailed comments were given at a speech at Electrostal outside Moscow in August (*Izvestiia,* August 28, 1987: an abstract is in CDSP, Vol. 39, No.34 [September 23, 1987]). See too, his comments in a meeting with the media, published in *Izvestiia* September 18 (abstract in CDSP, Vol. 39, No. 37 [October 14, 1987]).

82. NYT, November 5, 1987. See also *Moscow News,* November 4, 1987, for a piece by David Granin blasting Brezhnev and calling for a historical analysis of the mechanisms of the cult of personality.

83. WP, December 3, 1987, and RL 207/87. For a follow-up on Yurasov's revelations, see *Sobesednik,* November 22, 1988.

84. For a vivid description of the battle within the historical profession over the Soviet past, and of the courageous Afanasiev's role in the events of this year, see Dev Murarka, *The Nation,* October 24 and October 31, 1987. According to the *Baltimore Sun,* after a heated six-hour meeting Afanasiev failed to receive sufficient votes to be reelected to the Historical-Archival Institute's party commission. Pietila also deemed significant the fact that Afanasiev was not elected to the special commission appointed to review party history (BS, December 21, 1987). But early in January 1988 Afanasiev was out in public

swinging away at the Stalinists and even suggesting that it was time to review Lenin in a more objective historical light. He did not, however, win a seat to the June Conference.

85. The play was released in *Znamia* in December 1987. In the work, Shatrov reportedly portrays Alexander Kerensky in a positive light, shows Stalin insulting Krupskaia, and accuses Stalin of murdering both Kirov and Trotsky and deceptively assuring Zinoviev and Kamenev that they had nothing to fear. See the summary in WP, December 15, 1987. For related developments at the end of the year, see WP, December 19, 1987; NYT, January 6, 1988; CSM, January 7, 1988; RL 50/88 (February 2); CDSP, Vol. 40, No. 4 (February 24): 17 ("Culture Minister Hails Theater Experiment"); No. 5 (March 2): 10 ("Shatrov Puts Bukharin, Trotsky on Stage"); No. 7 (March 16) ("New Shatrov Play Hailed, Attacked"): 11; No. 9 (March 30): 16 ("Theatre People Rebuff Criticism of Shatrov"). Shatrov was bitterly attacked in the "Andreyeva Letter."

86. This, according to the summary in CSM, January 7, 1988.

87. This, according to WP, May 17, 1988.

88. For a discussion, see CDSP, Vol. 40, No. 23 (July 6): 22; Vol. 39, No. 29 (August 19, 1987); and Vol. 39, No. 32 (Sept. 9, 1987). See also WP, December 2, 1987.

89. Condee and Padunov, "The Frontiers of Soviet Culture": 1.

90. On June 28 radical economist Otto Latsis publicly called for a new look at Trotsky: NYT, June 29, 1988 (from *Komsomolskaia pravda*, June 28, 1988); CDSP, Vol. 40, No. 26 (July 27): 31.

91. NYT, June 8, 1988.

92. A major event in 1987 was a speech by Iuri Afanasiev, the new rector of the Moscow State Institute of Historical Archives, characterizing Soviet historiography as "stagnant and lagging" due to vestiges of Stalinism, particularly in the treatment of the October Revolution (RL 96/87: 2). Afanasiev has sponsored a series of lectures that have drawn much publicity. See, for example, RL 207/87 (June 3): 1-5.

93. RL 170/88 (April 18). The journal's new priorities include: estimating the number who suffered in the 1932-1933 famine; describing the repression of scholars under Stalin; reconsidering the economic debates of the 1920s; examining Russian colonial policy and publishing archival material. On the commission reexamining special holdings, see *Sovetskaia kultura*, March 15 and March 22, 1988.

94. On June 1, *Pravda* carried an article stating that "officials in charge of archives are more concerned with protecting the documents under their charge than making them available to researchers," but at the same time noted the physical deterioration of millions of restricted documents because of inadequate care. The writer described F. Vaganov, Director of the Chief Archives Adminstration, as an unreconstructed Stalinist suspicious of those who wanted to burrow around in the past.

95. See "Blank Spots in Soviet History," RL 119/88 (March 21).

96. *Pravda*, July 5, 1988.

4
Zakonnost—
Toward a Lawful Society?

Soviet publicist Burlatsky announced early in 1988 that "in the Soviet Union, greater attention is being focused on democratization—that is, on the expansion of civil and political rights and liberties and on their guarantees."[1] Until now the predictable Soviet response to Western criticism of shortcomings in civil rights was to point to the socioeconomic freedoms provided by the Soviet system (guaranteed work, free medical care, etc.). Now that the Soviet press itself is highlighting the existence of poverty and related social ills at home, the perhaps unintended consequence has been to make the official position on political freedoms even more difficult. We see then that perestroika, glasnost, and *zakonnost* (legality) are linked; changes in one are bound to force reconsideration elsewhere. It may be, however, that while economic perestroika requires zakonnost, the new emphasis upon individual rights and legal procedures will retard, even undermine, the attempt to overcome opposition to reform.

The conflict between *proizvol*, or arbitrary personal rule, and zakonnost reaches far into the Russian past and is intricately interwoven both with the evolution of political power and the struggle for individual rights before and after the 1917 Revolution. When Tsar Alexander II decided to emancipate the serfs, he also set up a commission to draw up a sweeping judicial reform (enacted in 1864) separating the functions of criminal investigator and prosecutor and establishing public trials, independent judges, and a professional bar. The statute on the courts was made possible by a quarter century of preparatory work done under the notoriously reactionary and uncompromising Nicholas I. These reforms were prompted by the recognition that emancipation from serfdom necessitated courts capable of handling litigation between social groups now equal before the law. But they also had their origin in the powerful argument that economic growth, necessary to restore Russia's great power status after defeat in the Crimean War, was unrealizable without laws specifying contractual obligations and courts capable of timely and honest enforcement of these laws. So economic growth and individual freedom were linked through the notion of legality and the effort to create an independent judiciary.

In the post-Stalin period, the struggle for legality and the legal profession's search for professional autonomy has a history at least as long (though not as well known) as that of the dissident movement. As one scholar notes, "Soviet law appears to have made major steps forward during the past 30 years. . . . The legal profession has achieved a high degree of professional training and competence. Soviet legislation has been systematized and codified. . . . Individuals now feel relatively secure against the recurrence of Stalinist terror."[2] In that sense the new concern for zakonnost is not new at all.

But in Brezhnev's declining years, there was accumulating evidence that rampant corruption had made deep inroads in the enforcement system. It was one matter that political dissidents found little protection from the KGB or the Communist party in the courts; it was, in many ways, far more ominous that graft, favoritism, and bribery made justice unlikely even in the day-to-day litigation that was of far greater concern to the average Soviet citizen.

As in prereform Tsarist Russia, the situation was especially lamentable in the provinces, where local "mafias" of party, government, police, and court officials ruled virtually unchecked over the citizenry, who knew better than to contest authority, however arbitrarily applied. Interestingly, this distrust of local authority is one of the reasons for the persistence today of anonymous denunciations, the continuing scourge of Soviet society. The citizens are afraid of victimization if they identify themselves in a letter of complaint. As one person wrote to *Literaturnaia gazeta*: "We're afraid! Yes, we're afraid that reprisals will be taken against us. We all have families and children, and we have all seen with our own eyes how the bosses get even with anyone who openly criticizes."[3]

It is the combination of economic stagnation, a corrupt and politically subservient court system, and declining civic morale that brings to mind a remarkable parallel between the era of the Great Reforms and perestroika today. Alexander II was a profoundly conservative individual dedicated to the preservation of autocratic power; yet he put his hand to legal reforms that significantly enhanced the rights of the individual in the Russian Empire.

Cause for Serious Concern

Speaking in September 1987 at a commemorative meeting honoring Felix Dzerzhinsky, KGB chief Chebrikov admitted "we have not yet managed to achieve a breakthrough in the struggle against such crimes as bribery, embezzlement, report-padding and the output of poor-quality goods, and against infringements on the life, health, honor and dignity of citizens. Drunkenness, drug addiction and parasitism . . . are cause for serious concern."[4] For decades, Soviet sociologists have pressed for recognition of environmental factors in crime and social malaise; ideologists have responded by pointing the finger to contamination by Western culture. Chebrikov has called for harsh law-and-order measures to deal with "carriers" of the disease. He continues to warn of the danger of Western subversion (and, in fact, one Western emigré organization has provided fuel for this argument by encouraging the use of dissident sources to collect information for Western intelligence agencies). But now, finally, the Soviet authorities also talk openly of the links between social and economic conditions, social injustice, "alienation" (a word only recently accepted as applying to the USSR), and crime. The press has launched a campaign exposing cases of police brutality (including beatings to induce false confessions), corruption, and false imprisonment and calling for greater independence of judges, increased accountability of the police,[5] and earlier involvement of defense lawyers in trial procedures. *Ogonek* has carried articles describing an armed robbery carried out by the police, the skull of a witness of a police beating being cracked to ensure silence, and glaring abuses of the system involving bowing to party pressure, particularly in the provinces. It is said that at least 5 percent of all cases before the courts involve significant procedural improprieties.

Most lurid were the series of exposés uncovering egregious violations of defendants' rights in Belorussia, where prosecutors knowingly convicted innocent citizens (executing one of them) in a serial murder case of thirty victims (the "Vitebsk affair"); concealed the confession of another murderer in order to cover up injustices committed in convicting an innocent man of killing his wife (thereby leaving the innocent husband to rot in a labor camp for fifteen years—the "Mogilev affair"); and fabricated murder cases against yet five other innocent citizens. In virtually all of these scandals, the investigators had previously been lauded in the local or national press for their successful careers. In all cases, too, beatings and even torture had been liberally applied to obtain confessions.[6] Atrocious conditions in prison camps have also been highlighted by the press.

It has been argued that a primary reason the Soviet legal system continues to be held in low repute is that "it continues to govern the people, but not their rulers."[7] Iurii Andropov, however, had earned his reputation while head of the KGB not only for crushing the dissident movement but also for leading a campaign against official corruption—a campaign graphically documented in Dusko Doder's *Shadows and Whispers*. Since Andropov assumed power, the leadership has continued this campaign (with a notable slackening under Chernenko), and it has made deep inroads into the power structure of the Central Asian republics (especially Uzbekistan) and into entire ministries working out of Moscow. Not surprisingly, according to *Nedelia* (April 22), Soviet criminal investigators are now turning up evidence of organized resistance to perestroika "from Uzbekistan to Moscow" by many implicated in corruption. As we saw in Chapter 2, there are rumors of a "mafia of senior officials providing protection" amidst the many small "mafias" of petty thugs running everything from cemeteries to protection rackets.[8]

Linking one's political opponents with all manner of corruption and peculation is, of course, a convenient way to discredit them (and, in the Soviet case, conservatives do the same by linking the reformist platform with "private ownership manifestations," that is, greed, acquisitiveness, and "money-grubbing interest").[9] In fact, many radical reformists seem to be calling for strong arm tactics both to clean up the cesspool of corruption and to neutralize the opposition. The writer Danil Granin, for example, in an interview with the *Christian Science Monitor*, complained of Gorbachev's "illusions" and warned of the "dangers of patience." Officials have already had three years to reveal their feelings about reform: "It's already clear who is willing to help and who is not."[10] In a much-read diatribe published in *Novyi mir*, Andrei Nuikin warned against "underestimating the bureaucrat" and complained that whenever the interests of the "class of bureaucratic managers" were threatened, "they act swiftly, decisively, and efficiently, without the slightest trace of formalism" (that is, without concern for legal procedure). To be sure, Nuikin called for the reduction of "coercive measures regulating social relations" and for enhancing the role of law. He drew a strong analogy between the present and the inception of NEP, when Lenin called for measures to rein in the Cheka. "Economic methods of regulation," he argued, "do not require political coercion." Ultimately, then, the market will reinforce political freedom (a remarkable statement in its own right!), but Nuikin's descriptions of the "avalanche of persecutions" of people trying to establish cooperatives or private businesses; of the "coup d'état" launched by Stalinists in 1929; and the "broad offensive" carried out, "while carefully camouflaging its plans with hypocritical praise for the announced reforms" in hope of "disillusioning people with perestroika," all suggest a "wrecking campaign" best dealt with, in the short run, by harsh measures:

> It is risky to spend too long coddling and trying to persuade those who are wavering. . . . The experience of social impotence is dangerous. I think there is nothing more dangerous right now for restructuring, for it threatens to turn glasnost itself into a pathetic farce. As it is, only a small fraction of the crimes, acts of tyrannical arbitrariness, violations of the rule of law, and corruption that actually occur find their way into the press. We must not permit such cases to go unpunished. . . . Of course punitive measures alone will not suffice . . . [but] we must not allow the revolution to be toothless.

Shortly before the June Conference Nicholai Shmelev hinted that a "Cheka of perestroika" may well be necessary. Nuikin allows that measures against the bureaucracy should "only be employed within the framework of the law and the rule of law," but in the same breath he insists that it is not "awkward to resort to undemocratic, repressive measures," for if the "forces of retardation" take power, they will ensure that "it is impossible to find a single healthy ear of grain for another hundred years in the field of public life!"[11]

So, for the time being, according to radical reformers, zakonnost may have to be sacrificed in the interests of perestroika. The same problem, we have seen, emerged with glasnost ("in a thaw, even the dung will melt"); but here the short-term need to defeat a well-entrenched opponent might well conflict with the long-term need to establish contractual, legally guaranteed relationships and procedures. More than that, it is hard to see how radical reformists can reconcile the call for a firm hand with the larger goal of *demokratizatsiia*. As one commentator explained it (in an article analyzing the purge trials of the 1930s), the purges began while the country was discussing a draft constitution; at the time, an article in *Izvestiia* insisted that investigation should precede arrest, that the defense should be admitted to the preliminary investigation, and even called for a habeus corpus act—all at the same time as calls were rife that the "vermin be destroyed." The message is clear:

> Today we are learning democracy, we are mastering the rules of political debate during another time of intense struggle. Our predecessors . . . were unable to master the situation, and were themselves consumed. . . . The absence of the very concept of the right to a personal opinion created the savage-mob syndrome that sanctified any high-handedness in the name of the people.[12]

For the time being, at least, Gorbachev has forcefully sided with the advocates of legality against those calling for the new Cheka of perestroika. As he put it just before the June Conference, "We don't need a new collectivization campaign." A brief review of ongoing measures to reinforce zakonnost in Soviet society follows.

Fresh Winds Blowing

In February 1987, officials announced that a review of the Criminal Code was under way.[13] On November 9, the justice minister announced that a commission working on the new criminal code had decided to eliminate internal exile and to reduce the number of capital offenses.[14] The highest-ranking judge in the Soviet Union has called for limitations on pretrial detention to six months (and then only in extremely serious cases), for immediate access to legal help for defendants, and for better training for lawyers. He has also called for measures to punish party "meddlers" in the judicial process. At least one official in the USSR has called for eliminating the infamous Article 190-1 of the RSFSR Criminal Code on anti-Soviet slander as "contradicting the spirit of glasnost."[15] And in his lengthy opening speech to the June Party Conference, Gorbachev spoke of the urgency of substantive reform of the legal system, which he said is "to date largely oriented not on democratic or economic but on command-style methods . . . with numerous bans and petty regimentation."

In calling for greater guarantees of the independence of judges (through longer terms) and for stiffer penalties for interference in court procedures, the leader had in mind the rights of individuals and equality before the law.[16] He urged "unswerving adherence" to the principle that "everything not prohibited by law is permitted." But, to return to the analogy with the Great Reforms, Gorbachev was also explicitly concerned with the economy: "With contractual relations increasingly permeating all economic ties, reliable operation of the legal sector assumes paramount importance."[17]

The issue of capital punishment merits closer attention. Abolition of the death penalty has become an issue much like the campaign to eliminate corporal punishment at the turn of the century—it has acquired symbolic dimensions, representing the effort to bring the country into the civilized world. Intellectuals and legal specialists in favor of the elimination of capital punishment insist that as a first step, the death penalty for "economic crimes" (embezzlement, speculation) should be halted immediately. In their view, all nonviolent crimes should be the first to be removed from the list of capital offenses. But on the pages of *Moskovskie novosti*, *Nedelia*, and *Ogonek*, where the debate has unfolded, letters to the editor indicate that the majority of readers continue to favor the death penalty. One letter writer had questioned seventy-nine people at his factory in Novosibirsk, and all were opposed to abolition.[18] This informal survey, and a poll carried out by the *New York Times* and CBS that found that only 35 percent of Muscovites (citizens of Russia's most cosmopolitan city) supported the right to demonstrate in the streets,[19] indicate that the observations of George Feiffer, made some twenty-five years ago in *Justice in Moscow*, continue to be valid. Feiffer spent a good part of a year sitting in local Soviet courts and observing popular justice (including the response of the crowd in attendance). He concluded that the society remained overwhelmingly draconian in its views on crime and punishment.[20]

Early in 1987[21] a high-ranking U.S. official lauded the Soviet Union for "positive actions," noting that "fresh winds" were blowing in the country, leading to improved compliance with the 1975 Helsinki accords on human rights. The Soviet Union has ceased jamming the BBC Russian language programs, as well as the Voice of America; permitted 100 former Soviet citizens to return permanently to the USSR; and for the first time allowed an organization openly critical of Soviet human rights' policies (the International Helsinki Federation of Human Rights) to meet in the USSR.[22] It has released from prison poet Irina Ratushinskaya and psychiatrist Anatoly Koriagin, allowing both to emigrate. Other prominent figures allowed to leave include pianist Vladimir Feltsman, Vladimar Slepak, Janis Barkans, Iosip Terelia, Serafim Yevsiukov, and Jewish activists Joseph Begun, Ida Nudel, Aleksei Magarik, and Alexander Lerner.[23] The Soviet Union has also released from prison up to 250 other prisoners of conscience. The number of people still incarcerated on political grounds, according to Amnesty International, is 540 (if political prisoners convicted of violent crimes are included, the number is 750); but a recent U.S. State Department report put the number at only 250.[24] In the past two years thousands of recent Soviet emigrés have returned home for visits, and far more Soviet citizens are now being given visas to visit family members in the United States.[25]

In December 1987, an unauthorized seminar on human rights met in Moscow. The event produced regular announcements to the press and "took on a public character . . . unthinkable even in the heyday of the human rights movement of the early 1970s."[26] Although the police initially cracked down on public demonstrations and refused the seminar participants access to public meeting halls, in the end they decided to let the meeting go ahead. More than 200 different reports were aired, advocating release of political prisoners, withdrawal from Afghanistan, abolition of capital punishment, and a public apology for the invasion of Czechoslovakia.

In mid-1988 Moscow authorities adopted a more tolerant stance toward public protests, allowing demonstrations to take place by environmentalists, nationalist groups, Jews, and Armenians. At first many thought this approach was window dressing for the summit but, surprisingly, it remained in force, convincing some that "it represented a significant step toward greater freedom."[27]

In November 1987, the Soviet authorities announced the formation of a Public Commission for Humanitarian Questions and Human Rights "to achieve conformity of Soviet legislation with the obligations assumed by the Soviet Union in the Helsinki Final Act and in UN human rights documents."[28] Its chairman is well-known Gorbachevets Fedor Burlatsky, and members include writers Ales Adamovich and Grigory Baklanov, academician Boris Raushenbakh, and a number of diplomats, lawyers, and church leaders.[29] The commission received considerable publicity and even carried off an international meeting in Moscow on human rights. According to Burlatsky, the commission wants to achieve a major reform of Soviet legislation on religion; to create a "foolproof mechanism" allowing investigation of complaints about the courts; to push for abolition of the death penalty; and to improve popular notions of justice (to encourage compliance with the law and compassion for others). The usually jaded Radio Liberty noted the similarities between Burlatsky's ideas and those promoted by the unofficial Moscow Human-Rights Committee set up early in the 1970s by Andrei Sakharov, Valery Chalidze, and others, which was crushed by the KGB.[30]

On June 30, 1987, the Supreme Soviet voted into law measures (effective

January 1) permitting popular referendums on local social and political issues and facilitating court appeal of decisions made by Communist party officials (requiring a court response within ten days).[31]

The notion of a "loyal opposition" has been aired with growing insistence. Writing in August in *Oktiabr*, Iuri Burtin offered a theoretical justification for opposition to Communist party leadership. Arguing that the Brezhnev era represented a defeat for democratic tendencies in socialism and a "moral rehabilitation" of Stalin, Burtin noted: "The transformation of a part—and, we stress, the best part—of the democratic movement of the time into an opposition movement, and of the energy of positive social reform into the energy of protest, is a sad and dramatic page in our history." Under these conditions, the journal *Novyi mir*, the flagship of reform under Khrushchev (and the journal for which Burtin worked), became "an opposition journal." Burtin concluded: "There are moments when the social activist, if he is a real citizen and patriot, has to go against the current, against the majority."[32] Such notions flow logically from Gorbachev's own statement to writers in 1986 that in the absence of an opposition party, writers had a duty to keep the leadership on its toes.

In the freewheeling discussions preceding the June Conference, many leading reformists pushed the idea of a "bloc" of grass-roots, proreform, informal organizations to promote perestroika, with the right to put forth local candidates to oppose those known to be resisting reform. In Estonia, just such an organization, The People's Front, emerged in the spring of 1988, reportedly with the blessings of the Estonian Communist party and an endorsement by Tatiana Zaslavskaia. At the June Conference, Leonid Abalkin loudly proclaimed that there could be no long-lasting change within a single-party state. A first reading of the proceedings of the Conference produces the impression that the leadership was determined to quash any notion that there is room for other political parties. Nevertheless, the view continues to be aired, and the notion of an informal coalition appears to be gaining strength.

The political abuse of psychiatry has long been of international concern. This year *Izvestiia* has admitted that "complainers" have been incarcerated in psychiatric hospitals, and *Komsomolskaia pravda* complained that doctors have administered medicine "that can make a healthy man sick."[33] A number of psychiatrists and psychiatric institutions linked with such abuses have now been publicly accused of accepting bribes; some individuals have been stripped of their positions and await criminal procedures.[34] In January 1988, Tass reported the adoption of a new set of legal rights for mental patients, the first major revision of such legislation in twenty-seven years. The new legislation, which took effect in March, gives families the right to sue for release; gives ultimate authority over special psychiatric wards now in the control of the Ministry of the Interior to the Health Ministry; and provides for the appointment of chief psychiatrists of republics, regions, and cities as court officials empowered to handle complaints from patients and their relatives. Reportedly, the new criminal code will make it a punishable offense to confine a healthy person to a mental hospital.[35] The Kremlin has also agreed to let a team of U.S. psychiatrists inspect mental hospitals reputed to torture political dissidents.[36]

Millennium of Christianity . . . in a ZIL

With the millennium of Christianity in Russia at hand, the Orthodox Church has been prominent in the media.[37] The Soviet government conducted "a very public rapprochement" with official church leaders, including a well-touted meeting between Gorbachev, Patriarch Pimen, and metropolitans of the church on April 29, 1988. Three monasteries have been returned to the Russian Orthodox Church (the Monastery of the Caves in Kiev, the Otpina Pustyn Monastery in Kaluga region, and a less well-known monastery in Iaroslavl). A case has been made in the Soviet press for rescinding a 1929 law forbidding the church from engaging in charitable activities (especially in hospitals, to ease the egregious shortage of nurses).[38] Soviet authorities have permitted the All Union Council of Evangelical Christians-Baptists to receive from abroad next year up to 100,000 copies of the Bible (the largest previous shipment was 25,000 copies in 1978).[39]

It is common to hear open criticism of violations of the rights of believers by authorities, and especially by authorities of the Council for Religious Affairs (essentially the Ministry of Religion). In an interview published in *Literaturnaia gazeta* in September 1987, renowned medievalist Dmitri Likhachev publicly complained that believers are treated like second-class citizens and called for the "full, effective separation of church from state, for a state that does not impinge upon the church."[40] All in all, developments in 1987 led one critical observer to concede that "the year . . . may in many respects be regarded as the most positive period in the history of the official churches in the Soviet Union since the October Revolution."[41]

Glasnost has also led to more open discussion of the present state of religion in the Soviet Union. A research journal carried a strikingly bold section on the condition of believers in the USSR, including an article by a U.S. specialist and, remarkably, criticism that he *underestimates* the number of believers in the USSR.[42] The journal *Nauka i religiia* (Science and Religion) late in 1987 released the first data on the number of religious communities and religious services in the country in the past twenty-five years. According to these data (which exclude unregistered, or illegal religious communities), believers constitute between 10 and 20 percent of the population (28 to 56 million individuals) in about 15,000 religious communities (defined as registered [legal] groups with more than twenty believers).[43]

Other recent surveys have provided local glimpses into the number of Muslims. In one rural community in Tadjikistan, one-fifth of all young people were firm believers (and one in three believed in life after death), 42 percent "wavered," and only 6.7 percent declared themselves confirmed atheists. In a town in the same district one-third of all sixth and seventh graders professed religious belief. Fully 70 percent of rural youth continue to observe major religious holidays; the gap between professions of belief and performance of religious rites is, according to the surveyors, a measure of the power of the family and of the interweaving of national tradition, culture, and religion, as well as a measure of the lack in rural areas of opportunities for socializing and of organized entertainment.[44]

For the first time in decades, church bells in a number of cities will chime to greet the celebration of the baptism of Rus. This event will have considerable symbolic importance in cultural as well as religious terms, for the arts of bell founding and bell ringing, for which Russia was long renowned, have been virtually lost, and in a few cities (especially Rostov) the struggle to save the remaining bells has rallied believers as well as all those concerned about the erosion of Russian cultural artifacts.[45] Many observers have detected "a nostalgia among the Soviet intelligentsia for religion and . . . the Judeo-Christian ethic."[46] This search for values may coincide with a new interest in the Kremlin in using Christian ethics to "stabilize" society and halt the progressive erosion of civic consciousness among the population. Serge Schmemann of the *New York Times* argues that the ongoing détente with the church is part of Gorbachev's "search for new sources of popular support against bureaucratic resistance."[47]

But if this is so, Soviet leaders will have to reach beyond the official church, which is notoriously docile and may be suffering a real "crisis of credibility." As Schmemann himself adds, recent changes reflect the "obvious fact that the domesticated and timid prelates have long ceased to pose a serious threat"; an institution incapable of mounting a major challenge is unlikely to possess the resources or popular support to be of much help in perestroika. In the words of one critic, Father Valery Lapkovsky, "The church should be the voice of those who have no voice. But the official church is not such a voice. They [sic] haven't even defended their own priests and believers. They won't fight for human rights, and that should be their duty."

Before the Revolution, the Orthodox Church was wholly subordinate to the state, lacked an active tradition of social work, and frequently cooperated with the state in suppressing other Christian churches, unofficial Orthodox sects, and other religions in the Russian Empire. Today, dissidents claim that the official clergy resist active pastoral work and have winked at suppression of other faiths (particularly fundamentalist Christian groups such as the Baptists and Pentecostals). Such critics sneer at the notion that reopening churches and monasteries is proof of improving conditions for believers. Another priest, who was recently dismissed from his post, noted that the top church officials "had sold themselves for a high position in society"; the huge ZIL limousine used to drive the aged Patriarch Pimen around during the ceremonies commemorating the Christianizing of Rus was the same kind used by the Kremlin leaders. Even within the church, sentiment has surfaced for the Patriarch to retire and make room for somebody more in touch with recent events.[48]

Glasnost has allowed groups of religious activists from various denominations to press their demands upon the government; it also enabled them to extract a letter from the Ministry of Justice (September 1987) declaring that a government commission was examining proposals to improve existing legislation. But the condition of unofficial religious groups remains parlous under Gorbachev. Although several believers incarcerated for their faith have been released, reports continue of harassment of Evangelical Christian Baptists, Pentecostals, Jehovah's Witnesses, and unofficial Orthodox groups.[49] For example, *Moscow News* reported an incident in the western Ukraine: Villagers there flocked to a site where "the Virgin Mary had appeared" but were beaten and arrested by local police. This report roundly criticized the behavior of local officials and attributed the high incidence of belief in that area to prevalent socioeconomic difficulties.[50] (Recent press criticism of local harassment of believers is yet another sign of the gap between the Moscow intellectuals and provincial officialdom.)

Located in the Ukraine, the Uniate Church recognizes the authority of the Pope but practices Eastern rites. Suppressed since 1946, it is the largest underground church in the USSR. In June 1988, the Orthodox Church announced plans to meet with the Vatican over the status of the Uniate Church. But at the same time, Metropolitan Filaret, who made the announcement, showed little willingness to consider legalizing this church.[51]

In the spring of 1988, the Russian Orthodox Church held a three day meeting "marked by an unusual sprinkling of blunt and candid complaints from the floor" and adopted (on June 9, 1988) new rules loosening central control over priests and returning to them the right to administer their own churches. The council also called for stepping up religious education, engaging in charitable work, and heard demands that it "repent" for its fawning subservience to Stalin.[52] Only time will tell if the official church is capable of acting independently as a revitalized force in society or if recent moves only fit a general pattern observed in culture, human rights, and elsewhere of liberalization in order to encompass, legitimate, and better control moderate forces for change.

The number of Jews allowed to emigrate in 1987 reached 8,155, the largest number since 1981, but only one-seventh the figure for the peak year, 1979.[53] In 1988, the number released continued to edge upward, by mid-year climbing to more than 1,000 per month for the first time since 1981.[54] How many more Jews would like to emigrate? Western estimates range as high as 400,000 (of the 1.8 million Jews in the Soviet Union); Soviet authorities aver the number is no more than 15,000.[55] In addition to Jews, as many as 15,000 Volga Germans have left for the West. Western diplomats say another 20,000 Germans and 14,000 Armenians will emigrate in 1988 (6,900 left in the first six months). Early in 1988 a Soviet delegation told U.S. officials that a provision added in recent years to emigration law, which prevented anyone without "immediate" family abroad from leaving, will be changed to include "distant" relatives.[56]

However, given Soviet—indeed, Russian—tradition (Tsarist authorities issued internal passports and assumed that travel abroad was a privilege rather than a right), and the lingering view of emigrants as traitors (reinforced, unfortunately, by widespread anti-Semitism and the fact that most emigrants have been Jewish), unlimited freedom to emigrate is not likely to result from glasnost. Yet dissidents argue that the freedom to emigrate ("the right not to participate in a society") is as basic as any civic freedom within that society. And a meeting between Soviet authorities and 250 members of the International Bar Association in June 1988 produced expressions of disillusionment with the "Soviet charm offensive" and the conclusion that "there is a legal revolution going on in this country, but it does not embrace the human rights of refuseniks."[57]

To this point, our discussion of religion has been Eurocentric (even while it neglects the role of the Lutheran and especially the Catholic churches in the Baltic). Limited attention has been given in the Western press to the impact upon Islam of any pending legislation modifying believers' rights or state-church relations. As one analyst pointed out, "the authorities can hardly afford to be perceived as allowing greater latitude to Christianity than to Islam." Yet the fact that Islam is a religion with a deeply embedded way of life (including, it should be added, suppression of women's rights), and social traditions that contribute to the nepotism and massive corruption affecting Central Asia, will give deep pause to Soviet leaders before major changes are made.[58] Once again, the theme of cooption emerges, for the authorities have long pursued a policy of tolerating a docile official Islamic hierarchy in order more ruthlessly to extirpate the uncompromising fundamentalist sects (especially Sufism, which has much support in the villages).[59] But at the very least, the fact that the leadership must develop a religious policy that serves official purposes without giving cause for complaints of discrimination against one faith (and ethnic group) over another adds to the very complexity of the issue. A good example here is Gorbachev's order to "call to account" party members who take part in religious ceremonies. He may well be indifferent or even supportive (for the reasons noted above) of a revival of Christian ethics and rituals, but feel compelled by circumstances in Central Asia to take a more rigid position.[60]

The Police Are Nervous

Many intellectuals within the country and observers abroad are convinced that the Soviet Union has "turned a major corner in the handling of human-rights cases."[61] Andrei Sakharov, Nobel Prize laureate and prominent activist, whose release from internal exile in Gorki in late 1986 was itself a landmark, has become a firm supporter of Gorbachev.[62] Human rights advocate Lev Timofeyev, who was released from prison in February 1987, observed that "the level of freedom here has become entirely different from the 1970s and 1960s. They could only dream about our scale of operations."[63] And the most recent U.S State Department report on human rights lauds "significant improvements" in the period from October 1987 to the following March.[64]

As of yet, skeptics point out, little has been institutionalized. Reformists, by mid-1988, were distinguishing between liberalization and democratization, warning that while democratization meant a fundamental redistribution of power, liberalization implied but a softening of the edges of the system. The danger of liberalization was that it could be retracted at any time (whether in the sphere of culture or in politics). So far, according to S. Frederick Starr, "whatever melioration has taken place in recent years has occurred de facto and not de jure."[65]

By the end of 1987, police crackdowns on demonstrations and other forms of harassment led some analysts to doubt the permanence of change. The semi-annual State Department report to Congress on human rights, cited above, included criticism of official harassment of demonstrators, selective interference with telephone service, and press distortion of accounts of protests. In December, eight demonstrators were arrested in Moscow for protesting against the KGB on its seventieth anniversary,[66] and a small number of activists have been arrested in 1988, whether for publishing independent journals, advocating Jewish rights, or working against nuclear power. Admittedly, these individuals, arrested on charges of disturbing the peace or offering resistance to police orders, have only been held a few hours or days—and at that in the local jail rather than in prison—but at least one individual, the Armenian nationalist Paruir Airikian, was held by the KGB for more than two months before being expelled from the Soviet Union in July 1988. More disturbing, the charges tendered against him were of slandering the Soviet state. This item in the Criminal Code was used to break the dissident movement in the 1960s, but many had hoped it had now been discarded.[67]

The novelty and fragility of the situation was well depicted by *Baltimore Sun* correspondent Scott Shane, who observed a demonstration on Pushkin Square in late May 1988. The police stood around awkwardly, using their megaphones only to urge the demonstrators not to trample on the grass. Surprised that no arrests had taken place, the activist Alexander Verkhovsky concluded that "perhaps something really is changing." As an afterthought, the bearded young man then added: "Of course the police are nervous. They're not used to this. But then, we're not used to it, either."[68] But an antidemonstration ordinance adopted in August 1987 remained on the books, and the new tolerance was not reflected in other cities, where recent demonstrators have clashed with the police.

How, then, are we to assess the state of human rights? The country has a long road to go before creating a public forum at which "the citizen may openly criticize the government's policies and officials, or disapprove of its presence in power, without exposing himself or herself to a charge of disloyalty, much less criminality."[69] Even a member of the Soviet Commission on Human Rights concedes that "human rights hasn't entered into our blood yet."[70] Peter Reddaway argued in early 1987 that "the Kremlin's record on human rights generally has been spotty, and has not yet approached the degree of liberalism the regime allowed between 1974 and 1979."[71] Reddaway also pointed out that as of yet no internal improvements have occurred in Soviet prisons.

Some even argue that creation of the new official Soviet Commission on Human Rights is a tactic "designed to block the activities of existing human rights groups" or to direct such activities through officially sanctioned channels, giving the party the credit for any advances made.[72] This would, of course, fit well with observations by Condee and Padunov on the recent trend in the cultural sphere to reabsorb unofficial groups. In a roundtable discussion printed in *Literaturnaia gazeta* June 8, legal reformers concurred that resolutions presented in the Theses submitted for Conference approval urging "perfection" of Soviet state legality were empty phrases without a genuine separation of powers within the Soviet political system. Many would support the assertion that "the durability of . . . improvements is in doubt as long as the Soviet Union remains a one-party state."[73]

Yet when all is said and done, the advances in human rights are palpable and undeniably of historic significance. The less harsh treatment of those subjected to persecution, the ongoing debate on the Criminal Code, the assault on the abuse of psychiatry, and the new treatment of religion and religious believers, along with the virtually astounding advances in freedom of expression, amount to a veritable revolution in Soviet political culture. It is only to be expected that progress will have ragged edges and that the all-important process of institutionalization of new rights will lag behind. It is also to be expected that Gorbachev, whatever his personal beliefs, will occasionally have to pull back, to lash out (or at least go through the motions of doing so) at those whose radical demands seem to threaten anarchy.

In my view, the longer Gorbachev stays in power, the more difficult it will be to reverse the course of change. Even if progress were to halt today, the Soviet Union would be a country far freer than it was but three years ago. The note of irritation with which Gorbachev responded to President Reagan's focus on human rights abuses during the May summit reflected, I believe, genuine frustration at the lack of recognition that conditions have improved as rapidly as anyone could have hoped, and far more so than most of us expected.

We should have a bit more patience; not only is Gorbachev dealing with entirely different traditions, but he also confronts a very volatile situation, with pent-up demands and enormous resentments, expressed in the vitriolic tone of public discourse, on the one hand, and fear of the consequences of a loss of control, on the other. We should keep in mind how far the Soviet Union has come; if anyone engaged in the study of Soviet affairs had predicted the kind of freedoms now exercised by the Soviet press, he or she would have been laughed out of the profession only three years ago.

Here the treatment of those involved in advocacy of minority rights will be most instructive. No other single issue is fraught with more danger for perestroika and for Gorbachev himself, for loss of control in the border regions would certainly create a powerful backlash and add momentum to Russian nationalism and the conservative advocates. Western analysts have long observed that Soviet citizens are generally supportive of law-and-order measures and unconcerned with the Western notion of the separation of powers or the procedures of the democratic process. Instead, they respect "doers"—regardless of how "it" gets done. This may well be changing with the emergence of a civil society and growth of a powerful middle class, but all indications are that public opinion is divided.

Ethnic disorders, combined with the ever-widening revelations about the past and the new candor about social ills besetting Soviet society, has, at least in the short run, severely disoriented many ordinary citizens and reinforced the feeling of decline prompted by economic slowdown. It may well be, in fact, that the perception of breakdown has run far ahead of the reality. This seems, in fact, to be the conclusion of a seminar sponsored by Tatiana Zaslavskaia in Novosibirsk in late April 1988. Warning that Soviet civil society was still nascent and that restructuring could cause serious social shock long before any positive effects could be felt, the reformers noted that there was a "powerful social base of millions of people who had moved away from one (rural) culture but still have not become part of a different (urban) culture." Such an unstable social base provides strong objective support for what the Conference speakers called the "third wind of Stalinism."[74]

Western analysts have shown little sensitivity to the real problem the Soviet leadership faces in cushioning the impact of this torrent of revelations. Here, Gorbachev confronts the same dilemma with zakonnost that is posed by economic perestroika. As Jerry Hough points out:

> Reform must be incremental . . . or the result will be chaos . . . yet [everything] is so interconnected that reform in one sphere may well fail without simultaneous and comprehensive changes in other spheres. . . . In addition, if reform is gradual, opponents have a long time to sabotage it. . . . The central concern must be how to sequence the various steps of reform in a way that solves this predicament."[75]

Absolute candor and pure democracy are fine goals; introduced suddenly they are likely to produce confusion, demoralization, and a backlash of frightening dimensions. It makes real political sense to focus first on developing the notions and practice of legality, along with individual responsibility and genuine participation.

Judging by the results of the June Conference, this progress is not likely to halt. The resolutions adopted at the Conference included one "On Legal Reform," reflecting many of the proposals made in reformist journals and the criticisms leveled by critics such as Arkady Vaksberg, Iuri Feofanov, Alexander Borin, Alexander M. Iakovlev (the legal expert), and Vladimir Kudriatsev. The resolution specifically endorsed the common law principle that "everything not forbidden by law is permitted";[76] called for the establishment of a Constitutional Supervisory Committee, which would function like the U.S. Supreme Court to ensure that government decrees do not violate the Soviet Constitution; proposed separating the functions of the office of the state prosecutor (placing official investigations under a new office in the Ministry of Internal Affairs); suggested that judges be elected by soviets at the next higher level (to insulate them from local party secretaries) and that attempts to influence judges be criminally punished; recommended increasing the number of people's assessors trying criminal cases (in effect, constituting a jury). The last part of the resolution urged measures to educate the Soviet population in juridical matters, presumably to overcome the historical legacy of popular indifference to the importance of legal procedures. Finally, the resolutions of the Conference separately pointed to the need to "eliminate abuses" by Soviet law enforcement agencies.[77]

Notes

1. *Moscow News*, No. 6, 1988: 7.

2. Peter B. Maggs, "Law," in James Cracraft, ed., *Contemporary Soviet Society* (2nd Edition: Chicago, 1988): 339.

3. *Literaturnaia gazeta*, No. 34 (1984): 11; cited in RL 52/88: 3.

4. *Pravda*, September 11; *Izvestiia*, September 12; cited in CDSP, Vol. 39, No. 37 (October 14, 1987).

5. WP, February 26, 1987. For stories about police beating crime suspects and party intervention to harass journalists or cover up police abuses, see CDSP, Vol. 39, No. 22 (July 1, 1987): 10, 19, and No. 37 (October 14, 1987): 20. See also the discussion in *Literaturnaia gazeta*, No. 4, 1987 (a meeting of writers and lawyers at the offices of the journal to discuss measures to reform the legal system).

6. For a review of these cases, which extend back into the early 1970s, see Valery Konovalov, "Violations of Socialist Legality in Belorussia," RL 174/88 (April 20, 1988): 1–5.

7. Maggs, "Law": 339.

8. On this, see WP, March 23, 1988; RL 177/88. For recent serious discussions of crime and criminality in the USSR see Louise I. Shelley, "Crime and Criminals in the USSR," in *Understanding Soviet Society*, ed. by Michael Paul Sacks and Jerry G. Pankhurst (Boston, 1988): 193–220; and Maria Los, *Communist Ideology, Law and Crime* (New York, 1988).

9. See the article by Elena Losoto in *Komsomolskaia pravda*, May 29, 1986.

10. CSM, July 21, 1988.

11. Andrei Nuikin, "Idealy ili interesy?" *Novyi mir*, No. 1, 1988: 190–211; and No. 2: 205–228.

12. Evgeny Ambartsumov, in *Moskovskie novosti*, June 19, 1988: 10.

13. See NYT, November 11, 1987, for a summary of the official Soviet announcement that a revision of the Criminal Code was planned.

14. NYT, December 6, 1987.

15. Alexander Iakovlev of the Moscow Institute of State and Law (Academy of Sciences): RL 382/87 (September 25). For related stories, see CDSP, Vol. 39, No. 46 (December 16, 1987): 24; No. 51 (January 29, 1988): 20 (on pre–trial detention and secrecy in investigations).

16. At the May session of the Supreme Soviet (where many other interesting topics were broached in a highly unusual session), a lengthy discussion centered upon the failure of the USSR's Supreme Court and the Soviet legal system as a whole to safeguard the rights of individuals: see RL 235/88 (June 7).

17. Gorbachev's speech, in English, can be found in *Moscow News*, No. 27, 1988 (Supplement: 1–16).

18. Valery Konovalov, "The Death Penalty in the USSR," RL 41/88 (January 25): 1–7. In the first half of 1987, 4,682 people were convicted of premeditated murder. During the entire year, some sixty–one people were condemned to death and three death sentences were carried out, in most of the remainder decisions were called final with no right to appeal. Of those cases on which information was available, five were for abuse of office or economic crimes, thirty–six for crimes of violence (aggravated murder, rape of a minor, attempted hijack of an airplane) and six for war crimes not subject to the statute of limitations.

19. Reported in the NYT, June 8, 1988.

20. *Justice in Moscow* (New York, 1966).

21. WP, February 22, 1987.

22. CSM, January 29, 1988.

23. For a partial list, see NYT, December 6, 1987. Nudel had been waiting seventeen years, as had Lerner and Slepak. Barkans is a Latvian nationalist; Terelia, organizer of the outlawed Ukrainian Church; Slepak, a founding member of Moscow Helsinki Watch.

24. The Amnesty International estimate of numbers was released in CSM, March 2, 1988. The State Department report is cited in BS, June 5, 1988. But other estimates of those still incarcerated are 3,500 or, less credibly, 10,000 (Anatoly Sharansky, based on "rumors circulating in the camps.") NYT, February 13, 1987. Peter Reddaway also talks of the release of "only a small proportion of the several thousands of political and religious prisoners." ("Gorbachev the Bold," *New York Review of Books*, May 28, 1987: 23.)

25. NYT, February 28, 1988.

26. WP, December 15, 1987.

27. NYT, June 8, 1988; BS, June 5, 1988.

28. *Izvestiia*, November 30, 1987; cited in RL 10/88 (January 12): 1–2.

29. RL 10/88: 4. But it also includes Andrei Grachev, senior official of the Propaganda Department of the CPSU, whose prominence led a skeptical Radio

Liberty researcher to call the commission the brainchild of Soviet propaganda officials.

30. RL 68/88 (February 17): 1–2. In an earlier interview published in *Sovetskaia Rossiia* (December 27, 1987), Burlatsky observed that the commission would be primarily concerned with international cooperation rather than violations of human rights in the Soviet Union, and that it would not deal with individual cases, another position he later altered (RL 10/88:5).

31. However, by October, *Izvestiia* was reporting that a special commission had been formed to deal with criticism of the law, particularly the absence of a provision for the right to appeal against a decision taken by a group of officials (RL 391/87: October 2).

32. Cited in CSM, December 4, 1987. See also, for another account, RL 377/87 (September 28): 2.

33. WP, December 3, 1987. See also the lengthy article in *Komsomolskaia pravda*, November 11, 1987, abstracted in CDSP, Vol. 39, No. 46 (December 16, 1987): 1–6, 28.

34. RL 61/87 (February 12), citing *Sotsialisticheskaia industriia*, January 31 and February 1, 1987. This is curious for, as Peter Reddaway has observed, the new minister of health, Evgeny Chazov, in his earlier position as director of the fourth section of the ministry, may have been directly involved in the abuse of psychiatry for political ends. A prominent reformer in this area has been A. Potopov, RSFSR minister of health. (This speculation is based upon conversations with Reddaway, and on a brief article in the WP, December 2, 1987: A28.

35. NYT, January 5, 1988; WSJ, February 12, 1988.

36. CSM, June 23, 1987: 6.

37. For details, see RL 381/87 (September 28). Commemoration of this event included appearances on television of religious leaders; press coverage of religious conferences; the stepped–up use of church spokesmen for diplomatic goals; and inception of a new journal, *Religiia v SSSR*.

38. See RL 179/88 (April 27): 1–4; Oxana Antic, "Government Policy Towards the Official Churches in the USSR in 1987," RL 54/88 (February 8): 1–7.

39. CSM, November 20, 1987. The information is from the American Bible Society, and the Bibles provided by the United Bible Societies. The Bibles will include 98,000 in Russian and 2,000 in Ukrainian.

40. Cited in RL 374/87 (September 28): 4, and 450/87 (November 11): 5.

41. RL 54/88: 1.

42. The specialist is William Fletcher, who has placed the proportion of believers in the population as high as 35 percent. From *Sotsiologicheskie issledovaniia*, No. 4, 1987; cited in RL 382/87 (September 25). The media have featured "dialogues" between believers and atheists.

43. RL 9/88 (January 11): 5. The data also indicated the number of christenings and religious weddings and funerals.

44. RL 150/88 (March 31): 1–3.

45. For interesting detail, see Oxana Antic, "Church Bells and Perestroika," RL 200/88 (May 16): 1–4.

46. RL 201/87 (May 26) "Soviet Writers and the Search for God,": 1–5; and 211/87 (June 5): 4.

47. NYT, June 19, 1988.

48. The above quotations from dissident priests are cited in BS, June 12, 1988.

49. For a survey, see Oxana Antic, "Policy Towards Unofficial Religious Groups Under Gorbachev," RL 138/88 (March 31): 1–8.

50. RL 374/87 (September 13). See also *Moscow News*, September 20, 1987. Calls for a more tolerant attitude toward believers are summarized in RL 360/87. Other examples of harassment of believers legally trying to register a new parish are described in RL 381/87 (September 28): 4.

51. NYT, June 5, 1988. Reuters reported (June 11) that Soviet President Gromyko promised that consideration would be given to allowing Roman Catholic bishops to practice in the Ukraine and Belorussia.

52. See NYT, June 10, 1988.

53. WP, January 6, 1988; BS, December 7, 1987. The number of Soviet emigrés in the United States alone is now estimated to be 171,500, concentrated in New York, Boston, Washington, and Los Angeles (NYT, December 5, 1987).

54. In April, 1,086 Jews departed; in May, 1,145; and in June, 1,470. The total for the first half of 1988 was 6,017 (WP, June 9, 1988 and July 2, 1988).

55. NYT, May 18, 1988.

56. NYT, February 22, 1988.

57. Irwin Cotler, a law professor at McGill University in Montreal; cited in WP, June 8, 1988.

58. The view that Islam is at the heart of many social ills (from corruption to the birth of deformed children) is advocated by S. P. Poliakov, head of the Central Asian Archeological Expedition of Moscow State University, but was strongly disputed as simplistic by many participants in a seminar held in September 1987 in Daghestan. Among those attacking the notion that Islam is a virus causing social ills was V. Pravotorov, chief editor of the journal *Nauka i religiia* (Science and Religion). On this see: RL 515/87 (December 11): 1–3.

59. The recently (June 3, 1988) deceased scholar Alexander Bennigsen was among the first to point out the strength of secret Sufi sects as a "parallel" Islam thriving alongside officially registered organizations (and particularly strong in the countryside). His views received support in an article on Islam by Igor Beliaev in *Literaturnaia gazeta* (May 20, 1987).

60. Here, I have in mind questionable party loyalty to Moscow in Central Asia: see RL 18/87 (January 14): 1–3.

61. NYT, February 13, 1987.

62. See his comments reported in the NYT, November 1, 1987. Sakharov has, however, been rebuked by some dissidents, who have hinted that his release from exile was won in exchange for support for Gorbachev.

63. Cited in NYT, May 24, 1988.

64. BS, June 5, 1988.

65. S. Frederick Starr, "Soviet Union: A Civil Society," *Foreign Policy*, No. 70 (Spring, 1988): 36.

66. WP, December 20, 1988.

67. NYT, June 7, 1988.

68. BS, June 5, 1988.

69. Archie Brown, "Gorbachev and the Fight for Soviet Reform."

70. Mikhail Krutogolov, cited in NYT, June 7, 1988.

71. "Gorbachev the Bold": 23.

72. Viktor Yasmann, "An Official Human Rights Organization in the USSR: 'New Thinking' or Propaganda?" RL 10/88 (January 12): 3.

73. Aaron Trehub, "Human Rights in the Soviet Union: Recent Developments," RL 67/88 (February 11): 1.

74. *Nedelia*, No. 18, 1988: 11; CDSP, Vol. 40, No. 21, 1988: 18–19.

75. Jerry Hough, *Opening Up the Soviet Economy* (Washington, D.C., 1988): 6.

76. It is a measure of how far we have come that when Gorbachev's close adviser advocated only last year that everything not explicitly permitted by law should be permitted, analyst Starr called it an "astonishing utterance" to be coming from Gorbachev's inner circle ("Soviet Union: A Civil Society": 37).

77. *Pravda* editor Afanasiev also told a news conference during the week of the June Conference that "while the KGB is needed, it should be more under the control of the party than now." WSJ, July 6, 1988.

5
The Economy

Right now we are like people who have been trapped by a mine cave-in and have just started to receive oxygen, which is being pumped in to us through a hose. We can't get enough of it. The danger is that we will forget, in our euphoria, that we are still trapped in the mine, and that the rock above our heads is starting to tremble and crack, sometimes quite ominously.

—Andrei Nuikin,
"Idealy ili interesy?"

The Rock Above Our Heads

The Soviet economy suffers from numerous well-known ailments: dwindling natural resources (and difficult access to those remaining); inefficient utilization of capital and labor (and dwindling supplies of both); overcentralization and organizational rigidities; insufficient horizontal ties between enterprises; inadequate transport and infrastructure; and outdated technology. An economic strategy based upon heavy industry and extensive rather than intensive methods has resulted in declining growth rates, ever-lower marginal returns on investments, huge government subsidies for basic necessities ($80 billion annually), and an increasingly disruptive repressed inflation, with excess money chasing scarce goods.

In his important new book, Gorbachev adviser Abel Aganbegyan summarizes for his Western audience the problems with the Soviet economy:

The current structure of the economy in the USSR is backward and conservative. Within it mining and agriculture occupy exaggerated positions, and in contrast manufacturing industry and the processing of raw materials are insufficiently developed. Even worse developed . . . is the service sector. . . . The quality, efficiency, competitiveness of goods produced is universally low. There is a high proportion of obsolete production. . . . Goods and services available [lag behind demand] and do not satisfy real social needs. . . . The branches providing for consumption and for . . . welfare needs have seriously fallen behind, as has the whole service sector.[1]

Such candor would have gotten Aganbegyan in trouble just a few years ago. Today it seems tame. The economic situation is very distressing, justifying the label "precrisis," for if present trends continue the country will be in a genuine fix in perhaps a decade.

But it should also be noted that the Soviet Union still has huge reserves of energy and resources; it has a highly educated population; grain harvests (despite seven disastrous years in a row) have more than kept up with population growth; and it has a gross output that surpasses the USA production in many smokestack industries. The Soviet Union does not have China's staggering demographic problem (reflected, most graphically, in arable land per capita ratios), nor does it have a crushing foreign debt.

Even if the economy is not in danger of imminent collapse, the task confronting the leadership is daunting. Nikolai Shmelev, an economist at the USA and Canada Institute, published a now famous article in *Novyi mir* (June 1987) in which he argued that the economy was in far worse shape than previously admitted, ridiculed earlier estimates of growth rates, and described corruption and demoralization as pervasive. Remarkably, Gorbachev cited this report approvingly (though disclaiming one passage arguing that a measure of unemployment, properly administered, is necessary to make workers apply themselves to their jobs).

Shmelev's paper,[2] given much attention both at home and in the West, was only one of a large number of trenchant criticisms of the Soviet economy aired in 1987 and early 1988. One critic went so far as to claim that although there were plans, there was no planning, but rather "inertial development" in the Soviet system.[3] Similarly, a Joint Economic Committee report to the U.S. Congress in October 1987, painting the condition of the Soviet economy in grim terms and describing the obstacles on the path to reform as formidable, was publicly said to contain much truth by Gorbachev. The attack on the agricultural system has been even harsher, extending to the very historical roots of the collective farm economy.[4]

The Joint Economic Committee report to Congress described Soviet plan targets for economic growth over the next Five-Year Plans as highly unrealistic. A Soviet economist wrote that official statistics have long understated the annual rate of inflation and that the cost of consumer goods has risen by 75 to 100 percent since the late 1950s.[5] Perhaps most remarkable was Gorbachev's own admission in February 1988 that Soviet economic growth from about 1975 (estimated at 2 to 3 percent) was achieved almost exclusively by the high world prices on oil and increases in retail sales of alcoholic beverages.[6] His chief economic adviser, Aganbegyan, calculated that in the fifteen-year period from 1971 to 1985, two-thirds of economic growth derived from new resources put into the economy (in labor and raw materials) and only one-third from improved efficiency. Moreover, he added, in the period from 1979 to 1982 "there was unprecedented stagnation and crisis," while between 1981 and 1985 there was virtually no economic growth.[7] The legacy from the past is a heavy one. As the authors of a lead article in a popular Soviet journal put it:

> Regrettably, aspects of the period of stagnation are dealing a heavy blow to our economy, and will continue to do so for some time. For years our economy lived off of the profits to be had by exploiting natural resources. Fuel, energy and raw materials made up more than seventy-five percent of our exports, with oil most prominent. As long as prices held up and production could be increased, such a policy was superficially successful. The foreign currency earnings permitted us to purchase ample machinery, produce and consumer goods. Now this source of "well-being" has seriously diminished. . . . This loss must be compensated for by reform. No small order! For years the costs of amortization (of plant) have been borne by the enterprise and equipment was not updated (especially in metallurgy, the railroads, and the light and food industries). But many billions were poured into huge hydro-electric stations, the Baikal-Amur Railroad, Atommash . . . and other "projects of the century." . . . Our environment has suffered a serious deterioration in recent decades.[8]

In the long run the apparent incompatibility between the Soviet economy and the so-called Third Industrial Revolution means that the Soviet economy simply must undergo a massive overhaul. As the overhaul will inevitably involve a reduction of central control, the political structure (party control) must also change. The introduction of unemployment, inflation and (aggravated) wage inequalities will also mean rewriting the "social contract" existing between people and state. The "gridlock dilemma," or issue of simultaneities (the notion that change, to be successful, requires changes in other sectors—see the comments concluding Chapter 4) means that change cannot be introduced incrementally, or at least not on a small scale.[9]

We Have Just Begun to Receive Oxygen

This, then, is the situation that confronts Gorbachev. In his first year Gorbachev acted more like a technologist than an economizer,[10] stressing industry, high technology, and reorganization rather than prices and incentives, and pushing for investment over consumption. He sought gains in reinforcing Andropov's campaign for discipline and against corruption, in making personnel changes, and in pursuing bureaucratic reorganization.

Gorbachev has publicly moved, in three short years, from a position of cautious tinkering to endorsement of an economic revival through major economic reform.[11] At the 27th Party Congress, Gorbachev gave a five-and-a-half hour speech focusing on economic reform and claiming that "the country's socioeconomic development is the key to all our problems." He called for more autonomy for plant and local farm managers and less interference from central planners; for improved banking and credit systems to make factories self-financing; for revision of the price system, to take into account consumer demands; for linking factory salaries with sales of goods; for a policy allowing state and collective farms "to use as they see fit" all produce harvested above government targets. At the Congress Gorbachev spoke of "radical reform" and used the term *prodnalog* (produce levy), explicitly linking his program to the NEP period (1921-1929) of relaxed controls, a mixed economy and, by implication, cultural pluralism. For the first time, the ruler of the Soviet Union spoke of "radical reform" and drastic measures needed to turn the economy around.

Perestroika gained structural definition[12] in 1987 with the June plenum and announcement of a long-term overhaul involving price changes, decentralization of decision making, market incentives, and a substantially reduced economic bureaucracy.[13] Beginning January 1, 1988, enterprises producing 60 percent of Soviet output become "self-financing" (*khozraschet*), allowing them to bargain with suppliers and wholesale customers, to use extra profits for wages and benefits, or to suffer bankruptcy for inefficiency. By 1991 all production is to be converted, the share of government in purchasing to be reduced to 30 percent, food and fuel subsidies phased out, small-scale cooperative enterprises encouraged to produce services, and millions of state and cooperative farm acreage to be farmed out to families or work teams, who will be responsible for all phases of the harvest and will keep all returns above set norms.

The new Law on Cooperatives,[14] given relatively little attention in the West, has been called "perhaps the boldest liberalization legislation on the economy . . . under the Gorbachev leadership."[15] Cooperatives flourished in the Russian countryside in the decade before World War I; in Siberia, dairy cooperatives achieved a high degree of organization and profitability. During the NEP period, moderates saw cooperatives as a stepping stone between private farming, individual enterprise, and socialism, as a way of demonstrating by example rather than by force the virtues of pooling resources and energies. Reformers today shrewdly regard cooperatives as institutions both vaguely socialist, hence ideologically palatable, and sufficiently flexible to permit individual initiative and a large degree of private enterprise. Gorbachev reportedly had to stand his ground at a heated Politburo meeting in February 1988 to overcome fierce conservative opposition to the new law. Conservatives are not fooled by the "cooperative" label, which they see as a mere cloak for the promotion of "money-grubbing private greed," as one critic nicely described private initiative.

The Law on Cooperatives gives cooperatives independent legal status comparable with state-run institutions, along with firm guarantees of inviolability of property and freedom from state interference. The state is excluded from oversight of management or operational issues, but losses incurred while fulfilling state orders must be fully reimbursed. The law also deals firmly with a problem that has received much attention in the press: harassment from local officials. Until now, cooperatives had been required to register with local authorities—to obtain permission to organize (according to these authorities). Now, the establishment of a cooperative is not contingent upon such permission and hindrance from local authorities is punishable by law. Cooperatives will have the right to terminate their activities, amalgamate, and declare bankruptcy—in short, to resort to "virtually all the alternative forms of action available to businesses in the West when they face new developments in their markets or in their financial position." Annual and five-year plans are to be drawn up "independently" and ratified by general membership meetings. Prices on goods and services produced entirely by the cooperatives will be set by supply and demand. Taxation of cooperatives is a contentious and as yet unsettled issue; it caused an unprecedented upheaval in the Supreme Soviet (where deputies, in May, demanded repeal of a steep progressive income tax on new businesses that would have taken 90 percent of all earnings over 1,000 rubles per month).[16] A new tax law was to be prepared by July 1, 1988.

Trade with the West remains an unsettled aspect of perestroika.[17] Soviet leaders have historically vacillated between autarkic policies and the advantages of mutual interdependence. The realization that a country having only raw materials to offer in exchange for manufactured goods would be in a disadvantageous position on the world market has traditionally been reinforced by a fear that dependence upon Western products or finance could result in foreign interference in internal Soviet affairs or the imposition of unwanted terms.[18]

Gorbachev's policies reflect this ambivalence. On the one hand, he has argued that the Soviet Union has to modernize from within, and he has explicitly stated that borrowing leads to dependence, that international organizations such as the IMF can exploit to impose conditions. On the other hand, the appeal of foreign aid to "help ease the transition pains" of perestroika is tempting, and since 1986 the foreign trade apparatus has twice undergone a major overhaul in order to facilitate international contacts. Moreover, a major tenet of the New Thinking is the interdependence of the global economy and the virtues of fostering international trade, which, we are now told, is not a zero-sum game in which one party to the action must, by definition, lose if the other gains.

Still, to date "perestroika is a rather disorganized process as far as the foreign trade system is concerned." Since May 1986 the Ministry of Foreign Trade has undergone two major reorganizations (connected as much with an attempt to clean up pervasive corruption as with the desire to facilitate trade). At that time the Ministry lost its monopoly over foreign trade, was deprived of control over customs, and was placed under the supervision of a commission attached to the Committee of Ministers. In January 1988, the Ministry of Foreign Trade was amalgamated with the State Committee for Foreign Trade Relations to form a new Ministry of Foreign Economic Relations, headed by the former chairman of the State Committee. A comparison of the two shake-ups led Western analysts to conclude that the most recent moves were not a logical follow-up to the earlier changes but rather signaled a continuing political struggle over the status of these institutions. In the meantime, measures similar to those carried out in Eastern Europe fifteen years ago have been introduced to foster trade by allowing major ministries and enterprises to deal directly with foreign partners. As of January 1987, twenty ministries and seventy enterprises were empowered to operate directly with the outside world and maintain their own accounts. James Giffen, president of the U.S.-USSR Trade and Economic Council, said: "They are going to change the method of doing business. They want to be part of the international trading economy. If all this comes about [it] would have a tremendous impact on the political relationship." Of equal importance are measures designed to facilitate joint ventures, which are seen as a way to acquire Western technology, expertise, and market skills, to upgrade the production process, and to spur exports.[19] The Soviet leadership has also been lobbying (against U.S. opposition) for membership in the international trade and tariff organization, GATT, both to gain reduced tariffs and to expand general Soviet familiarity with world trade.

As Gorbachev's views on the economy have evolved, so has his emphasis upon the need for radical political change, pithily expressed in his frequently cited comment that "we need democracy as we need air." The interaction of politics and economics should come as no surprise, for as economist Robert Campbell has observed, "A distinguishing feature of the Soviet social order is the high degree to which politics and economic management are fused in a single system." As he points out, the Stalinist economic model was one "designed by geniuses to be run by idiots," i.e., "reconciling dynamic change in the large with individual passivity."[20] However, the emergence of a civil society, marked by more discriminating, skeptical, individualistic attitudes and greater contact with Western life, has put new demands upon a system already encountering increasing difficulty in meeting its targets. Stalinist planners "distrusted fine calculation, feared decentralized values and perspectives" and were unwilling "to see leverage in the hands of individuals."[21] By emphasizing the "human factor," and especially popular participation, Gorbachev has both acknowledged the new demands of civil society and (in conjunction with carefully designed structural reforms) added a major component to perestroika. In so doing, he has reasserted the link between politics and economics, but reversed the relationship.

By the summer of 1988, Gorbachev was on record as strongly endorsing both

Chinese (agricultural) and Hungarian (industrial) reforms. The historian, ever aware of the looming figure of Peter the Great, can only be gratified to learn that recently Gorbachev has also shown a strong interest in the "Swedish model"—a country with "high levels of economic efficiency and social justice" that went through a painful restructuring of its own in 1982 to regain international competitiveness. According to one source, Gorbachev is particularly interested in Sweden's experience with "participatory management, employee training and the cooperative movement"; in Scandinavian skill at converting technology into marketable products; and in a "strategy of innovation and investments in research and development, training, and organizational development rather than more traditional investments in plants and equipment."[22]

Still Trapped in the Mine

The Basic Provisions adopted by the June plenum may be the "most extensive such measures since the Khrushchev reforms, perhaps even since the New Economic Policy of the 1920s."[23] According to Aganbegyan, they are "one organic whole for economic restructuring."[24] Yet, the opinion in the West is that "there is not yet a blueprint that an economist could say would work";[25] even some of Gorbachev's most ardent supporters concede that "we are still having colossal problems building a general conception for restructuring."[26] The impact of the Basic Provisions approved by the June plenum "on the structure and performance of the Soviet economy and on consumer welfare is likely to be limited."[27]

What, then, has perestroika brought? According to Shmelev, very little. In April 1988 (in response to hundreds of letters sent to *Novyi mir* concerning his strident article "Advances and Debts"), Shmelev wrote of "mounting anxiety about the fate of perestroika"; pointed to widespread resistance, to the persistence of long lines and empty shelves in the stores, to fears of price increases and of a major budget crisis linked to the war against alcoholism, and lamented the "widespread failure to recognize that there are no real alternatives to perestroika, and that economically we have not yet stepped back from the edge of an abyss." Shmelev even cited one factory director's call for an "extraordinary commission" (or Cheka—the original name of the Soviet secret police) to run perestroika: "Is this too stiff a measure? Perhaps so, but we've got to do something, or once again [all these reform efforts] will come to nothing."[28]

One of Gorbachev's first large-scale measures was to declare a "campaign" against alcohol consumption; this move both responded to an egregious problem and fit the Andropov-inspired drive for "acceleration" through heightened discipline, moral measures, and the heavy hand of the state. The first result of the anti-alcohol campaign was to create yet one more bureaucracy, the All-Union Voluntary Society for the Battle for Sobriety, formed in 1985 and enrolling, by September 1987, 14 million members in 450,000 "grass-roots" organizations.[29] The organization, of dubious spontaneity, is now under investigation for overstaffing, formalism, and other shortcomings.

Whatever the social consequences of the anti-alcohol campaign (see Chapter 6), the effects upon the budget have been catastrophic, costing up to 45 billion rubles and leading to a "dangerous deficit." The production of homegrown brew is increasing, despite a new law (June 1987) increasing fines for consumption to 300 rubles (and two years imprisonment for repeaters). Officials complained that violations of rules on selling alcohol were common and that efforts lagged in combatting *samogon* (moonshine) production. In 1987 the number of people charged with producing home brew totaled 390,000).[30] At least one factory illegally producing moonshine has been uncovered. In Shmelev's estimate, before the antidrinking campaign, about two-thirds of revenues from the production of spirits went to the state and one-third to moonshiners; now the proportion has merely been reversed.[31] Moreover, as Gertrude Schroeder points out, because liquor plays such a large role in family budgets, the anti-alcohol drive has offset improvements in the availability of food, clothing, and services.

Finally, with the increase in moonshine production, demand for sugar in the stores has increased by as much as 30 percent (or by 1 million tons in 1987 alone), leading in turn to shortages in condiments and nonalcoholic beverages (previously in abundant supply) and to rationing (imposed in April 1988). The alternative to rationing, one official said, was to spend an extra $1 billion in foreign currency to import more sugar. In fact, early in 1988 the Soviet Union entered the world market (Cuba was unable to help) to purchase 1.4 million tons of raw sugar for delivery in March and another 800,000 tons in June. To add insult to injury, rationing has led to ever more ingenious subterfuges; in Odessa, residents report that samogon producers now require customers to include a rationing coupon along with the price of a bottle of vodka.[32]

Pravda reported[33] that in Karelia, Poltava, and Krasnodar official sales of alcohol had risen sharply in 1987 and that anti-alcohol commissions had "virtually ceased activity" in many areas. The relaxation of rules on the sale and production of alcohol is probably a response to popular discontent as well as to the upsurge in illegal sales, which both take revenues away from the state and represent a substantial health threat. In some areas, authorities concerned with plan fulfillment have been lax in enforcement; the Agro-Industrial Committee was blasted for actually increasing production of wine and cognac.[34] Perhaps as a result, the number of recorded instances of drunkenness on the job *rose* from 117,000 in 1986 to 250,000 in 1987.[35]

Overall the "outlook for the economy [in the short run] is not particularly bright."[36] In 1986 the national income reportedly rose by 4.1 percent (or by 4.2 percent if calculated in terms of GNP), a major improvement over the 3.5 percent average growth rate of 1981-1985.[37] According to Western intelligence estimates, "the Soviet economy performed far better in the first full year under Mikhail Gorbachev's leadership than it has for a decade."[38] However, several

Western scholars have questioned these figures; one organization studying Soviet economic performance calls them "unbelievable" and claimed that growth was only 1.5 percent, "the worst performance of the Soviet economy since World War II."[39] Industrial growth in 1986 was reported at 4.9 percent,[40] but recent reports in the Soviet press attribute most if not all of this growth to excess production of surplus goods (steel, farm combines, shoddy footware).[41]

If earlier reports pointing to gains in 1986 were true, the situation has since then taken a turn for the worse. A new CIA/DIA report concludes that "Gorbachev's ambitious program . . . ran into trouble in 1987."[42] Poor weather, transportation bottlenecks, and the disruptions created by the reforms resulted in an increase of GNP of less than 1 percent. Industry grew by 1.5 percent and the machine-building sector, regarded as critical for perestroika, was stagnant. In seven out of ten branches, performance was down from 1986. Only the energy sector, responding to higher investments, did well.

Agricultural output was also down in 1987, but from a record harvest the previous year. Given very poor weather, which led to low early estimates, the 211 million-ton grain harvest and an excellent forage crop were substantial achievements (although heavy frost cut fruit output by 30 percent). But, the expert contributions to the report to the Joint Economic Committee of Congress late in 1987 concur that the outlook for agriculture is not bright: "Some progress may be made, but the many measures intended to accord priority to improving the living conditions of farm workers—and thus hopefully their work attitudes—are likely to founder on the shoals of insufficient investment."[43]

The CIA/DIA report also concluded that despite quality-control reforms (*gospriemka*), there had been "no major improvement in overall product quality." In fact, quality-control standards, imposed in 20 percent of factories, were apparently relaxed after the first quarter of the year in order to help meet plan targets, but "continued to exert a dampening influence upon production."

At the enterprise level, managers were "confused by contradictory directives from above, struggled to find reliable suppliers, and meet contract obligations." According to a survey conducted in mid-1987, 80 percent of enterprise managers believed that their freedom of action was no better than, had perhaps even diminished since, 1984.[44]

The new wage system (effective January 1, 1987), increasing differentiation and encouraging layoffs, caused much public concern about unemployment and created the "first legions of the unemployed." Losses in work time from supply interruptions and idle equipment increased, and forfeited pay bonuses resulting from such interruptions demoralized the workforce, leading even to strikes and disturbances.

Such is the picture drawn by the CIA/DIA report, and it finds support in the comments of Soviet economists. Abalkin has said on several occasions—most recently at the June Conference—that the reforms are not working. Abalkin asserted that the growth in national income in the past two years had been lower even than growth during the reviled Eleventh Five-Year Plan period (1981-1985). By comparison with the period of *zastoi*, he argued, indices of resource utilization, the supply of consumer goods, and the technology gap between the Soviet Union and the West had all deteriorated. In a lecture published in March, Aganbegyan candidly discussed health, housing, and food supply problems, all basically unimproved at the three-year mark for perestroika.[45] An American reporter in a mining town in Kazakhstan wrote in July 1988 that amid palpable political changes taking place, enormous problems loom:

> The city's shops sadly reflect the continuing inability of the Soviet economy to get on track. Meat is a rarity. Butter and other dairy products are in short supply. The 500 workers at the nearby Saransky Mine-Construction Company found the quota of automobiles available for their purchase this year cut to just 4 (from 16 the previous year). Many frustrated workers—and enterprises—now farm their own plots of land to supply vegetables and fresh produce that the tangled economic system is unable to provide.[46]

Shmelev too concludes that there have been no palpable changes for the average Soviet citizen, instead the sentiment is widespread that conditions have actually worsened: "Lines in stores and empty shelves exist as before: the production of food from state sources has increased only marginally, the quality of domestic consumer goods has not changed, and imports (even including essential items such as tea and coffee) have declined markedly." Shmelev warned that if major gains are not achieved in the next year or two, the fate of perestroika will be in real danger.[47]

And what of foreign trade? In 1987 hard currency purchases from the West declined by 15 to 18 percent; there has been a fall in real volume of trade estimated at 30 percent since 1984. As one study observed, Western suppliers have "been geared up . . . to increase sales to the USSR, only to find their expectations dashed." The Soviet leadership, irrespective of the difficulties of perestroika, has been dealing with highly unfavorable international conditions because of a sharp fall in hard-currency earnings from oil and gas (making up 80 percent of their earnings). Oil prices are at less than one half their 1983 level, and each fall of $1 in the cost of a barrel of oil costs the Soviet Union over half a billion dollars in earnings. The losses have been compounded because oil is priced in dollars; consequently, Soviet purchasing power for goods in yens and marks has fallen sharply (the purchasing power of a barrel of Soviet crude oil in West Germany has declined by one third since early 1985). The Soviets have responded to the situation by paring imports (thus, as Shmelev observed, coffee is hard to find) and by expanding the volume of their staple exports (the volume of oil sales to the West is up by 25 percent since 1985), but everyone recognizes that given the growing problems the USSR faces in producing energy, this solution is only short-term. Joint ventures have also advanced slowly; to date only 20 agreements have been reached out of 300 proposals. Most of the deeds concluded or pending are, according to the CIA/DIA study, "relatively small endeavors, involving simple production processes, and little foreign capital." So, joint ventures will do little to advance the Soviet goal of utilizing foreign expertise to enhance production processes or management techniques.

Many observers have noticed a basic contradiction between the long-range Soviet goal of utilizing joint ventures ultimately to produce manufactured goods of export-level quality and Western reluctance to encourage competition on the market. The terms now set by Soviet law for joint ventures are hardly likely to entice Western companies at this time. As Shmelev bitingly commented:

> We've got to be bold enough to repudiate the present requirement that 51 percent (of all enterprises) be in Soviet hands, the unacceptably high rate of taxation, the regulations forbidding Western businessmen to run their own operations and, finally, we must allow not only for an export, but also, primarily, for a domestic market orientation for such enterprises. Try for a minute to put yourself in the place, say, of an American businessman. If in the United States he has to pay a tax of 34 percent, and in Southeast Asia 20-25 percent, but we are ready to take 44 percent from him, why in the world should he invest his money with us? Perhaps in hope of an opening to our markets? But we ourselves make it clear that the output of such operations must be aimed not at our domestic, but at the export market. And he knows that in the export market there are already enough competitors to go around without our presence.[48]

In sum, foreign trade is likely to remain an important part of perestroika, but obstacles to its promotion are several: the confusion occasioned by the massive personnel turnover following the anticorruption drive and overhaul of the ministry; acute shortages of foreign trade expertise on the spot (of the seventy-seven enterprises now empowered to deal directly with Western firms, most are far from Moscow); the absence of personal networks to facilitate trade negotiations; continued secrecy over Soviet economic data; the decline in oil prices (and the traditional Soviet response of paring imports); the ongoing struggle over the status of the Ministry of Trade; and the terms governing such trade and operations, even under the new legislation. Making Soviet currency convertible would enormously facilitate trade relations (and is a prerequisite to joining GATT), but recent official statements indicate that such a move is not envisioned before 1995 at the earliest.[49]

You Can't Be a Little Bit Pregnant

Each of the basic elements of perestroika faces formidable obstacles.[50] A consensus exists that "even if Gorbachev had the enthusiastic support of the entire country, which he doesn't, many of the changes mandated . . . would be extremely difficult to carry out."[51] Throughout this text, discussion pops up of opposition to perestroika. Recently in *Moscow News*, Soviet analyst Zbigniew Brzezinski listed three obstacles to reform: institutions, traditions, and the complexity of the reform process itself. Jerry Hough believes that "the biggest obstacle to radical economic reform in the Soviet Union is not political or bureaucratic opposition, but the immense inherent difficulty of achieving the goals of the reform itself."[52] Aganbegyan concedes that even in the best of circumstances he does "not think that in 15 years it is possible for the USSR to reach the highest standards of living in the world. . . . Our backwardness compared to the most developed countries in the world is too great to be overcome before the end of the century." Instead, he counsels, the Soviet people should look forward to the 100th anniversary of the Russian Revolution (2017) in the hope that socialism can outproduce capitalism.[53]

CIA analyst Gertrude Schroeder concludes that "taken as a whole" the package of reform measures is "impressive" and "represents a comprehensive package, embracing nearly every aspect and sector of the economy." But she continues that it is hard to "visualize" the nature of the system the planners want to put into place and argues that "its overall design is not that required for a system of market socialism or of worker self-management as those terms are usually understood." More ominously, she adds, "Gorbachev's reform documents leave the pillars of the traditional economic system prominently in place—state ownership, central planning (albeit changed in form and reduced in detail)," administrative tutelage, rationing of goods, state control over prices, and enterprise incentives oriented toward plan and output targets rather than "following signals from the market."[54] Still, it is noteworthy that she, a foremost authority and harsh critic of the "treadmill of Soviet reform," does believe that the Gorbachev economic reform is superior to that of the 1960s and is "mildly optimistic" that the reform may have some beneficial effects.[55]

Is there any consensus about the long-term future of the Soviet economy? Western economists are generally skeptical that the market can coexist with state planning (as one Soviet economist put it: "You can't be a little bit pregnant") and believe that without price reforms in the near future the entire package is doomed to fail. Another concern of Western economists that has not been picked up by the press is that wholesale trade reform is not scheduled to take place until 1992; but without free trade in supplies or a capital market, enterprises will likely cling to state orders and traditional behavior rather than pursue riskier ventures.[56]

Price reforms, which will certainly lead to sharp increases in the costs of basic goods and to increased inequality, are fraught with danger. As Aganbegyan said when asked why it was taking so long to implement price reforms: "We have to be very careful, because if we stumble, no one will pick us up."[57] In other words, unlike Hungary, if experiments get out of hand and disorder ensues, there will be no "fraternal power" next door to move in and restore order.

In May 1988, Gorbachev indicated that price reforms would be introduced in 1991 at the earliest; this delay would have been a political concession to allay widespread anxieties (in fact, in April Shmelev had argued that a short-term postponement of financial and price reforms might be politically necessary, given popular fears)[58] but would have spelled disaster for the reform package.[59] In his speech to the June Conference, however, Gorbachev seemed to indicate that price reforms were back on the near-term agenda.[60]

Finally, what of the competence of those giving Gorbachev advice and shaping the economic reforms? This issue is difficult for a nonspecialist to gauge, but as a discipline, Soviet economics is in poor repute among Western specialists and even at home.[61] Furthermore, it is unclear whether the run-of-the-mill Soviet economist really sees the situation in as drastic terms as do leading Soviet reformers and the markedly reform-oriented Soviet press.[62] Western economists are dismayed by the inadequacy of the Soviet conceptualization of the entire reform "package" and by the crudity with which price and marketing measures have been devised.

The virtually unanimous opinion seems to be that half measures cannot work. Even leading Soviet reformers are apprehensive; in January 1988, Popov and Shmelev were writing pessimistically that the new measures would hamstring rather than liberate workers and managers, and the assessment in the Soviet press of the results of the new Law on State Enterprises has been virtually uniformly negative.

Herbert Levine, however, comments that Soviet economic journals today are full of discussions of the linkage between substitution of wholesale trade for centralized supply and the reform of the pricing system as well as the financing and credit system. He adds that:

> One hallmark of the Gorbachev reform program is the recognition given to the fact that an economy is a complex interrelated system. When the economic mechanism is changed, attention must be paid to the interrelations among its various parts. Yet there is also the necessity of transition. Not everything can or should be changed at once. . . . [What then is the minimum level of simultaneity required to keep the process of reform moving forward?] Soviet discussions abound with references to this simultaneity issue.[63]

For these reasons, we must keep in mind that the reforms presented to date are the "initial package" and that, whatever their inadequacies, Soviet planners seem to be well aware of the difficulties of carrying out such a large-scale reform. As Leonid Abalkin said to an audience at the Kennan Institute in March 1988, perestroika is not a short-term campaign but an evolutionary plan to be carried out over many years.[64]

There is also widespread consensus that simultaneously pursuing short-term economic growth (*uskorenie*, or acceleration) and long-term restructuring is a mistake. Shmelev forcefully argues that *gospriemka* (quality control) and *uskorenie* are incompatible and that the latter should be abandoned: "Surely, indiscriminate growth, increases in output of anything and everything, growth for the sake of growth—is this really what we need today?"[65] Shmelev argues that as long as the bottom line for the enterprise remains the *val* (or measure of value-added output), no enterprise director acting rationally will seriously undertake restructuring. Put more bluntly, "either the *val* will crush the new economic mechanism, or the reverse will take place."[66] Such reasoning leads Shmelev to the conclusion that other drastic measures should be taken to compensate for the drop-off in production that inevitably occurs during any period of serious reorganization.

This brings us to the nub of the problem. Reform, as Ed Hewett reminds us, involves a trade-off of pain and payoffs: "The pain comes first and the payoff comes later." Gorbachev has been trying to have the best of both worlds by pursuing both long-term modernization and short-term growth, and key sectors are being told to do everything at once: retool, improve quality, save resources, change the product mix, and increase output.[67] As long as growth figures remain the only measurement of progress, pressure will grow to meet targets and the traditional "campaign" or "storming" behavior so characteristic of Soviet industry will be reinforced. Moreover, as the Soviet press has pointed out, much of the growth of the economy achieved in 1986 involved the production of goods already in excess supply.[68] Thus, Gorbachev has two alternatives. The first is "retrenchment," or essentially giving up on achieving a major decentralization, reducing obligatory plan targets, and increasing authority for enterprises, and instead renewing emphasis upon discipline and organizational shake-ups. The second is "taking the long view," or downplaying short-term growth (especially fulfillment of plan targets) and accepting short-term disruptions as a necessary part of the reform process. There are, in fact, some indications that the Gorbachevtsy are moving in the latter direction.[69] Hewett goes so far as to argue that the first real signs of progress will be "things most people regard as signs of trouble: unemployment, reductions in the growth rate, maybe even negative growth rates, strikes. . . . When I see growth rates go up, when I see no signs of social unrest, no firms failing, then there's no reform. It's as simple as that."[70]

It's as Simple as That

How, then, can conditions be improved? The economic reform did not originally envision shifting resources to the consumer sector in the near future,[71] and if, as Schroeder notes, Gorbachev's stance is "to demand hard work and creativity in return for pledges of future substantial material rewards,"[72] the going will be rough indeed. Everyone seems to agree that a shift in the allocation of resources away from the military (which, by most estimates, including some recently published in the Soviet press, presently consumes from 14 to 19 percent of Soviet GNP, but may, according to Anders Aslund, consume as much as 30 percent) is a prerequisite of successful reform,[73] and achieving such a shift obviously underlies Gorbachev's push for arms negotiations. A recent CIA-DIA study of the Soviet economy concludes that "the Soviets could reap some benefits from arms control, given the provisions of the recently signed INF treaty and the type of reductions envisioned from a START accord." Savings would result from reduced deployments of modernized weapons, and from releases of thousands of troops and of workers in defense plants.[74] But slashing the military budget, important as it is, will be no cure-all. Colton argues that the short-term results of slashing the military budget would be small, perhaps one tenth to one-fifth of a percent a year in annual growth.[75]

Several Western analysts have argued that it would have been far better for the Soviet leaders to begin with agricultural rather than industrial reform, to put changes in the countryside at the forefront of perestroika, as in China and Hungary. As Robert Campbell points out, the failure to take decisive action in this sphere is puzzling because "this is an area in which radical institutional change could be introduced on a broad scale in an isolable context without changing the traditional planning system elsewhere," and, he might have added, without great outlays.[76]

Surprisingly, although Gorbachev first came to Moscow with responsibility for agriculture and is known to favor radical measures in that area, since becoming general secretary he has given less attention to that sphere in his public pronouncements.[77] Some have expressed perplexity at Gorbachev's reluctance to do so; others trace this reluctance to ideological objections put forth by conservatives.[78] He has given high priority to shifting resources within the agricultural sector away from farms and into infrastructure (such as roads and storage facilities) and food processing, to reducing conflict within the agro-industrial sector through reorganization, and to streamlining the movement of produce from farms to retail outlets. As elsewhere, he has emphasized the transition from "administrative means" to individual incentives. New laws on contracts permitting group and family leasing for up to twelve to fifteen years create conditions for "small-scale private agriculture" and are, according to Alec Nove, "an important step forward."

Events in the first half of 1988 may be the first sign that Gorbachev is taking heed of Western advice, or of the Chinese example. Speaking at the Fourth Congress of Kolkhoz Workers (the first in decades) in March, Gorbachev referred favorably to the Hungarian reforms, and in a visit to Hungary in July, he spoke even more explicitly of emulating the Hungarian model. A new Model Statute for Collective Farms codifies changes under way since the plenary session of the CPSU in May 1982 (notably, family contracting, or *semeinyi podriad*, by which land is distributed for long-term use to individual households); brings the operation of collective farms in line with the new Law on State Enterprises (thus encouraging autonomy, self-financing, and self-management); and introduces the produce levy (*prodnalog*), according to which collective farms are free to sell surplus at market prices outside the state network. Most important, according to Gorbachev, "the time when the district party committee issued commands and orders on what to plant, when to plant it and what direction to cultivate in, on when the reaping of wheat or barley should begin, etc., has gone, never to return."[79] Interestingly, Gorbachev drew comparisons with China in a speech to the Kolkhoznik Conference in March 1988 (speaking of family contract groups, and long-term rentals of both land and equipment), but he suggested that reforms in the USSR would differ in one respect: the small size of plots given families in China, and now retarding further progress there, would be assiduously avoided.[80]

Problems of delivery of supplies to contract groups, resistance from local officials, and continued use of traditional command methods in ensuring deliveries from collective farms (despite exhortations from Gorbachev to allow farms to dispose freely of their surplus) indicate that "deeply rooted negative attitudes towards successful private activity" remain intact (to the degree that in 1987 local officials went so far as to bulldoze private greenhouses).[81] According to pioneer of the contract method Vasily Shvets, an economist jailed in the early 1980s for promoting individual farms, local conservatives have devised an interesting way to resist perestroika: "Without giving people any clear explanations, introduce (the rental contract) everywhere. . . . The idea is almost guaranteed to fail." According to Shvets, in the province of Tselinograd, out of 104 farms he visited in the spring of 1988, only four had introduced "genuine" rental contracts.[82] At a Central Committee meeting in May, Gorbachev stated firmly, "Our demand on everyone is to open the road to contracts, to leases, and to help people with initiative. . . . People want to take the new path, but many others are impeding them because they still have doubts. . . . We put [it] this way—no one can refuse to allow a person to switch to a contract . . . those who [do] and impede the changeover to new methods [must be removed from office]."[83] Yet, he added, the excesses of the collectivization campaign, when "people were driven into collective farms, to put it crudely," must be avoided.

Once again the dilemma emerges: how to press reform from the center while avoiding the bullying tactics ("administrative methods") of the past; how to convince local party officials to keep hands off while holding them ultimately responsible should anything go seriously wrong; how to convince local officials to cooperate in reforms that have as a goal a diminution of the power of these officials, or even a loss of position. (On a typical state farm introducing contract methods, managerial staff was cut from seventy to twenty.)

Another bone of contention is the applicability of the Law on Cooperatives to collective farms, which are, of course, cooperative enterprises (at least on paper). The Supreme Soviet session of May 24 to May 27 debated this topic. Local authorities may indeed decide that "Moscow is far away" and proceed as if the old order were still intact, continuing to suppress efforts at reform or local initiative, but Gorbachev at the June Conference called for adjusting the new Collective Farm Statute to bring it in line with the Law on Cooperatives. If the new law is rigorously implemented, collective farms will be free from mandatory state orders and will be allowed to engage in any legal economic activity, lease their land out, and decide upon the size of private plots allocated to members. Such changes would represent a truly historic turn of events.

In a speech on July 29, 1988 to a plenum of the Central Committee, Gorbachev urged adoption of a proposal to lease farmland to small groups of people, or "even families," for up to fifty years. The proposal was "hotly debated" in the press, but then endorsed by the agricultural ministry (*Gosagroprom*) on August 27, only a day after *Pravda* carried a major article depicting the horrors of the collectivization campaign sixty years ago. It now seems that the limited "privatization" of agriculture is sure to come to pass in the near future.[84]

A few years ago James Millar suggested another measure to help the country through the difficult transition period; namely, "large-scale but short-term" imports of consumer goods to minimize price increases, increase "total satisfaction," and "offset the impact of redistribution [caused by price and wage reforms] upon the losers."[85] Of course Soviet hard currency has dwindled in recent years as prices on oil, gold, and diamonds have declined; and the Soviet Union has found it increasingly difficult to produce enough oil both to meet its own needs and to export. But the Soviet Union has a relatively small foreign debt and its credit rating is excellent on international money markets. The decision not to take this path has been a political rather than a narrowly economic one—the leadership fears becoming politically beholden through large debts.

But without improvements greater than the very gradual increments projected for the post-1990 period, it is hard to see how perestroika can proceed as the initial gains achieved by the campaign for discipline in the workplace run their course. Western economists even argue that initially the disruption caused by the changes under way could depress growth rates to less than 2 percent per year for the next few years.[86] Soviet economists recognize that it will be at least four to five years before gains can be realized from perestroika, and many Western economists talk of a ten-to-fifteen year transition period.

Gorbachev himself was complaining by 1987 that the momentum of "human factor" initiatives had been lost; perhaps in recognition of this problem, the 1988 plan substantially increased resources allocated to consumer and housing services over those originally called for in the 1986-1990 plan in order to stimulate consumption, which rose by only 0.7 percent in 1987.[87] It is unlikely, however, that investment reallocations alone will do the trick. Unless the reforms are "front-loaded" with substantial, short-term imports of consumer goods, Gorbachev is unlikely to convince anyone to work harder (especially since personal savings rose by 2.7 percent in the same period, exacerbating the problem of excess demand, or "repressed inflation," and rendering wage increases useless as a stimulant to work). Interestingly, the proposal to turn to imports of consumer goods recently received the endorsement of Shmelev in the bitter article cited often in this text. In May 1988, the Soviets signed a $2 billion credit agreement "on very favorable terms" with a group of banks in West Germany to allow them to modernize the food and consumer industries.[88]

But proposals to stimulate worker productivity by flooding the market with high-quality goods bought on credit come at an unpropitious time. According to several assessments published this year, Soviet credit ratings are extremely good; only four years ago, the USSR's total overseas debt was $20 billion, small for the size of its economy. But since then, the country, according to the *Wall Street Journal*, has been "going into the red," is borrowing from Western banks at a rate of $700 million per month, and by the end of 1987 had a gross debt of $38.2 billion.[89]

Thus, there seems to be an emerging consensus that the pain can be reduced and the payoff advanced by two "front-loading" measures: substantial agricultural reform and an improved supply of high-quality consumer goods from the West, or even from the Far East.[90] Agricultural reform, given that sector's enormous inefficiencies, would provide a flow of goods and services at relatively little pain. Sold at high prices, imports would both soak up excess purchasing power (made worse by the elimination of 45 billion rubles worth of liquor sales in 1985-1987) and provide the missing stimulus for greater effort at the workplace.[91]

Notes

1. *The Economic Challenge of Perestroika* (Bloomington, In., 1988): 4.

2. "Avansy i dolgi," *Novyi mir*, No. 6 (June 1987): 142–158. See also a report on his talk describing collectivization as a total failure and attacking the Stalinist type of economic system as catastrophic and the labor camps as wasteful and inhumane (CSM, June 16, 1987).

3. For the debates, and especially a roundtable published in *Literaturnaia Gazeta* (June 3, 1987) see RL 237/87 (June 23): 1–8. The comments here were by Nikola Petrakov, who argued that because there was no planning in reality, opposition to market socialism on the grounds that it would mean a loss of central control was fallacious. The fallacy of the central goal, he said, was based on the proposition: "I issue directives, I grant approvals, therefore I plan." See also NYT, June 4, 1987. For other harsh criticisms of the economic system, see Aganbegyan's comments in *Ogonek*, Nos. 29 and 30, 1987, and the numerous sources listed in Anders Aslund, "Gorbachev's Economic Advisors," *Soviet Economy*, Vol. 3, No. 3 (July–September, 1987): 246–269.

4. See RL 237/87 (June 23): 5, for a summary. See also Anatoly Streliany, "Raionnye budny," in *Novyi mir*, No. 12, 1986: 231–241. In 1988 Gorbachev's own comments on the situation in agriculture have become markedly more strident.

5. The official estimate is 8 percent from 1960 to 1985. See RL 374/87 (September 18) citing articles in *Literaturnaia gazeta* and *Moscow News* (September 20). The economist was Oleg Bogomolov.

6. *Pravda*, February 19, 1988.

7. *The Economic Challenge of Perestroika*: 3, 10–11.

8. V. Belkin, P. Medvedev, I. Nit, "Reforma: Model' perekhoda—shag pervyi, vtoroi, tretii," *Znanie—Sila*, No. 12, 1987: 5.

9. On this, see Marshall Goldman (citing Leonard Silk), *Gorbachev's Challenge* (New York, 1987): 43.

10. According to Thane Gustafson, there are two broad programs concerning how to change this situation. "Economizers" believe that the economic mechanism and incentives must be improved, call for economic signals rather than administrative commands, and push for decentralization and/or market forces. "Technologists" place the blame for poor performance on bad machines, poor planning, weak investments, and inadequate innovation. It has become clear that a third platform exists as well: that of the conservatives, who argue that the system is essentially good but the people are bad, and who look for change in stepped-up discipline at the worksite, campaigns to improve morality, and assaults on official corruption.

11. When Gorbachev assumed power in 1985, the direction of the Twelfth Five-Year Plan (1986–1990) was already set, and his opportunities to make major changes limited. Thus, it is unclear whether Gorbachev became radicalized in the process of trying to stimulate growth or if he was simply concealing his true goals until opportunity knocked.

12. For a nontechnical overview of the economic situation and reforms, see Marshall Goldman, *Gorbachev's Challenge* (New York, 1987). Important recent studies include Aganbegyan, *The Economic Challenge of Perestroika*, and Ed A. Hewett, *Reforming The Soviet Economy: Equality versus Efficiency* (Washington, D.C., 1988). For more detailed studies of individual areas, see Joint Economic Committee of Congress, *Gorbachev's Economic Plans*, Vols. 1 and 2 (Washington, D.C., 1987).

13. WSJ, August 7, 1987. The New Economic Mechanism includes the "Basic Provisions for Fundamentally Reorganizing Economic Management," (*Pravda*, June 27, 1987; approved by the Supreme Soviet June 30, 1987); and supplemented by ten decrees approved by the Central Committee and the Council of Ministers (July 10) and an eleventh decree (August 3, 1987); a new "Law on the State Enterprise," (*Pravda*, July 1, 1987) and 1986 decrees on the wage and salary system, reorganizing foreign trade, expanding private enterprise, and measures (1985–1987) to reorganize the bureaucracy and reform incentives in agriculture. The best summary and analysis of the economic reform to date is by Gertrude E. Schroeder, "Anatomy of Gorbachev's Economic Reform," *Soviet Economy*, Vol. 3, No. 3 (July–September, 1987): 219–241.

14. The law was approved at a session of the Supreme Soviet on May

24–27; it became effective July 1, 1988; the text was printed in *Pravda* June 8, 1988.

15. RL 111/88 (March 15): 8.

16. NYT, May 26, 1988.

17. This section draws heavily from the following: CIA/DIA, "Gorbachev's Economic Program: Problems Emerge," report to the Joint Economic Committee of Congress (April 13, 1988): 1–67; RL 129/88 (March 21); RL 58/88 (February 9); NYT, February 15, May 16, and June 5, 1988.

18. Not an unfounded fear: on this see the summary of recent congressional discussions on trade and human rights (NYT, February 10 and June 5, 1988).

19. CIA/DIA, "Gorbachev's Economic Program": 41.

20. Robert Campbell, "The Soviet Economic Model," in *Gorbachev's Russia and American Foreign Policy*, ed. by Seweryn Bialer and Michael Mandelbaum (Boulder, Co., 1988): 67–69.

21. Ibid.

22. Testimony to Gorbachev's interest in Swedish strategy comes from Leonid Abalkin in a talk at the Kennan Institute and at Duke University in spring 1988. The comments here are drawn from an editorial by Professor Thomas H. Naylor of Duke University in the CSM, June 27, 1988.

23. John E. Tedstrom, "On Perestroika: Analyzing the Basic Provisions," *Problems of Communism*, Vol. 36, No. 4 (July–August, 1987): 93.

24. WSJ, August 7, 1987.

25. Robert Campbell, in BS, November 1, 1987: 2A.

26. WSJ, August 7, 1987.

27. John E. Tedstrom, "On Perestroika: Analyzing the Basic Provisions": 98. However, the author continues, "We should remember that drastic and sweeping changes in the Soviet economy are not possible overnight," and the Basic Provisions are a positive step toward a new, decentralized, and more efficient system.

28. Nikolai Shmelev, "Novye trevogi," *Novyi mir*, No. 4, 1988: 160–166.

29. Radio Moscow–2, September 25, 1987; cited in RL 382/87.

30. RL 382/87 (September 25); *Pravda*, November 15, 1987.

31. "Novye trevogi": 162–163.

32. Reported in the NYT, April 27, 1988. The data on imports came from Reuters, June 2, 1988.

33. September 14, 1987.

34. On the anti-alcohol campaign, see also David Powell, "A Troubled Society," in the new edition of *The Soviet Union Today: An Interpretive Guide*, ed. by James Cracraft (Chicago, 1988): 358–362.

35. CDSP, Vol. 39, No. 48 (December 30, 1987): 17.

36. Gertrude Schroeder, "The Soviet Economy Under Gorbachev": 345.

37. Reported in RL 76/87 (February 26): 1–5.

38. The CIA/DIA study report (March 1987) is cited in RL 127/87 (March 27): 1.

39. PlanEcon, "The Dark Side of Glasnost: Unbelievable National Income Statistics in the Gorbachev Era," *PlanEcon Report*, Vol. 3, No. 6, February 13, 1987. A brief comment by the organization's director is in WSJ, March 10, 1987.

Others, such as Ed Hewitt of the Brookings Institution and Philip Hanson of the University of Birmingham agree that something is wrong with Soviet figures. Several Soviet economists have pointed in the same direction this year (see RL 127/87: 2–5). See also NYT, March 29, 1987; CSM, February 26, 1987.

40. *Pravda*, January 18, 1987.

41. Shmelev, "Novye trevogi": 161, 166. See also the discussion by Abel Aganbegyan in *The Economic Challenge of Perestroika*: 35–36.

42. CIA/DIA, "Gorbachev's Economic Program": 1.

43. *Gorbachev's Economic Plans*, Vol. 1: 3.

44. Cited in Shmelev, "Novye trevogi": 161.

45. "Slagaemyie perestroiki," in *Nauka i zhizn'*, No. 3, (March 1988): 2–15, summarized in RL 176/88 (April 25): 1–4.

46. Jeff Trimble of U.S. News and World Report, writing in *Moscow News*, No. 27, 1988: 5.

47. "Novye trevogi": 161–163 (the translation is from RL 199/88 (May 11): 2.

48. "Novye trevogi": 170.

49. On the question of foreign trade, see the detailed comments by Jerry Hough in *Opening Up The Soviet Economy* (Washington, D.C., 1987): 54–97.

50. *Moscow News*, May 15, 1988: 7.

51. Philip Taubman, "Gorbachev's Gamble," *New York Times Magazine*, July 19, 1987: 38.

52. *Opening Up The Soviet Economy*: 45–46.

53. *The Economic Challenge of Perestroika*: 39–40.

54. Schroeder, "Anatomy": 233.

55. I am borrowing here from Herbert S. Levine's comments on Schroeder's "Anatomy": 245.

56. On the need for a capital market, even for stocks and bonds in Soviet society, see the lucid comments by Shmelev, "Novye trevogi": 169–173.

57. In "Reforms in China and the Soviet Union," *Brookings Review*, Vol. 6, No. 2 (Spring, 1988): 17.

58. "Novye trevogi": 174.

59. WP, May 28, 1988.

60. As reported on National Public Radio, June 28, 1988.

61. Aslund, "Gorbachev's Economic Advisors": 260. This article provides an excellent introduction to the status of the profession in terms of institutional structure.

62. On the press, see Aslund, "Gorbachev's Economic Advisors": 264–265. It may well be that media support is creating a false impression about the depth of concern for the state of the economy among economists themselves.

63. "Comment on Gertrude Schroeder's Paper," *Soviet Economy*: 243.

64. "Restructuring the Soviet Economy," "Meeting Report," Kennan Institute for Advanced Russian Studies.

65. "Novye trevogi": 161.

66. Ibid.: 166–167.

67. CIA/DIA, "Gorbachev's Economic Program": 22.

68. See, for example, "Novye trevogi": 161.

69. See the CIA/DIA study, "Gorbachev's Economic Program": 46.

70. "Reforms in China and the Soviet Union": 17.

71. Schroeder, "The Soviet Economy Under Gorbachev": 317, 344–345.

72. "The Soviet Economy Under Gorbachev": 345.

73. See, for example, Goldman, *Gorbachev's Challenge*: 11–12.

74. "Gorbachev's Economic Program": 36.

75. Colton, *The Dilemma of Reform in the Soviet Union* (New York, 1986): 201.

76. "The Soviet Economic Model": 86.

77. On this, see Goldman, *Gorbachev's Economic Challenge*: 32–41 and 58–64.

78. See the WP, April 3, 1988: B3, and comments by Ed A. Hewett and Harry Harding in "Reforms in China and the Soviet Union," *Brookings Review*, Vol. 6, No. 2 (Spring, 1988): 15–17.

79. *Pravda*, May 15, 1988.

80. RL 131/88 (March 24): 4.

81. "Meeting Report," Kennan Institute for Advanced Russian Studies (November 3, 1987). For a brief discussion of the woes of Soviet agriculture and of ways to remedy many of them, short of eliminating the collective and state farms, see D. Gale Johnson, "Agriculture," in *The Soviet Union Today: An Interpretative Guide*: 198–209; or the lengthier volume by D. Gale Johnson and Karen M. Brooks, *Prospects for Soviet Agriculture in the 1980s* (Bloomington, In., 1983). See also the multiple entries in *Gorbachev's Economic Plans*: Vol. 2: 1–140, especially the overview by Carl W. Ek (1–8) and the article by Penelope Doolittle and Margaret Hughes, "Gorbachev's Agricultural Policy: Building on the Brezhnev Food Program": 26–44. For recent developments concerning the rental contract, see the various articles in CDSP, Vol. 40, No. 20 (June 15): 1–9.

82. *Izvestiia*, May 19, 1988.

83. *Pravda*, May 15, 1988.

84. CSM, August 29, 1988.

85. "An Economic Overview," in *The Soviet Union Today: An Interpretive Guide*: 183.

86. Cited in NYT, September 15, 1987.

87. CIA/DIA, "Gorbachev's Economic Program": 22, 30.

88. WP, May 10, 1988.

89. WSJ, December 7, 1987.

90. Once again, this suggestion was made by Shmelev ("Novye trevogi": 167–168).

91. On this, see the essay by Jan Vanous, research director of PlanEcon, in WP, April 3, 1988. Hewett makes the same argument.

6
Popular Mood

Restructuring Is a Capacious Word

"Dear editor," wrote B. Bogdanovich from Minsk, "is it really possible to foster a communist consciousness using a commodity-money system, which can only produce a consumer society, mass culture and narrow petty-bourgeois views? After all, a person's consciousness is determined by his existence in society. Or maybe Karl Marx's dictum is out of date?"

In reply, the journal *Argumenty i fakty* (Arguments and Facts) turned to a specialist with a degree in economics, A. Cherepenko. Of course Marx was not out of date, he wrote, but the formula had a more profound meaning than Mr. Bogdanovich had been able to grasp. To put it bluntly, one could not simply wish Communist relations into existence. As Marx pointed out in his early *Philosophical Manuscripts*, as long as a division of labor exists, it is frivolous to hope to operate without money. The well-known social ills that have gained a foothold in our society are not the consequence of the normal spread of monetary and commodity relations, as much as the result of the restraints imposed upon their spread, which lead to their distorted, anomalous development in the "shadow" economy. All of this happened, Cherepenko continued, above all because of the persistent gap between word and deed in the past decade, when there was much talk about rewarding effort while, in reality, all manner of leveling was pursued. That's what caused the apathy about work, the total indifference to the final product, and the urge to "grab" something for oneself in the unofficial economy.[1]

The "human factor" has received much attention from the leadership. Gorbachev has argued repeatedly that perestroika can only work if accompanied by a massive change in popular psychology, a "restructuring" of attitudes toward self, authority, and work. He intends "to persuade Soviet citizens to take responsibility for their actions" and to help fight corruption by supplementing "monitoring from above" with "monitoring from be-low."[2] His strategy has come increasingly to reflect the notion that economic stagnation was rooted in social problems and that economic reform is inseparable from sociopolitical change. In an often cited statement, the leader said: "Restructuring is a capacious word. I would equate restructuring with revolution . . . a genuine revolution in the minds and hearts of people."

If one considers the general structure of the reforms, the economic reasons for emphasizing the human factor are readily evident: "Given that labor discipline has been terribly lax in recent years, the tightening of discipline has become a relatively inexpensive way of increasing productivity."[3] The planners are asking the population to accept a greater degree of wage differentiation and a possibility of "labor force disruption" (i.e., unemployment) while offering only very modest improvements in living standards for the first five years. Actually, the disruption caused by major change could well spell an initial decline in well-being. The law encouraging small-scale enterprise is by all accounts also meant to "coopt the flourishing underground economy" and to tax unearned income, which may amount to 12 percent or more of Soviet earnings.

In turn, reformers insist, the state must address and correct the "low value and status accorded to the individual."[4] Attitudinal transformation depends upon restoring "social justice," the sense of fair play and probity in social intercourse that has all but vanished. Previously Soviet ideology propounded a view of a homogeneous society with various gradations of skill and reward, but no antagonistic economic or social groups; it was for this reason that the party could speak for the general will, for the whole society. Reformers, led by Zaslavskaia, now speak frankly of "competing interests" and "classes" in Soviet society and find the roots of the economic slowdown precisely in social processes.[5] The failure to address the issue of social classes led to the much decried "gap between word and deed" of the *zastoi* period. Now, for the first time, Soviet authorities openly apply the Marxist concept of "alienation" to their own people.[6]

Popular malaise stems at least partially from the economic slowdown, combined with spectacular success achieved in educating Soviet society—providing skills and aspirations beyond the capacity of the society to absorb. During the early years of Soviet industrialization, millions of white-collar positions were created, conferring social mobility on virtually an entire generation; the move from peasant to worker, or from unskilled to skilled worker, was also perceived as an advance.[7] Education, however limited, was a virtual ticket to promotion. But now, many well-educated citizens are competing for scarce jobs conferring status, power, or wealth. Life is becoming a zero-sum game—your neighbor's gain (whether we are talking literally of neighborhoods or of classes, ethnic regions, or republics) is your loss.

At the same time, the traditional explanations of failure (the aftermath of World War II, Russia's historic backwardness and the distance necessary to travel to catch up, the perfidious activities of the capitalist powers) lost their persuasiveness for a people who had been told by Khrushchev that they would catch up to the West in their own lifetime. As contacts (direct and indirect) with the West and—just as important—with other East European countries multiplied, "there was a shift in the standards by which regime performance was evaluated."[8] To add insult to injury, the awareness is dawning that not only is the distance growing between Western and Soviet living standards, but many smaller non-Western nations (Korea, Malaysia, Taiwan) have caught up with or surpassed Soviet standards. Awareness also exists of the gap in basic rights: In a poll of 400 citizens on the street, three-quarters acknowledged they were aware the Soviet Union had signed an international agreement on human rights at Helsinki; of this number 90 percent believed that these rights, and those provided in the Soviet Constitution, were not being honored.[9] Ed Hewett argues that it was shame at the contrast beween the West and the USSR, and dismay at the widening gap, that created the rising tide of anger in Soviet society leading to Gorbachev's ascent.[10]

Finally, if Zaslavskaia and others insist that economic processes have their roots in social processes, other reformers argue that social diseases ultimately stem from misguided economic policies. In his unremitting attack on the Gorbachev anti-alcohol drive, Shmelev was so bold as to publicly attribute the "massive increases" in problem drinking since the 1960s to a deep moral crisis caused by popular "weariness with the lies and pointlessness [*bestolkovost*] of it all, with effort and energy spent to no manifest good either for self or for others."[11] To him, rampant alcoholism is part of a larger crisis permeating the spiritual, political, and economic spheres but can be traced back to policies and structural distortions in the economy in particular:

First of all, we must make it clear that whatever is economically inefficient is immoral, and in contrast, whatever is efficient is moral. The economically inefficient circumstance of widespread deficits is, I am profoundly convinced, the underlying cause of pilfering, bribery, deep-seated bureaucratism, all manner of amoral, clandestine, profiteering, of animosities. The economically inefficient planning mechanism of extensive [*zatratnyi*] growth has resulted in the mindless plundering of our national resources, of an immoral use of our natural wealth. The refusal to attach a value to land and water has had staggering consequences, such as the degradation of entire regions of the country. The economically inefficient restraints put upon popular enterprise and activism in the workplace, the policy of wage leveling, the protracted struggle against all forms of individual and cooperative labor—such are the underlying causes, I am sure, of the exacerbation of social problems such as popular apathy [*bezdel'e*] and drunkenness which threaten the future of our nation.[12]

Reformers argue that the level of alienation and anomie in society has reached threatening dimensions and that a matter of first urgency is to restore a relationship between effort and reward at the workplace. This objective involves more sharply scaled differentiation in wages among workers (contrary to popular Western views, wage differences do now exist). But if workers are to accept such changes, it will also involve, in the view of the reformers, a major reduction of privilege in the party bureaucracy.[13] Finally, social justice doctrine urges self-management, namely, the election of factory directors. All in all, as Lars Lih points out, "this requires . . . a situation where the results of one's actions have visible consequences for one's own well-being."[14] But to this date, according to a Soviet sociologist, "most people feel restructuring only in terms of greater work pressure."[15]

If Soviet citizens are to be persuaded to pitch in, Gorbachev will have to tap the deep currents of resentment that exist against corruption, favoritism, and waste. He will also have to convince the population that sacrifices are being imposed impartially and universally, and for a larger cause.

Living Standards

As Shmelev notes: "The country is awash with all manner of rumors, which are all the more agitating given popular distrust of government initiatives, stemming from past experience. And matters are not helped by the present situation, i.e., the absence to date of any tangible changes in daily life."[16]

Soviet living standards[17] remain abysmally low, estimated in the late 1970s at 34 percent that of the United States, one half that of France, West Germany, and Austria, slightly more than one-half that of Japan and the United Kingdom, and about two-thirds the Italian level.[18] Since then, the gap has probably widened rather than narrowed. In terms of food, beverages, and tobacco, Soviet per capita consumption is about 50 to 75 percent that of the West (with a far higher proportion of calories coming from carbohydrates). The Soviet Union spends less than one-fifth the U.S. sum spent on housing, and less than half of what is spent in Spain and Japan. Outlays for the health-care system are about one-third that of the U.S. amount, and allocations for transportation are very low compared to the West: The Soviet Union has about the same mileage of railway track as the United States, despite the fact that it is larger than China and the United States combined, and only one adult Soviet citizen in twenty owns a car. The service sector is grossly underfunded: Moscow, the city of privilege, has only one-quarter to one-third the number of retail stores to be found in a typical major American city and one-half as many restaurants. In terms of gross national product, the output of services accounts for only 20 percent, compared with 47 percent in the West.[19] (See Table 6.1).

TABLE 6.1
Cost of Living: Moscow and Washington
(amount of work required to purchase listed item)

Item	Moscow	Washington
Loaf of bread	11 minutes	18 minutes
One chicken	189 minutes	18 minutes
Bar of soap	17 minutes	3 minutes
Bus fare: two miles	3 minutes	7 minutes
One grapefruit	112 minutes	6 minutes
One liter of milk	20 minutes	4 minutes
One liter red wine	257 minutes	37 minutes
Postage stamp	3 minutes	2 minutes
Man's haircut	34 minutes	62 minutes
One head of cabbage	7 minutes	7 minutes
Three ounces of tea	36 minutes	10 minutes
Pair of jeans	56 hours	4 hours
Pair of men's shoes	37 hours	6 hours
Washing machine	177 hours	46 hours

Source: World Topics Yearbook 1988 (Tangley Oaks, Illinois, 1988): 488. The original figures were calculated by Keith Bush, "Retail Prices in Moscow and Four Western Cities in October, 1986," (RL Supplement 1/87 [January 21, 1987]: 1-30).

Such comparisons have their limits; they ignore the substantially cheaper cost of housing, medical care, and other benefits in the Soviet Union, the psychological importance of job security, and the uncounted benefits of hidden income (some 40 percent of Soviet citizens reportedly have "extra earnings").[20] Goldman argues:

> The Soviets have had some impressive achievements on the social front. . . . They have eliminated most overt forms of unemployment and inflation, boosted literacy rates to a reported 100 percent, and instituted a safety net to prevent homelessness and some of the other extreme forms of poverty that occur in the West.[21]

But such comparisons also understate the size of the gap in living standards and the difficulties encountered in simply getting by in the Soviet Union. Not only are durable goods far more expensive, but the quality of goods and services is notoriously poor. Moreover, Soviet citizens spend endless hours in line—something like 50 to 65 billion labor hours per year, or two to three hours per day, according to women interviewed. Irregular access to basic goods leads not only to severe health problems in many children (for example, rickets from constant shortages of dairy products) but even to life-threatening situations. The unavailability of antibiotics, or even sedatives to ease the pain of terminally ill patients is a massive problem; anyone who has lived in the Soviet Union has been besieged with tearful requests to bring back medicine for friends or children. As Minister of Health Chazov complained at the June Conference: "Is it possible to tolerate the fact that there isn't enough medicine? Medicine means more to sick people even than bread."

The Soviet school system has massive inadequacies in facilities for physical activity, such as swimming pools and recreational courts; the talent so visible in international competition is recruited through special schools catering only to the especially gifted, where money is lavished upon facilities. Such facilities are also in dire shortage for adults wishing to participate in sports. Not surprisingly then, recent statistics show that at least half of the population is overweight, including 40 percent of all minors 15-16 years old. Two-thirds of the population engages in no physical activity whatsoever, and 70 million Soviet citizens are regular smokers.[22]

The health-care system itself is dilapidated, inequitable, and grossly underfunded—perhaps in a state of severe crisis. In this area matters have gotten much worse since 1983, when Loren Graham commented that "the Soviet Union can serve as an object lesson in what may happen to a nation's health if funds are taken from medicine and health care over a long period of time and devoted to the military."[23] Murray Feshbach claims that the number of unsolved issues in this sphere are greater than in any other area of Soviet life and that 90 billion rubles (in labor) are lost to the country every year from inadequate care. To provide just a few illustrations: In Moscow one-third of all instruments and equipment are in disrepair; of 4,000 district hospitals throughout the country more than 1,000 lack indoor plumbing and 2,500 have no hot water; of recent graduates of medical schools, 40 percent cannot read a cardiogram. In Turkmenia, only 40 percent of the population gets its drinking water from pipelines; many carry it from open drainage ditches. Feshbach asserts that the country's entire water system needs replacement; even excluding this cost, he estimates that the price tag of measures needed to overcome the health crisis is more than 80 billion rubles, or a fourfold increase in present annual outlays. The spread of infectious diseases has become so ominous that the leadership has appointed an Extraordinary Commission (another Cheka!) to combat epidemics. It is to the credit of the leadership that the health problem is finally being addressed, but the dimensions of the problem are massive indeed.[24]

Here the issue of social justice is also salient: Recent public discussions of a proposed law on health-care showed strong support for retention of socialized medicine (as well as for fee clinics and cooperative nursing homes), but also for turning over all health facilities (i.e., clinics for the privileged in the political, military, and internal security system) to the Ministry of Health, and for the right to personally select one's own doctor.[25]

Housing remains substandard (in Aganbegyan's terms, "the worst social problem of the country") and in short supply; the goal of reformers is to provide minimally satisfactory dwellings for all citizens by the year 2000. For such a target to be met, the existing supply will have to be *doubled* (or 40 million new flats built).[26] Pensions are, for many of the 33 million receiving benefits in 1980, niggardly: Those who receive the minimum benefit are consigned to a condition of near starvation. There is a massive shortage of nursing homes: Names on waiting lists number in the hundreds of thousands—and how long can one wait at an advanced age? The quality of care in homes for the elderly is, to put it mildly, inadequate: These homes are in such bad repute that many families in need of help nevertheless stay away from them. Callous treatment of the disabled is a hot topic of glasnost: There are, to mention just one fact, few wheelchairs in the Soviet Union. I never saw one during a three-year stay, or in many subsequent visits, and a recent issue of *Sobesednik* complained that disabled citizens, including veterans, had to build contraptions for themselves if they wanted to get around. What can one say about a nation that puts men and women on the moon but can't muster the resources to build wheelchairs? (To be sure, a recent issue of *Izvestiia* discussed the problems veterans in Moscow have getting around in their wheelchairs, and problems of access presuppose, of course, the existence of such chairs.)[27]

Although the past fifty years have seen, in Mervyn Matthews description, a decline in the incidence of poverty from a condition affecting the "overwhelming majority" to one encompassing "a sizeable minority,"[28] the quality of life, measured by material standards, remains grossly inadequate by Western standards and inexcusable given the national wealth of this great country. It is encouraging that the press now often uses the word "poverty" (*bednota*) rather than "underprovisioned" (*maloobespechennyi*). In 1988 new data were made available in the Soviet press on the living standards: A study of 62,000 families determined that 10 percent could not get from one paycheck to the next and that 25 percent had no savings at all. Soviet and Western analysts concur in setting the poverty line at about 70 rubles per capita (per month)—the minimum wage. The study showed that about 20 percent of the Soviet population earned just about that amount. When this study appeared in the press, it provoked irate letters claiming that the budget estimates of what was needed to get by were preposterously low and that the actual extent of poverty was grossly understated. A discussant on Radio Moscow-1 June 1 concluded from this same study that more than half of the Soviet population lived in poverty.

The Soviet poor include a large number of young couples with children, single mothers (at least 8 million), and pensioners. There are 58 million pensioners who receive an average payment of 75 rubles monthly; in this group there are at least 14 million receiving "considerably less" than 70 rubles. There are, in addition, according to *Moscow News*, 4 to 5 million families earning less than 50 rubles per capita per month.[29]

Alcoholism has long been recognized as a severe problem in Soviet society, but its increasing dimensions in recent decades have caused real concern. It is estimated that between 1970 and 1980 a 9 percent population increase was accompanied by a 77 percent increase in alcohol sales. One Soviet specialist reported in 1980 that 37 percent of workers were problem drinkers. Alcoholism is also spreading rapidly to the female population and is partially responsible for the high incidence of child mortality. More than half of all crimes and automobile accidents are connected with alcohol abuse, as are one-fifth of all premature deaths in the country. Losses at the worksite caused by alcohol have been placed at more than 50 billion rubles annually.[30]

In 1986 consumption of spirits was down 50 percent from 1984, and alcohol-related crimes were down by 26 percent.[31] Deaths by accident, poisoning, and trauma reportedly dropped by 22 percent. In 1987 the number of alcohol-related deaths on highways dropped 37 percent, and unauthorized absences from work declined by 30 percent in industry. Crimes committed while under the influence of alcohol dropped by one-third compared to 1985. Some even claim that wife-beating, and marital discord in general, have declined with dwindling consumption of spirits,[32] and that increases in fertility and life expectancy are also tied to declining alcohol consumption.

But in many areas (the police list nine republics and twenty-four regions of the RSFSR), there was an increase in drinking-related crimes, and Lt. General Logvinov of the Ministry of Internal Affairs complains that "the campaign against drunkenness has lost some of its urgency of late." Popular resentment of the campaign is high: Police have been put on duty outside liquor stores to prevent windows being broken by angry people waiting in lines,[33] and 250,000 people—a quarter of a million!—were arrested in 1987 for "hooliganism" in the area of liquor outlets. There were 40,000 cases filed of individuals charged with "speculation" in alcohol, and 31,000 alcohol dens were broken up. The number of people charged with home brewing supports the contention made by Shmelev (Chapter 5) that the only effect of the campaign has been to reverse the proportionate flow of income between home brewers and the state. In 1985 proceedings were launched against 80,000 individuals for producing *samogon*; in 1986 the figure was 150,000; in 1987, 397,000; and in the first two months of 1988, 120,000![34]

The Soviet press reports that the "social profile" of the producer of illegal alcohol is also changing, from elderly women in the countryside to people in all walks of life and those living in urban areas.[35] Among the 370,000 home brewers arrested in 1987 were 7,000 Communist party members; one out of ten were young men under 29, and 15,000 had a university education. In addition, alcoholism has now taken on new, "unsightly forms" as the population has been turning to perfume, brake fluid, various cleaning solutions—even, in one fatal case, to cattle growth stimulators. The result: in 1987 11,000 people died from drinking chemical preparations.

Returning to the Political Fold

Analyzing the current public mood[36] is a difficult task. Most recent studies emphasize the powerful impact of urbanization, education, and the mass media in transforming Soviet society—eroding the traditional distinctions between worker and peasant on the one hand and between blue-collar and white-collar workers on the other. The new civil society has its social roots in a mobile, urban middle class that shares with workers an emphasis on family, leisure activities, and consumption.[37] In my mind, too, the traditional distinction between society and state (or *obshchestvennost* and *vlast*), which was never terribly helpful, has become entirely meaningless. The middle classes (scientific, cultural, and administrative) have been deliberately recruited into the party, and thus, have become deeply implicated (through the "process of inclusion" launched by Khrushchev) in running the country and sharing the perks of doing so.[38] We should also consider Jerry Hough's assertion that the changes in the composition of the working class that have taken place over the past generation are so substantial that many working-class people are "middle class in psychology."[39]

At the same time, the Soviet population is differentiated not only according to generation, education, and occupation, but also by ethnic affiliation, residential patterns, and other factors. In particular, the difference between rural and urban, provincial city and metropolitan area, is enormous. Thus, a poll of Soviet citizens traveling abroad found out that residents of Moscow and Leningrad were most likely to be aware of and to support glasnost; residents of the Baltic states and the Caucasus were most skeptical; and residents of Central Asia were the most indifferent. Better educated people were more responsive, as were women.

We have, then, three propositions: (1) Traditional categories for understanding Russian and Soviet society are meaningless as a powerful urban middle class has emerged and distinctions between blue- and white-collar have eroded; (2) social, economic, and ethnic differentiation remain powerful factors; and (3) by admission of Soviet social scientists, there are powerfully conflicting "interests" with contradictory needs and agendas pressing upon the national leadership.

At the second Novosibirsk seminar (the first, held in 1983, produced the now famous *Novosibirsk Report*), Soviet sociologists provided the following alignment of social forces in the age of perestroika: those engaged in manual, "preindustrial" labor and "various declassé elements" are against both economic and political reform (and sympathetic to various authoritarian, nativistic appeals); skilled workers support democratization but are skeptical of economic reform; skilled specialists, scientists, and those engaged in the arts and humanities are behind both political and economic change; bureaucrats (in both political and economic sectors) are opposed to radical change; and enterprise managers agree with economic but not political reform.[40]

The middle class, if defined in terms of education, is a key player in the drama of perestroika. While only 6 percent of the population belongs to the party, one-third of urban males with a higher education belong. Moreover, the scientific community has skills that are vitally needed if, as Aganbegyan claims, scientific and technological change are to be the locomotives of perestroika. But "a diverse body of Soviet sources, from sociological studies to Soviet films and fiction," demonstrate that it was precisely among the better educated, younger sectors of the population that disillusionment, apathy, and even alienation were spreading under Brezhnev. If early studies of emigrants (notably the Harvard University survey of World War II refugees) found regime support positively correlated with education, today the reverse seems to be true: "The more highly educated the respondent, the weaker their support for state control over the economy and the greater their commitment to individual over collective rights."[41] Soviet studies of the mass media likewise show the highest resistance to official versions of events in Soviet newspapers to be among the better educated classes and a greater tendency for this group to turn to alternative sources of information. By most accounts, both perestroika and glasnost have found the most receptive audience in this admittedly quite diverse social stratum; freedom of information, public input, respect for the rights of the individual, a concern for nature—all have an obvious appeal. Thus Gorbachev has returned a key segment of society to the political fold, lining it up behind his goals.

Hough asserts that even the bureaucracy is far from monolithic or unambivalent about change. Nor is the Communist party a single-minded beast. As Archie Brown writes: "There is much greater diversity of opinion within the 19-million strong CPSU (and still more, of course, within Soviet society as a whole) than is generally appreciated in the West."[42] Robert Tucker, too, states that "we have credible information that there are in the middle rungs of the Soviet establishment itself . . . people who have come to feel that . . . the economy is at an impasse and that fundamental changes are essential." These people are not "visionaries," but factory managers and others looking for release from stifling central control and confident that their skills would be needed in a reformed economy. This "potential constituency for change" wants peaceful evolution rather than upheaval, with, as "a sine qua non . . . strong political leadership from above."[43]

Comments in the press by Soviet sociologists indicate that these middle rungs of society are, nevertheless, by no means solidly behind perestroika. Both managerial and engineering personnel are highly threatened by the proposed changes, and administrators in several sectors (especially the military-industrial complex) are convinced that "everything is fine . . . and that no changes in the economy are necessary."[44]

One as yet unexplored topic is the potential threat that "social justice" poses to the middle classes, reportedly Gorbachev's chief constituency for perestroika. It is accepted wisdom that one of the reasons Khrushchev was turned out of office was that he alienated the burgeoning new middle class. He did this not only by his country-bumpkin antics, but by pushing affirmative action measures, especially in education. Thus, the issue of equity versus efficiency is not a new one in Soviet society, and it has no easy solution.

A related theme is that of generational differences. Jerry Hough finds "fundamental changes occurring in the composition and psychology of the Soviet people." Citing earlier observations by Edward Crankshaw, he believes that the best of the Brezhnev generation were either repressed or wiped out in the war; the survivors were "either too stupid to be considered dangerous . . . or brought sycophancy to a fine art." They were the "insecure youth" of the first quarter of the twentieth century who turned to "essentially nativistic rejections of modern western society." In contrast, those in their fifties now, the "ruling generation," were deeply influenced by the "great events of their youth"—the westernizing experiences and "unfulfilled promises" of the Khrushchev era—and evince a strong nostalgia for the period. As for those now coming of age, "the lives of today's youth in a large Soviet city are far closer to the lives of the young in a large American city than to that of their great-grandparents in a rural Russian village."

Hough's comments, though germane, must be qualified. Soviet sociologists point out that more than half of the Soviet population were born in villages—a fact suggesting to them social dislocation and the existence of a massive social base for authoritarian, nativistic movements.[45] Moreover, reformist Igor Kon, discussing the social constituency for neo-Stalinism, identifies a significant group among those brought up in the Brezhnev era, recruited through the Komsomol, who now find their interests and way of life threatened.[46]

The young are themselves a divided constituency. Soviet sociologists have detected widespread antipathy to official ideology among young people.[47] A youth journal published a poll revealing that one-half of young people professed not to believe in the Communist system or to have serious reservations about it.[48] Another survey revealed that only one-third of Soviet students believe that Marxism-Leninism plays a major role in shaping people's world views.[49] But the recent attention given to the sensational documentary *Is It Easy To Be Young?* has created the false impression that the entire generation has chosen the "exit" option (through drugs, religion, and punk fads); an impression no truer in the USSR today than it was of the 1960s in the United States.[50]

The "collective amnesia" about the past among young people could work to reinforce the "myth of a golden age" under Stalin, to give credence to the idea that the suffering imposed was both necessary and on an acceptable scale. The impact of the unfolding revelations could powerfully disorient or, alternatively, create a huge constituency for perestroika (reinforcing the perennial tendency for youth to reject the previous generation's values and to align belief and reality). The long-standing gap between "word and deed" and the practiced duplicity of Soviet society have led to disillusionment and a corrosive cynicism, producing initially skeptical responses to the Gorbachev platform (when young people bother to listen). But this attitude may well be changing as Gorbachev remains in power, as his message becomes persistently more radical, and as his sincere determination to change the country becomes more evident.

Rewriting the Social Contract

Dusker Doder related a revealing (but probably apocryphal) anecdote concerning worker morale late in the Brezhnev era. A friend of his, an engineer at a machine-tool plant in Moscow (before perestroika) was beaten up when he tried to force workers to show up for work. Of 320 workers, there were forty absences every day, and another forty workers who showed up intoxicated; thus, at any time one-quarter of the work force was out. After being physically trounced at the workplace, he felt there was nothing he could do.[51]

Correspondents are virtually unanimous that the sense of crisis felt by the leadership is not shared by the populace. Shmelev himself writes that while common people are fearful of price increases and suspicious that the government will confiscate their savings, few believe life is now intolerable: "The press is basically full of propaganda of various achievements (largely passing), which tends to smooth the rough edges, to blunt the acuteness of the tasks facing the country. Neither the populace nor the ruling circles as a whole have yet comprehended the full seriousness of our situation."[52]

It appears that a crackdown on discipline has yielded increases in labor productivity, if only in forcing workers to show up, and sober at that. But nobody argues that this route can be a long-term substitute for general increases in factory productivity, for restructuring initiatives, transforming management practices, reforming price structures, and decentralizing the economy as a whole. (As even defenders of centralized practices admit, "Planning millions of products at the level of the national economy is like trying to make out the names of city streets and house numbers on a globe.")[53]

Moreover, analysts of perestroika agree that up to the present the material incentives projected to reinstill discipline and effort have simply been inadequate.[54] The basic criticisms are that general promises of improvements in housing and consumer services are unlikely to motivate skeptical workers, that individual performance must be correlated with reward, and that enabling conditions should make possible a close relationship between effort and output (i.e., workers should have materials to work with). Finally, economists say that without adequate price reforms, in a situation of repressed inflation (excessive personal savings) wage differentiation alone is unlikely to produce the needed results. The population now has at least 260 billion rubles put away in savings (and a further large, but unknown, sum "stuffed in stockings"). Why work to put away more useless money?

"Stormy protests" erupted last year at the giant Kama truck factory over the introduction of quality-control measures (which not only often threaten bonuses, but are also often unachievable, given the workers' lack of control over the supply of raw materials or quality of components delivered to them).[55] In 1987, bus drivers in a small city south of Moscow went on strike in protest against a new performance-linked pay system.[56] The CIA/DIA report on the Soviet economy cited extensively in Chapter 5 alludes to widespread work stoppages throughout the country.

Many common people are notably nervous about the possibility of future unemployment and the implications of price increases on basic necessities. Following Gorbachev's Murmansk speech (October 1, 1987), Russians, fearing price increases, began to hoard food and other items.[57] There has been much concern about the threat of unemployment subsequent to the economic reforms, about the impact of price rises[58] upon the poor and elderly, and about the possibility of increased inequality (both individual and regional) as a result of the new law on private enterprises.[59] Many see price increases as a violation of the notion of social justice so important in discussions today. Increases on staples will affect the poor (perhaps 40 percent of the population) and especially the elderly living on fixed pensions (now consuming bread and potatoes), who will not benefit from promised, compensating wage increases. But, as Gorbachev pointed out at Murmansk, subsidies also disproportionately benefit the wealthy, who are heavy consumers of meat and milk.

Reformers promise that displaced workers will be given new jobs, but others talk about unemployment as a permanent cost of efficiency.[60] On future unemployment, T. Anthony Jones writes:

> Regardless of Gorbachev's fate . . . the social contract in the Soviet Union is in for a major overhaul in the next few years. In addition to . . . policies designed to get the economy moving, there are also long-term trends in the use of new technologies that will fundamentally change the relationship between the state and civil society. . . . The emphasis upon profitability and efficiency, however, has already given rise to a heated debate on the social consequences of such a move. The very foundation of the social contract, the guarantee of full employment, is being put in jeopardy . . . displaced workers will have to find alternative work. Some will move to less skilled, lower-paid jobs in manufacturing and construction, but many will have to take jobs in the service sector. . . . Reallocation will not only produce a change in occupation, it will also mean a significant decline in income. Not only are service workers paid less than those in manufacturing, but the gap has been steadily widening [at present the difference is 30 percent]. . . . Many workers will have to scale down their aspirations and settle for a future less bright than . . . envisaged. So . . . will their children. . . . Even if the reforms are scrapped however, the continuing introduction of new technology will have the same effect.[61]

There can be no question that deep-seated and comfortable work habits and routines will be difficult to uproot, and not only among workers. And, it might be added, not only among Soviet citizens: Given a choice between moderately comfortable jobs with little pressure, full security, and ample leisure on the one hand, and potentially profitable but risky ventures on the other, how many in any country would choose the latter? Workers are worried about their security and standard of living, and they may well make an "instinctive calculation that the danger of losses outweighs the hope of gains."[62] It is possible, too, that traditional "anticommercial" attitudes persist along with notions equating egalitarianism with social justice.

A joke exchanged among Russian workers during the Polish crisis of 1981 was that "the Poles want to be paid American wages but continue to work the way we do in Russia!"[63] In fact Soviet workers seem to be angling quite rationally in their own best (short-term, at least) interest; namely, for better salaries at no added risk of unemployment and for a greater abundance of goods at stable prices. But it should be added that recent strikes against the implementation of *gospriemka* have not been directed against the principle of improving the quality of goods as such, but against the imposition of demands that simply cannot be met, given the irregularity of supplies in the wholesale market and the lack of control over components delivered to the factory. (As one worker was cited in *Moscow News*: "Give us good bricks, and we'll build you a good house!")

Historians have repeatedly shown that in certain circumstances people can transcend their own perceived, immediate material interests (the 1917 Revolution was at least partially about emerging notions of dignity and personal worth among the workforce). Given the real signs of social distress and alienation in Soviet society, it would be wrong to dismiss entirely the notion of social degradation (a corollary of environmental despoliation, both representing the squandering of natural resources) advanced by Shmelev (see Chapter 3). But the shocking indifference with which the intelligentsia responded to the nascent free-trade union movement just a few years ago suggests that the traditional chasm between *narod* (folk) and *obshchestvennost* (educated society) continues to affect perceptions. The image of the sullen and irrational Russian worker of the past lingers on, reinforced by many Soviet intellectuals in contact with Western journalists. Thus, the picture we receive of workers and their concerns is colored by the middle-class prejudices of those who write for the media. And those who would conclude that workers are set against perestroika must explain the extraordinary popular discontent that surfaced at the dismissal of Yeltsin in Moscow.[64]

Not Every Kind of Truth Is Useful to Us

If perestroika has unsettled many workers, glasnost makes a segment of the population very upset. Letters have been printed expressing anger at public discussion of painful issues like drug abuse (30,000 arrests annually, 75,000 addicts on the police blotter)[65] and prostitution. One person complained: "Okay, so it's the truth, but not every kind of truth is useful to us."[66] An engineer commented after a free-ranging public discussion at the October Theater in Moscow: "More meetings like this and there will be no standards remaining."[67] On capital punishment: "I'm a staunch supporter of harsh punishments. Use of the death penalty must be greatly expanded. Those damned driveling liberals must be rebuffed" (A. V. Murzich, lawyer from Riga).[68] On conditions in prisons: "Deprivation of freedom is not enough: let the vermin wallow in filth and eat rotten potatoes." (V. G. Lyashov, Moscow Province).

No subject has provoked more bitter controversy than the revelations about Stalin as war leader, about the cruelties of collectivization and the barbarities wreaked upon the party opposition, most of whom are now being rehabilitated. Many seem to agree with N. Andreyeva ("I Cannot Betray My Principles") that "the now commonplace subject of repression has become excessively magnified in the perception of some people." For example:

Comrade Mironov, a resident of Baku, is writing this to you. Here's what is bothering me: this business about Comrade Stalin's personality cult. Do our writers and correspondents really have nothing else to write about, if all they can do is wag their tongues about nothing but Stalin, Stalin, Stalin? I myself am a disabled veteran of the Great Patriotic War. . . . Stalin . . . shot those people who prevented him and the entire Soviet people from living a correct and honest life. The people lived well, and there was plenty of everything. Vodka used to cost 3 rubles 62 kopeks . . . now it costs 9 rubles and 10 kopeks. . . . And to top it all off, Stalin is being criticized. . . . After this letter you can arrest me.[69]

Who are the letter writers so upset by glasnost? Sociologist Bestuzhev-Lada identifies them as former employees of the security apparatus, veterans of World War II, those of the older generation who have never adjusted to the shock of the 20th Party Congress, and many who recognize the truth but believe that making it public would irreparably damage the country. Finally, there are those who are genuinely exasperated by economic inefficiency, shoddy work, social injustice, embezzlement, crime, and alcoholism but who see the way out in return to an "iron hand."[70]

Soviet media expert Ellen Mickiewicz concludes that in the past the leadership relied heavily upon letters to gauge public opinion but has recently discovered that letter writers tend to be older, to belong to the Communist party (6 percent of the population) and to engage in but a limited range of occupations.[71] Bestuzhev-Lada cautions, too, that such letters "express the opinion of but a small minority." And, he adds with a sigh of relief, "they are an inevitably declining percentage, since many are already past retirement age." So we should not rely too heavily upon letters. In rebuttal, however, one can argue that such *frontoviki* (front-line verterans) are opinion-makers who play an important role in the community. As a study in *Sovetskaia Rossiia* noted:

> It is likely that people of this generation (over 60), even if they have retired, still play a [greater] role in determining our overall attitudes than do the "children" or the "grandfathers." Many of them engage in public activities at their places of residence, are members of various commissions set up under Soviets, etc. One mustn't underestimate their impact.

Not coincidentally, this is the generation of *frontoviki*, whose attitudes toward life were shaped in combat in World War II, and who still dominate many Soviet institutions.[72]

Soviet subscription lists also offer an informal poll on glasnost, and the circulation of *Ogonek*, once stagnant, has jumped from 400,000 to 1.3 million for 1989. Likewise, subscriptions to *Novyi mir* and *Znamia* have doubled.[73] In Odessa in the summer of 1988, all of the periodicals in the forefront of perestroika (*Ogonek, Sobesednik, Argumenty i fakty*, etc.) were continually sold out at the newsstands. A reporter stood by a newsstand near Children's World Store in Moscow and tabulated sales: *Moskovskie novosti* was sold out in ten minutes; *Literaturnaia gazeta* in fifteen minutes; fifty copies of *Ogonek* sold out in twenty minutes; and the dailies *Sovetskaia Rossiia* and *Sotsialisticheskaia industriia* were gone in an hour. *Pravda*, which has been notably more conservative in outlook than other papers, had to extend the subscription period by two weeks at the end of the year in order to boost the number of orders. Several commentators have noted, however, that many journals, regardless of political philosophy, have successfully pumped up subscriptions by grabbing a hot item to publish (whether Mario Puzo's *The Godfather*, Vladimir Nabokov's *Lolita*, or some more stately, yet long suppressed, Soviet work). Moreover, paper shortages affect print runs; with the radical increase in subscriptions, *Ogonek* had to sharply curtail its newsstand sales (its editors estimate it could sell 2.5 million copies instead of the 1.7 million now printed).[74]

Is It Fair?

Realizing rather belatedly that letters, upon which they had long relied to assess public opinion, were highly skewed sources, the leadership has decided to use polls. These polls, however flawed, have revealed a popultion with conflicting, often inconsistent views on work, life, power, and social change. Unsurprisingly, one sentiment widely held is "frustration by the gap between raised expectations and grim reality."[75]

A poll taken of over 1,000 Soviet citizens traveling in the West discovered that aside from greater latitude for self-expression, only a quarter had seen concrete results from the reform period in their own lives, and nearly a half felt that new policies had had no effect upon them personally. One in four stated that they were more interested in current events or in their work. Another telephone poll conducted within the Soviet Union found few people able to define glasnost, and even fewer able to point to tangible effects of the policy.[76]

A poll of workers at 141 factories in the Urals revealed that only 14 percent saw significant positive results of restructuring at work. Sixty percent had "no formed opinion of the advantages" of the reforms, and 75 percent were unable to describe how the program of restructuring would translate into changes in the workplace. Only 5 percent expected changes within the next year, 24 percent expected them within the current five-year plan, 15 percent in the subsequent five-year plan, and 23 percent believed results would take even longer.[77] An "informal opinion poll" (based on letters to a newspaper) concluded that generational differences existed in attitudes toward the economy: Concerning the establishment of cooperatives (i.e., nonstate enterprises), of those aged 45 and under, 87 percent were in favor; of those aged 45 to 60, 79 percent were undecided; and of those aged 60 to 75, fully 81 percent were opposed.[78]

A poll conducted jointly by French and Soviet researchers in October 1987 of 1,000 residents of the Moscow area (and thus better educated and more affluent than the average Soviet citizen) showed that 72 percent expected higher prices in the store; 65 percent approved of the establishment of new cooperative restaurants and other services; 42 percent disapproved (27 percent approved) of the release of dissidents, but 73 percent believed those who wish to leave the country should be allowed to do so. Only 9 percent favored abolition of capital punishment, but 53 percent favored (and 27 percent opposed) the withdrawal of troops from Afghanistan.

As noted above, the issue of social justice has emerged as a major topic of glasnost. One poll surveyed those who enjoy a modicum of authority. Conducted in Siberia, this poll showed reluctance on the part of collective farm chairmen to seek promotion, and even a desire to escape from the responsibilities and pressures of their post, because the social prestige accompanying such work was not commensurate with the burdens.[79]

A telephone poll of 548 Muscovites in mid-1988 addressed the issue of privilege squarely.[80] When asked: "Is it fair that some people in our society receive (through legitimate and honest means) very high incomes?" the answers were 61 percent affirmative and 25 percent negative. Those in principle against a high level of inequality were over 60 and/or had less education. Those in the military and engaged in law enforcement tended in general to be more in favor of privileges (though everyone disliked the word itself). The pollsters learned that "most people are in the dark about the details of the system of privileges"; many felt they could not respond because they lacked precise knowledge, and some were entirely unaware of the eight special privileges listed in the sample (only one-third of a fuller list compiled by the sociologists). Thus, as glasnost probes the issue of reward and privilege, popular resentment could rise quickly.[81]

One of the most dramatic moments of the June Party Conference was Ligachev's aggressive speech when he, to boisterous applause, told the assembled delegates that the only privilege they had as professional party functionaries was that of serving society. By all accounts Ligachev's speech was widely resented, and the *Moscow News* poll tells why. When asked, "Do you think our society can be called a society of social justice?" only 23 percent replied "yes" and another 21 percent leaned in that direction. Twenty-five percent said "no," and another 19 percent said "rather no than yes." Interestingly, among those who found the society fair, besides the military and managers, a disproportionate percentage were poorly educated and above age sixty. In contrast, specialists in both the sciences and humanities, as well as the young, had a stronger perception of injustice. Among those aged 21 to 29, only 11 percent called the society fair. Which privileges are fair? The poll listed eight perks (see Table 6.2).

More than half of all polled believe that all the privileges listed above, except for the use of chauffeured cars (which, by the way, keeps more than 50,000 young, able-bodied men out of the productive sector), are unjust. Many people added on their own that use of chauffeured cars by wives and children was improper. I found very surprising the rather high acceptance (29 percent) of differential access to quality health care; this result does not fit with the views often heatedly expressed by Soviet citizens in conversation with Americans that income or position in society should not affect access to health care or education. As one commentator to this poll noted, if health care is to be a scarcity item, administratively distributed access is less democratic than individually paid access: "If there are only differences in earnings and no privileges, then should my child fall ill, I'll buy nothing, I'll be able to pay for him to be treated at the best resort. But today we have resorts and medical institutions which no ordinary citizen can get his child into, no matter what."

Who deserves privilege in Soviet society? The pollsters listed ten groups, unfortunately excluding the KGB (see Table 6.3).

The poll, then, shows society fairly evenly divided about how fair Soviet society is, generally against the perks now provided the elite, but accepting of privileges given specifically to national political leaders, the military, and (to a lesser degree) the cultural elite. Remarkably, one-third of all young people believed all privileges given Komsomol leaders were unmerited; the same proportion of workers held identical sentiments about perks for trade union leaders. The sharp demarcation in attitudes between the elderly and the young suggested two things to a commentator: First, "since tomorrow there will be more educated people . . . and our young people will constitute the majority of the population . . . more people will consider our situation unjust than do so today." And second, since the older generation will be around for another ten to fifteen years, their antimarket, anti-private initiative and generally pro-Stalinist views (in favor of the system if not the person) had to be accommodated.

TABLE 6.2
Which Privileges Are Fair: Muscovites Respond

Privilege	Fair	Unfair	Don't Know
Chauffeured cars	42	44	14
Better housing	21	67	12
State-owned dachas	24	65	11
Exclusive health care	29	60	11
Food packages, goods in special stores	9	84	7
Preferential access to travel tickets	36	52	12
Preferential access to cultural amenities	11	80	9

TABLE 6.3
Who Deserves Privilege?
(on a scale of 2, undeserved, to 5, deserved)

Privileged Groups	Average Mark
National political leaders	4.3
Military	4.1
Diplomats	3.7
Soviet delegates	3.6
Noted cultural figures	3.6
Economic managers	3.2
Party apparatus	3.0
Ministerial executives	2.8
Trade union executives	2.6
Komsomol executives	2.6

Finally, Soviet polls have provided glimpses of public opinion on foreign policy issues. Insiders have long known that unpublished polls show a Soviet citizenry much more willing to accept official claims in the area of foreign policy than in domestic affairs. This discrepancy can be explained by the public's inability to verify the description of events abroad by access to alternative sources. Glasnost has not extended to foreign policy; scattered results from polls indicate strong patriotic sentiments prevail. The joint French-Soviet poll of Muscovites also considered foreign affairs. When asked to name a declared enemy of the Soviet Union, 52 percent pointed to the United States[82] and 22 percent to West Germany. Thirty percent described relations with the

United States as bad or very bad (and only 5 percent believed relations were good). Only half of Soviets polled knew of the Berlin wall; of that half 44 percent believed it should be torn down and 32 percent opposed such a move.[83]

Popular reaction was mixed to the broadcasts of "Space Bridge" programs cohosted by Phil Donahue and Soviet commentator Vladimir Posner; some respondents welcomed mutual open criticism, but many others attacked television officials and called for increased censorship and jamming. There were similar reactions to televised speeches by Gary Hart, George Shultz, and Margaret Thatcher. One journalist reported that letters demanding increased jamming arrived at a rate of 500 a week.

Conclusion

Obviously, nothing definitive can be inferred from such polls. Polling is so new and unfamiliar to Soviet people that the techniques used are very rudimentary, responses tend to be guarded, often disingenuous, and sometimes even hostile: In the fall, pollsters were turned into the police in Moscow for causing a disturbance, or committing provocative actions. Even the curious sample provided above should serve as a caution against quick and facile platitudes about the Soviet people. Nevertheless, the very complexity and variety of the response to the present changes are testimony to the transformation that has taken place in Soviet society in the past quarter-century.

Notes

1. *Argumenty i fakty*, No. 12 (March 19–25, 1988): 8.
2. Lars Lih, "Gorbachev and the Reform Movement," *Current History*, Vol. 86, No. 522 (October, 1987): 310.
3. John Tedstrom, "On Perestroika: Analyzing the Basic Provisions": 98.
4. Leonid Abalkin, *Voprosi ekonomiki*, No. 12, (December, 1987): 3–13.
5. Interview with Tatiana Zaslavskaia, *Izvestiia* (March 8, 1988): 3. In the early 1980s, a heated debate occurred in the journals *Kommunist* and *Voprosy filosofii* over the possibility of antagonistic social contradictions in a socialist society. The upshot was the forced retreat, in October 1984, by supporters of Anatoly Butenko, who had argued that such contradictions, evident in the Soviet Union, were generated by socialism itself rather than remnants of the past. See Gail Lapidus, "Gorbachev's Reforms: Redefining the Relationship of State and Society": 23–25.
6. According to Elizabeth Teague, the term "alienation" was first applied to the USSR in Zaslavskaia's Novosibirsk Report of 1983. Georgy Razumovsky used it in the important speech delivered to mark Lenin's birthday on April 22, 1988, and Gorbachev first spoke of alienation in a meeting with Soviet newspaper editors May 7 (reported by Tass on May 10). See RL 202/88 (May 11): 3. The text of Gorbachev's talk is in *Pravda*, May 8, 1988.

7. For evidence, see Jerry Hough and Merle Fainsod, *How the Soviet Union is Governed* (Boston, 1979): 564–565.

8. Lapidus, "Gorbachev's Reforms": 11.

9. WP, December 22, 1987. This poll revealed the difficulties of conducting opinion surveys in the Soviet Union. Many respondents were plainly afraid to answer the questions, some were hostile and even summoned the police. On the other hand, according to the report in the Soviet press, the 270 who did respond were vehement and emotional in expressing their opinion that human rights were not honored.

10. "Reforms in China and the Soviet Union," *Brookings Review*, Vol. 6, No. 2 (Spring, 1988): 15. See also Hough, *Opening Up The Soviet Economy*: 24–25; and Tucker, *Political Culture and Leadership in Soviet Russia*: 135. The shift in popular mood took place sometime in the mid-1970s and was first described by John Bushnell in "The 'New Soviet Man' Turns Pessimist," in Stephen Cohen et al., *The Soviet Union Since Stalin* (Bloomington, In., 1980): 179–199.

11. "Novye trevogi," *Novyi mir*, No. 4 (April 1988): 169.

12. "Novye trevogi": 175.

13. The acrimonious, only partially public debate about party privileges launched in *Pravda* on the eve of the 27th Party Congress, and involving Yeltsin (who is against such privileges), was one indication of the depth of feeling on this issue.

14. Lars Lih, "Gorbachev and the Reform Movement": 310.

15. The sociologist was Vilen Ivanov, director of the Sociological Research Insitute of the Soviet Academy of Sciences, cited in Taubman, "Gorbachev's Gamble": 40.

16. "Novye trevogi": 170.

17. For a virulently anti-Soviet, but reasonably accurate, depiction of conditions, see the special issue of *Survey*: "Social and Economic Rights in the Soviet Bloc," ed. by G. R. Urban, Vol. 29, No. 4 (August, 1987). The issue includes substantial materials from the Soviet press, and from Soviet critics such as Zaslavskaia. See also Horst Herlemann, ed., *Quality of Life in the Soviet Union* (Boulder, Co., 1986).

18. According to World Bank Information, of 125 countries studied, thirty-eight had a per capita GNP of less than $1 per day; all eighteen industrialized countries were in the $9–$40 range per day; Eastern Europe was in the $5–$15 range (Mervyn Matthews, *Poverty in the Soviet Union* [London, 1986]: 1. See 1–28 for a historical survey of poverty and a comparison of Russian living standards with the West from 1913 to the present).

19. This information is culled from Herlemann, *Quality of Life*.

20. Matthews, *Poverty in the Soviet Union*: 29.

21. Marshall Goldman, *Gorbachev's Challenge* (New York, 1986): 4.

22. Figures cited in *Pravda*, December 8, 1987.

23. "Science Policy and Organization," in *The Soviet Union Today: An Interpretive Guide* (1983 edition): 221.

24. These comments were culled from a talk by Feshbach at the Kennan Institute, October 5, 1987; from *Moskovskie novosti*, March 13, 1988: 9; *Literaturnaia gazeta*, January 27, 1988 (on infant mortality and health conditions

in Turkmenia). See also "Social and Economic Rights in the Soviet Bloc," esp. 47–72 and 145–214; Christopher Mark Davis, "Developments in the Health Sector of the Soviet Economy, 1970–1990," in Joint Economic Committee, *Gorbachev's Economic Plans* (Washington, D.C., 1987), Vol. 2: 312–335.

25. *Pravda*, December 8, 1987.

26. *The Economic Challenge of Perestroika*: 17. See also Michael V. Alexeev, "Soviet Residential Housing: Will the 'Acute Problem' Be Solved?" in *Gorbachev's Economic Plans*, Vol. 2: 282–296.

27. A new pension law has long been under review, and pensions were recently increased for collective farmers. Other recent discussions of the handicapped (a new subject in the Soviet press) can be found in *Ogonek*, No. 9, 1988: 12–15; and *Izvestiia*, February 14, 1988. Professor William McCagg recently led a conference on the problems of the handicapped in the USSR, the papers of which should soon be published.

28. Matthews, *Poverty in the Soviet Union*: 12. Poverty, as he discusses at length, is difficult to compare across cultures or even to measure objectively within a single nation. But his studies, as well as my own personal observations, suggest that deep–seated poverty is the lot of well over 40 percent of the Soviet population. Matthews claims too, that in terms of per capita income, the wealth of the Soviet citizen as a ratio of citizens in Western countries has scarcely increased since the 1920s (i.e., the sacrifices of the 1930s produced little gain relative to the West).

29. For a survey of recent Soviet discussions of poverty, see RL 256/88 (June 20): 1–6. See also *Moscow News*, No. 14, 1988: 12; and, on the life of pensioners: *Sobesednik*, No. 33, 1987: 10. The Soviet survey discussed here was published in *Sotsialisticheskaia industriia*, June 1, 1988.

30. Here we should be cautious. Soviet drinking is a highly visible problem because there are few indoor bars, men tend to drink in company on the streets, and the "Irish" (as opposed to "French") tradition of drinking calls for heavy, but episodic, bouts rather than daily consumption. A careful study of Soviet emigrants discovered that "though depressing, the problem of Soviet alcoholism/absenteeism is not drastic. . . . The notion of an economy paralyzed by alcoholism is not supported by this study." (Paul R. Gregory, "Productivity, slack and time theft," in *Politics, Work and Daily Life in the USSR: A Survey of Former Soviet Citizens*, ed. by James Millar [Cambridge, Ma., 1987]: 273).

31. The Society for the Struggle Against Alcoholism in the Soviet Union had enlisted some 14 million members in 450,000 grass-roots organizations by September 1987 (Radio Moscow–2: September 25; cited in RL 382/87).

32. See Goldman, *Gorbachev's Challenge*: 2; Aganbegyan, *The Economic Challenge of Perestroika*: 35; David Powell,"A Troubled Society" in James Cracraft, ed., *The Soviet Union Today: An Interpretive Guide* (2nd edition: Chicago, 1988): 361.

33. *The Guardian*, December 15, 1986.

34. *Izvestiia*, March 3, 1988.

35. *Izvestiia*, December 3, 1987.

36. For an attempt to measure public opinion through surveys of recent emigrants, see Brian D. Silver, "Political Beliefs of the Soviet Citizen: Sources of

Support for Regime norms," in *Politics, Work and Daily Life in the USSR*: 100–141.

37. Gail Lapidus, "Gorbachev's Reforms: Redefining the Relationship of State and Society." Paper prepared for the American–German Conference on the Gorbachev Reform Program, The Kennan Institute, Washington, D.C. (March 20–22, 1988): 9.

38. On the notion of "inclusion" see Lapidus, "Gorbachev's Reforms": 3.

39. Jerry Hough, *Opening Up The Soviet Economy*: 23–24.

40. *Nedelia*, No. 18 (May 2, 1988): 11. Unfortunately, the article gives no clue how this assessment was deduced.

41. Lapidus, "Gorbachev's Reforms": 11.

42. Archie Brown, "Soviet Political Developments and Prospects," *World Policy Journal*, Vol. 4, No. 1 (Winter 1986/1987): 56.

43. *Political Culture and Leadership in Soviet Russia*: 135–136.

44. See, for example, *Moskovskie novosti*, April 10, 1988.

45. *Nedelia*, No. 18 (May 2, 1988): 11.

46. *Moskovskie novosti*, April 10, 1988.

47. CSM, June 30, 1987.

48. *Sobesednik*, No. 39, cited in RL 391/87 (October 2).

49. *Sotsiologicheskie issledovaniia*, No. 4, 1987, cited in RL 382/87 (September 25).

50. On the young, see *Pravda*, November 9 and December 21, 1987, for a discussion entitled "Is It Easy to be Young?"

51. *Shadows and Whispers*: 45.

52. "Novye trevogi": 163.

53. *Pravda*, May 30, 1988 (translated in CDSP, Vol. 40, No. 22 (June 29): 24.

54. See, for example, John Tedstrom, "On Perestroika: Analyzing the Basic Provisions," *Problems of Communism*, Vol. 36, No. 4 (July–August, 1987): 98.

55. RL 472/86 (December 17).

56. RL 379/87 (September 17). The city was Chekhov; the drivers were protesting being penalized for not meeting the timetable when they were saddled with antiquated buses. By 1990 some 75 million Soviet workers will be converted to similar performance-linked pay systems.

57. A front-page appeal in *Pravda* October 29 did nothing to stop panic buying. Food supplies reportedly have improved in the past two years, but primarily through farmers' markets at deregulated prices (NYT, October 30, 1987).

58. On prices see NYT, June 28, 1987. Raising prices means attacking a powerful bureaucracy (the Goskomtsen, or State Committee for Prices), tampering with a basic tenet of ideology, and introducing the possibility of "potentially explosive inflation." (In Eastern Europe food price increases have set off demonstrations; in 1962 food price increases in the USSR led to a violent protest in Novocherkassk.)

59. For discussion of income distribution and the new law, see RL 230/87 (June 19): 1–7; and RL 389/87 (September 24): 1–5.

60. Measures to cushion unemployment are also being discussed. See *Izvestiia*, January 20, 1988: 1–2.

61. CSM, August 10, 1987: 12.

62. Lapidus, "Gorbachev's Reforms": 32.

63. Doder, *Shadows and Whispers*: 40.

64. For example, 5,000 auto workers at the Leninskii Komsomolets plant refused to rubber-stamp a report on the reasons for firing Yeltsin, and officials, fearing a strike, sent the workers home (NYT, November 25, 1987).

65. *Izvestiia*, September 2, 1987 and February 29, 1988. According to these reports, police confiscate forty-two tons of narcotics every year, which is "less than 15 percent" of the total in circulation.

66. RL 472/86 (December 17), 'from *Izvestiia*, February 15, 1986. On the "telebridge" see RL 129/87 (April 8).

67. NYT, October 2, 1987.

68. *Ogonek*, No. 49 (December, 1987): 26–28. Everyone seems to have something to say today in the Soviet Union. Newspapers are inundated with letters, although many dissatisfied citizens, according to *Ogonek* editor V. Korotich, continue to send their complaints directly to the "higher instances . . . i.e., the [security] 'organs'." "Don't bother," Korotich adds, "nowadays those 'organs' just pass your complaints right along to us. So send them to us, it'll be quicker!" (*Ogonek*, No. 11, 1988: 6).

69. *Izvestiia*, April 16, 1988: 3 (translated in CDSP, Vol. 40, No. 16: 1).

70. *Nedelia*, February 1–7, 1988: 14–15. See also the issue for March 28–April 3: 8–9, for letters in response to these comments, and Bestuzhev-Lada's follow-up letter, April 11–17: 10–11.

71. Ellen Mickiewicz, "Policy Isssues in the Soviet Media System," in *The Soviet Union in the 1980s*, ed. by Erik P. Hoffmann (New York, 1984): 114.

72. *Sovetskaia Rossiia* (July 24, 1987), cited in CDSP, Vol. 39, No. 41 (November 11): 5.

73. WP, December 20, 1987.

74. From CDSP, Vol. 40, No. 8, 1988: 25; translation of *Moskovskie novosti*, No. 8, February 21, 1988: 2.

75. Alexander Goldfarb, "Testing Glasnost," *New York Times Book Review Magazine*, December 6, 1987: 49.

76. RL 104/88 (March 15): 1–5; O. Maslova, "Kak my predstavliaem sebe demokratiiu i glasnost," *Argumenty i fakty*, No. 8, 1988.

77. On the last question, 33 percent had no opinion. The study was in *Izvestiia*, September 4, 1987; cited in CDSP, Vol. 39, No. 36 (October 7):7.

78. *Sovetskaia Rossiia*, July 24, 1987, cited in CDSP, Vol. 39, No. 41 (November ll): 5. The indication of generational differences is a hint that the Politburo is receiving a disproportionate amount of mail against the reforms.

79. Cited in CSM, July 3, 1987. Only 9 percent sought promotion, while 30 percent would prefer less demanding work.

80. *Moscow News*, No. 27, 1988: 10–11. It could plausibly be argued that any telephone poll, in fact any poll of Muscovites, is skewed in favor of the society's better-off citizens.

81. I personally remember the smoldering rage of my own father-in-law, a factory worker who was not particularly materialistic, when, in the mid-1970s, I took him to a store in Riga stocked with deficit items available only to those

with special certificates, and he walked around, glaring at the items he had been denied all his life.

82. For a survey of recent opinion polls on how Soviets view the United States, see WP, December 6, 1987. Roughly the same percentage of Soviets and Americans believe coexistence is possible (84 percent and 80 percent respectively); reportedly 6 percent of Soviet citizens view the American administration favorably, but 80 percent think positively of the American people. . . . For a brief, but interesting report on a postsummit poll of Pittsburg residents on how they see Gorbachev, see WP, December 16, 1987 (David Broder editorial). A similarly brief survey of other polls on American views of the USSR and the perspectives of coexistence is in CSM, December 4, 1987. See also CSM, November 27, 1987: 2.

83. NYT, November 1, 1987.

7
The Environment

We Have Delivered Nature a Serious Blow

One recent Western survey of the Soviet press concludes "that the impression created over the past year [is] of a country teetering on the brink of an ecological catastrophe."[1]

The events at Chernobyl in April 1986 are known throughout the world. Many readers are no doubt also familiar with the outcry over the pollution by pulp mills of fabled Lake Baikal, and even with the controversy over, and final scuttling of, the colossal project to divert the course of Russia's northern rivers into the Volga in order to provide water for the arid south. But there have been many other less well-known environmental disasters in recent years.

In September 1983 in Lvov province in the Ukraine, an earthen wall holding back waste salts from a fertilizer plant broke, and a billion gallons of thick brine poured through a breach 180 feet wide in a 20-foot-high wave, sweeping down fifteen miles to the Dniestr River; the millions of tons of salts contaminated water supplies downstream, including those of Odessa 600 miles away, and killed hundreds of tons of fish.

In 1980 Soviet engineers built a dike to plug up a lagoon, the Kara Bogaz Gol, which was purportedly contributing (along with industrial drawoff) to the dropping level of the Caspian Sea. The dike, some 1800 feet long, cut the flow of some 4 million acre feet of water per annum, but replenishment of the water supply to the Kara Bogaz was to be guaranteed by a lock that would prevent formation of a dry salt lake and maintain the chemical balance of the water. The Kara Bogaz, covering an area about the size of Connecticut, was not only drawing off water from the Caspian but also depositing valuable chemicals, found nowhere else in the USSR, that have long been commercially exploited. It was expected that with the lock (which was never built), the lagoon would survive another twenty-five years; instead it virtually disappeared in three years (in 1983 scientists reported that a foot of mud remained). Moreover, evaporation exposed noxious salts, which were then spread by wind over the irrigated oases of Central Asia. The chemical industries that exploited the underground brines have been disrupted, and the wind-blown salts are now reaching the grain areas of the Kuban. It now turns out that the level of the Caspian Sea had bottomed out in 1977, and was dependent not upon the Kara Bogaz, but rather upon long-term cycles. Because of the project, however, the level of the Caspian itself has been rising so fast that a major port has been flooded and nearby oilfields threatened.[2]

An "emergency ecological situation" exists in the vicinity of the Aral Sea, where the level of water has dropped 54 percent in twenty years, sandstorms have increased, the soil has become saline, and the population has been drinking untreated water from drainage canals. The main cause is the reduced volume of the Syr Darya and Amu Darya rivers, brought about by profligate farm irrigation practices ("the water is free, why not let it pour forth?"). Journalists report that because of the unremitting sowing of cotton in the area (which has caused serious health problems now being exposed), stands of timber, once making up 15 percent of irrigated land, have disappeared, and "now, hot dry winds race across Central Asia." The Kyzyl Kum and Kara Kum deserts now join at the bare bottom of the Aral Sea (because the Syr Darya now peters out before reaching the sea), and salty sand now covers the once fertile Amu Darya Basin: "The winds which used to bring rain from the glassy sea, now come with trains of millions of tons of salt, poisoning the land and the air ever farther to the south." Doctors in the area have discovered dangerous levels of salinity in women's breast milk. One journalist vividly depicted the death of a sea:

> We walked along the former sea floor to the former harbor, where on the sand, side by side like beached whales, lay the rusting mummies of a fishing fleet. A strong steady wind blew from the north, bringing a salty taste to our lips—far off in that direction, every day the mass of strong salt solution, lifeless but still called the Aral Sea, continued to shrink and recede.[3]

"The Volga Groans" is the title of an interview with F. Shipunov, head of the Biosphere Research Laboratory of the Academy of Sciences. The Volga basin provides 25 percent of the country's industrial and agricultural output; historically the Volga River has served as Russia's central artery of commerce and human transportation. But "the mighty Volga no longer exists." In the past fifty years vast forest tracts along the river have disappeared and 300 reservoirs have been built along with thousands of miles of canals and huge dams. But no concern has been shown for preserving this, "one of the largest ecological systems on the planet." The Volga has been "converted from a mighty river into a chain of slow-flowing bodies of water. . . . All of its physical, chemical and biological properties have changed." More than one-third of its 150,000 tributaries have simply disappeared, the water-exchange ratio reduced to one-twelfth its previous level, and the upper reaches of surviving tributaries have receded by dozens of miles. Most of these tributaries are "clogged up, polluted, deforested, dug up, or drained." Seventy percent of the fish in reservoirs are infested with parasites because of the poor series arrangement of reservoirs and the inadequate water flow this arrangement causes: "Anyone who has been on the Volga cannot help seeing how bream infected with tapeworms cannot swim down into deep water and are writhing on the shores, sandbars, piers and docks, as if asking people for help. Not getting it, they die in droves." Because of the reduced self-purifying capacity of the river, "long stretches have become unsanitary bodies of water . . . with large accumulations of toxic chemical substances." In addition, because the many power stations have no fishways, only 400 of 3,000 natural spawning grounds for sturgeon now remain. In fact, "the entire series of hydroelectric stations was erected in violation of elementary ecological conditions." Consequently, high levels of groundwater salinity have developed, and about 25 percent of land under irrigation in the Volga basin is salty or swampy. This estimate does not take into account the 4.8 million hectares of fertile land immersed and 6-8 million additional hectares with greatly reduced productivity. Because of the concentration upon water management (consuming 80 percent of all investments in agriculture, on 5 percent of the plowland, exclusively in the southern portion of the Volga basin) in the past thirty years, 10 million hectares of plowland in the neglected northern section have been lost.[4]

Pollution hasn't overlooked smaller rivers either. In Georgia, the majority of the republic's 26,000 rivers have been transformed into "open sewers for animal and human waste and industrial effluents." The worst are the "tamed rivers": those whose course has been diverted, which have been connected with primitive irrigation systems and blocked with cement. Lake Cherepashy, near Tbilisi, has been closed to recreational use since 1983 because of the high coliform count (from the discharge of household sewage into the rivers feeding it). In Latvia, the Lielupe River, which has many health resorts along its banks, is utterly filthy.[5]

Then there is White Russia, where "barbaric methods" have been used to extract potassium ore since it was discovered thirty years ago. A journalist flying over the region of Polesye this winter saw caved-in mines every-where, which created "huge black lakes, sludge settling ponds, poisonous mud ponds. . . . We felt as if we were flying over the surface of the moon. . . . The picture was terrifying: a dirty-gray desert." The land over the worked-out mines is settling, groundwater is rising to the surface, and the local inhabitants are breathing in poisonous salt dusts borne by the winds. Millions of tons of brine have been flowing from mountains of salt, and the volume of (inadequately) stored brine is 47 million cubic meters, enough to dwarf the "Lvov Canal" disaster should it ever break loose, which is "entirely possible": According to one source, the dikes of the effluent dam are threatened because of subsistence caused by salt removal under the reservoir.[6]

Speaking in 1987, the country's leading official in charge of protecting the environment, Iu. Izrael, reported that "air pollution in cities posed the greatest danger." Minister of Health Evgenii Chazov reported that in 104 cities pollution levels exceeded permitted limits[7] and that total emissions of harmful substances into the atmosphere amounted to 65 million tons per annum from stationary sources and 40 million tons from motor vehicles (compared to 150 million tons in the United States). Total emissions of sulfur dioxide surpassed 20 million tons. Up to 6.5 cubic kilometers of untreated waste is discharged into rivers, lakes, and seas every year; fertilizer concentrations were at dangerous levels in many reservoirs. The Sea of Azov, Lake Balkash, and Lake Issyk-Kul are suffering similar problems. Creation of large reservoirs has led to substantial eutrophication; the establishment of large Siberian "seas" has resulted in the large-scale destruction of trees as well as the poisoning of these seas by the by-products of wood decomposition. A poorly planned flood control project seems to be creating a "real cesspool" at the mouth of the Neva, which flows through Leningrad into the Gulf of Finland. And a combination of offshore drilling as well as discharged effluents continues to severely pollute the Black and Baltic sea coasts; beaches in Odessa and the Crimea are frequently closed to swimmers. The Black Sea coast itself has been eroding away for years as a result of overbuilding and utter neglect of conservation measures.

The aftereffects of the nuclear disaster at Chernobyl in 1986 continue to be felt.[8] Recent Soviet estimates claim that the radiation emitted was fifteen times less than originally stated and that this level of radiation would cause only 200 to 600 additional deaths in a life span.[9] Such assertions found support in a Western report released this year which, however, was not universally accepted.[10] The significance of the economic and ecological consequences are beyond dispute.[11]

Finally, the worsening pollution of the world's deepest freshwater lake, Baikal in Siberia, has long been an issue in the Soviet Union—the effort to save Baikal is said to have begun the environmentalist movement in the USSR. Since 1969 the Central Committee has passed four resolutions aimed to protect the lake, but it continues to be polluted by paper mills situated on its banks and along its tributaries.[12] Even the fact that Russia's most popular writer, Valentin Rasputin, hails from the Baikal area and has often pointed to it as an egregious example of the ongoing despoliation of nature in the USSR has had limited effect, except to make Baikal the object of renewed media publicity in the past two years.[13]

Few observers, then, would disagree with statements like the following, common fare in the age of glasnost:

> In recent decades we have delivered nature a serious blow. Over large expanses the soil cover has been damaged and the natural fertility of the land undercut. Many lakes and rivers have been polluted . . . or are undergoing dessication. In certain regions extremely perilous ecological conditions have arisen. Even so, measures to protect the environment have been put on the back burner; even the most urgent needs are not receiving a commensurate response. The debt incurred over many decades to nature must now be paid back, and paid back in full without tardiness, which will of course also require the diverting of substantial resources from other needs.[14]

Heady Times for Environmentalists

And yet, "these are heady times for Russia's environmentalists."[15] At a speech this year to the Congress of Journalists' Union, *Pravda* editor Viktor Afanasiev observed that earlier, the environment, like the space program, had generally been a "forbidden zone" for journalistic criticism. Under Gorbachev it has become a symbol of the waste and detrimental impact of ill-designed showcase projects carried out under Brezhnev, as well as an object lesson in the nature of bureaucratic resistance to reform. Concern for the environment, evident in scholarly journals well before Gorbachev, became a major public issue with the fiery speeches delivered at the 1986 Writers' Union Conference, where Sergei Zalygin compared the earth with its 5 billion inhabitants to a "communal apartment with one sewage pipe for all."[16] Some fierce attacks have been directed by Zalygin, Shmelev, and others at the "gigantomania" of past years—at the megaprojects designed to alter the course of Siberia's rivers (abandoned, finally, in August 1986),[17] to run a railway through some of the roughest terrain and through one of the most forbidden climates in the world (e.g., the Baikal-Amur railway, or BAM), and so forth. The ministry of water resources (Minvodkhoz) has been the special target of reformers. With a budget of 10 billion rubles (equal to the entire sum spent on health care) and almost 2 million employees, this ministry has become a self-perpetuating catastrophe, swallowing up resources to carry out "prestige" projects with huge carrying costs, of dubious benefit or, often, of positive harm (the "myriad" of hydroelectric power stations, for example, which have flooded millions of hectares of the country's most fertile land). Ironically, the Minvodkhoz pleaded budget constraints in deleting the lock from the Kara Bogaz project and continues to resist efforts to restore the damage done to the Gulf, calling such efforts too costly.[18]

The grass-roots following in the growing environmental movement is heterogeneous; it ranges from those concerned with the excesses of hasty industrialization and concerned with local preservation to ethnic minorities resisting Russian plans to alter their region and to Russian nationalists seeking to restore mystic roots in the primeval landscape.[19] The movement has also gained momentum from the Chernobyl accident, which even helped to spawn serious doubts about the Soviet nuclear energy program. This year, in a bid to gain popular support, the Komsomol has taken up environmental themes—an action signifying the depth of public concern.

The link between environmental concerns and ethnic grievances must be of particular concern to the Soviet leadership. In July 1987 several hundred Armenian scientists accused the authorities of implementing "biological genocide," and in October several thousand people marched in Erevan in protest against pollution. In Tartu, Estonia, students at a meeting called a project to mine phosphorite in that republic a "typical example of colonialist economic thinking."[20] And in Uzbekistan, long-suppressed reports that pesticides applied to the cotton crop are causing serious health problems for the children of the republic (who often help pick the crop) have exacerbated relations between Russians and Central Asians (although it was the Moscow press that first brought out the facts). Georgian intellectuals have protested the building of a new railroad across the Caucasian mountain range, and local residents in Tskhinavali, also in Georgia, met to protest against contaminated drinking water, which had caused an outburst of typhoid fever.[21] In Lithuania this year, the Writers' Union passed a resolution criticizing the republican government for tolerating economic activity harmful to the environment. And in neighboring Latvia, petitioners gathered 30,000 signatures in protest against construction of the Daugavpils Hydroelectric Power Station; another 12,000 to 15,000 protesters demonstrated in Riga in April 1988 against planned construction of a new subway system.[22] In the Ukraine, following Chernobyl, protests against a new nuclear power station in Chigirin have led to suspension of work, and local scientists have publicly called for a reassessment of nuclear energy in the region. In the Ukraine, protests are mounting over apparent government plans to "sidestep public opinion by enlarging capacity at existing plants"[23] and against construction of the Danube-Dniepr Canal.

Some impressive successes have been scored in the past year, and protests are growing in force.[24] Resistance to nuclear power has increased immeasurably, as letters pour in to Moscow "from the Ukraine, from Belorussia, from all over the country." Late in 1987, public protests forced Moscow to cancel construction of a nuclear plant in the foothills of the Caucasus near Krasnodar (after 25 billion rubles had reportedly already been spent).[25] Two dozen plants already in operation, and all plants under construction, are now "bitterly contested" by local residents: "It's a chain reaction" one scientist lamented.[26] "Environmentalists thus find themselves in the forefront of . . . democratization."[27]

The Debt to Nature Must Be Paid Back

The Soviet Union has a long history of environmental legislation, dating back to the 1920s but especially rich during the past thirty years. Soviet ideologists have frequently referred to this legislation as "testimony to the long-standing commitment of the Soviet Union to environmental conservation."[28] Moreover, they have added that socialist systems have an inherent advantage over market economies in coping with environmental problems in that there is no private profit motive to govern resource usage, central planning is inherently more rational, and property rights maximize social welfare.

The second claim has been effectively disposed of by critics who point not only to the demonstrated record but also to the "generic" insufficiencies of central planning (for example, the lack of adequate information and imperfect plan coordination); overlapping administrative jurisdictions; lax enforcement of environmental laws; inconsequential fines imposed upon offenders; lags in developing waste disposal technology; irrational pricing structures (treating natural resources as free goods); and, especially, the institutionalized priority given to production over conservation.[29]

As for legislation, given the record of despoliation, Soviet claims to a long lineage of environmental laws lays such proponents open to ridicule along the lines of the smoker's joke that "quitting is easy, I've done it hundreds of times." Nevertheless, at least one analyst sees real promise in the Gorbachev switch to intensive rather than extensive growth strategies, which "are intended to alleviate, if not solve" many of the problems resulting from past practices.[30] And "the impression that legal enforcement is totally wanting should not be given."[31] Some industrial enterprises have been closed down for violating the laws and criminal sentences have been passed out. Highly efficient gas scrubbers and dust traps have been installed and emissions stabilized or reduced in many cities. "Positive signs" have been reported in the quality of the Ural River, where major pollution-control efforts with recycling waste and water supplies are under way.[32] In the past few years, the documents of the 27th Party Congress and the resolutions of the 19th Party Conference placed strong emphasis on environmental protection. Moreover, in the decade from 1975 to 1985, the Soviet Union more than doubled the area of land designated as preserved or reserved.

A good case can be made for the argument that the outright scuttling of the river diversion project represents, like the Baikal controversy of the late 1960s, a major turning point in Soviet environmental history. The decision by the CPSU Central Committee and the Council of Ministers "focused attention on utilizing existing regional water resources more economically and efficiently rather than on the massive scale and prohibitively costly diversion projects." Moreover, "a critical . . . evaluation of the economic worth of large-scale and often environmentally harmful projects has surrounded the recent chapters in the river diversion debate. Finally, "better and more comprehensive cost accounting approaches and ecological considerations have practically sounded the death bell to large dams and reservoir projects."[33]

On January 16, 1988, Tass announced a joint resolution of the Politburo and Council of Ministers for "the radical reorganization of environmental protection in the USSR." In addition to the formation of a union of informal environmental groups and the establishment of a publishing house to deal with environmental issues, the resolution established the USSR State Committee for Environmental Protection, in charge of both formulating and implementing environmental policy and responsible for working with international bodies to ensure compliance with agreements. Previously, environmental policy had been handled by no fewer than nine state committees and seven ministries. Tass also announced plans to draw up a draft law on environmental protection to be submitted by 1989. In one analyst's view, the formation of "a unified environmental protection agency . . . presumably in the face of ministerial resistance, is a victory for the scientists, writers, and other concerned citizens who pressed for action on environmental problems during the years of official indifference and hostility." It is also a measure, this analyst continues, of the intensity of the ecological crisis in the country.[34]

But the prodevelopment forces are well entrenched, especially in the bureaucracy, now 18 million strong, with a budget, according to Gorbachev, of over 40 billion rubles. One American observer compared the official mentality to that of the U.S. Army Corps of Engineers: "Every time they see a river, they want to pave it."[35] Izrael indicated in 1987 that watchdog agencies were largely powerless to prevent despoliation of the environment. At the same time, legal means for enforcing environmental protection measures remain, for the time being, toothless. Izrael complained of "ecologically illiterate economic management" and noted that firms have "virtually no economic interest in environmental protection activity."

Most important, Izrael expressed fear that with self-financing and stricter economic accountability, the temptation to pollute would be even greater.[36] In fact, in order to pay the "bill" now due from past sins, substantial resources will have to be diverted from other areas to stem the deterioration. But from where? The consumer? Investment in modern technologies (also long past due)? Although public concern about the environment is mounting, it will be very hard to reverse long-standing traditions of resource exploitation, and just as hard to convince the public that improvements in living standards will have to again be deferred. For Soviet citizens who have long waited for hot water and other amenities, and who (I can testify personally) have little notion that resources are exhaustible, learning to conserve will be painful. And it will be just as painful, politically, to increase consumer rates for utilities.

Here the problem emerges once again of how to combine long-term goals with the need for short-term gains in productivity. The April 1986 accident at Chernobyl "called into question not only the RBMK graphite-moderated reactor technology used at Chernobyl, but also the whole ambitious program to base almost all new electric power capacity and much new heat supply in the western Soviet Union on nuclear technology."[37] Some political scientists have concluded that Chernobyl was a landmark for Gorbachev as well, convincing him of the need for greater glasnost, for structural reforms, and even of the fragility of life on earth.

At the same time, "as the Twelfth Five-Year Plan unfolds, the risk grows that shortages of power will constrain other targets for industry." In fact, a quick look at the Soviet energy picture shows that "a redesigning and slowing down in nuclear power plant development could not come at a more inopportune time. Oil and gas are already absorbing major amounts of capital. To now slow nuclear power expansion as well as to direct additional funds into alterations in the system is most unwelcome."[38]

The Soviet Union has powerful incentives to continue developing nuclear power and is pushing ahead with its program, bringing several new stations on line after only the briefest of reviews at the end of 1987.[39] Chernobyl, it is said, "was a failure of personnel, not of policy."[40] Just two months after Chernobyl, the Supreme Soviet announced a decision to increase generation of nuclear power from 167 billion to 390 billion kilowatt-hours within the next five years. The proportion of nuclear energy in power generation is to rise from 11 percent in 1985 to 21 percent by 1990 (thus, to make up 6 percent of "overall primary production").[41]

An End to Gigantomania?

Soviet environmental concerns both stem from and interact with all other facets of Soviet life under Gorbachev: economic perestroika; the attempt to rein in bureaucracy and the struggle against "gigantomania"; freedom of self-expression; the rejection of the dogmas of progress and, implicitly of core Marxist values; ethnic concerns and the problems of running a colonial empire in a century of self-determination; an emphasis on scientific input and policy formulation; and a resurgent Russian nationalism and search for roots (in Russian nature and history).

The environmental movement has come to the fore not only because the scope of looming—as well as past—disasters could no longer be overlooked, but also, it must be added, because the emergence of a concern for the preservation of nature has everywhere been historically connected with the rise of middle classes. As Starr points out in "Soviet Union: A Civil Society," "fundamental shifts in Soviet society are going forward, and these increasingly define the national agenda." The waning of a peasant society has paradoxically given rise to new views of nation, history, and now nature, similar to those marking much of Europe at the turn of this century: a cult of the peaceful countryside and the old peasant life, the harmony of old village ways in times of rapid change and unrest, and a romanticization of landscape (quite alien to peasant cultures!).[42] As in Europe, environmental concerns took a backseat during early stages of industrialization, and a time lag existed between the period of industrial, agricultural, and urban development and the appearance of major environmental problems.[43] What is unique about the new Soviet view of nature is that it is occurring in a context fundamentally different from that obtaining in Europe at the turn of this century; Soviet society is already experiencing an acute ecological and economic crisis, a pent-up release of resentments and grievances, and an aggravated search for core, unifying values. The Soviet environmental movement is both a reflection of these changes and a key element in the new national agenda, now defined by "civil society" rather than by the narrow political elite alone.

Environmental concerns have been given a boost by glasnost because Gorbachev sees instrumental value in highlighting the past despoliation of nature. Analysts believe that Gorbachev is "using environmental concerns as a vehicle for allowing, if not indeed encouraging, the expression of pent-up criticisms of bureaucratic mismanagement and corruption." In the process, "a quasi-democratic dialogue critical of the Soviet Union's management of the environment is being heard within ever wider circles of Soviet society."[44]

Finally, the environment also fits well into Gorbachev's New Thinking in foreign policy, exemplifying the notion of the "interdependence" of the globe. In an interview with political commentator Flora Lewis, Valentin Falin, head of the Soviet press agency Novosti, speaking of the arms race, commented that irreversible damage was taking place to the environment, that ecological dangers loomed large, but that "neither [the United States nor the Soviet Union] has the resources to take the necessary measures now; we're putting them into the arms race." According to Lewis: "It is clear that the Chernobyl accident had a deep impact on Mr. Gorbachev's thinking, forcing him not only to a new awareness of the danger of war but also of the unpredictability and uncertainties of the modern world."[45] In fact, Soviet prominence on the world stage in addressing issues such as energy supplies, population growth, and environmental protection has been evident for at least twenty years, but has been little noticed by Western observers.[46] In Europe, diplomats point out that it is precisely in the area of environmental concerns that the most progress has been made in devising cooperative measures. "Everyone focuses on security issues and human rights," says Aira Kalela (a Swedish official). "But when we met in 1985 on the 10th anniversary of the Helsinki Accords, the diplomats agreed that the environment was the area in which there had been the most progress over the past 10 years."[47] The feeling is that if gains could be made during the Brezhnev era, talks should "thrive and multiply" with the atmosphere fostered by New Thinking.

Notes

1. NYT, December 27, 1987.

2. These summaries of the Kara Bogaz and "Lvov Canal" incidents are based upon my annual survey of events in the USSR in *World Topics Yearbook* (1983 and 1984), and upon a recent report in RL 48/88 (February 3). See also CDSP, Vol. 35, No. 42: 1–3, 14, and Vol. 36, No. 16: 14–15.

3. *Literaturnaia gazeta*, November 18, 1988:12; CDSP, Vol. 39, No. 51 (January 20, 1988): 11.

4. *Sovetskaia Rossiia*, November 18, 1987: 4; from CDSP, Vol. 39, No. 50 (January 13, 1988): 15.

5. On Georgia, see CDSP, Vol. 39, No. 52 (January 27, 1988): 18.

6. *Literaturnaia gazeta*, March 2, 1988: 11.

7. *Literaturnaia gazeta*, April 29, 1987.

8. For the trial of those responsible for Chernobyl, see RL 384/87 (October 6). For recent surveys of events pertaining to Chernobyl, see RL 249/88 (June 22); NYT, April 25, 1988 and May 23, 1988; RL 175/88 (April 25); and CDSP, Vol. 40, No. 2: 19; No. 6: 22; No. 8: 29. For the ecological consequences, see Theodore Shabad, "Geographical Aspects of the Chernobyl Nuclear Accident," *Soviet Geography*, Vol. 27, No. 7 (September, 1986): 504–526.

9. CSM, April 27, 1987: 18. A Soviet official attending a conference on nuclear safety sponsored by the International Atomic Energy Association asserted that Soviet citizens had received a radiation dose only 2 percent above normal, and that the incidence of cancer in future years would be only "hundredths of a percent" above normal: RL 391/87 (Oct. 2): 7. Many questions remain unanswered concerning Chernobyl, including the reason for the second radioactive release, the motivations for the experiment that triggered the accident, and whether this experiment was conducted without approval of superiors, as claimed. David Marple claims that officials from the state committee supervising the atomic energy industry were at the fourth reactor building at the time of the accident. See his "The Chernobyl Disaster" in *Current History*, Vol. 86, No. 522: 325; and RL 390/87 (October 2).

10. The report, released by three California researchers and sponsored by the U.S. Department of Energy, argues that except for people living within a 30-mile radius of the reactor (400 deaths, a 2 percent increase in risk), there will be hardly any effect, and that the increased risk of cancer is slight: in the Northern Hemisphere a .004 percent increase in risk (0 to 28,000 deaths). For the people of Europe the dose received "is equivalent to a few years' exposure of natural background radiation," and subsequent mortality is "statistically insignificant." The United States will have 0 to 20 additional deaths from cancer. Others, however, predict up to 100,000 additional deaths. The difference in estimates stems from two indices: the uptake of cesium 137 (a fission by-product) by plants, and the so-called cancer-risk coefficient (probable number of fatalities per unit of person-rem exposure to radiation). Critics of DOE studies argue that the parameters used are far too low (CSM, August 31, 1987, 3). For a much more pessimistic view of future (and present, unacknowledged) casualties, see Marple, "The Chernobyl Disaster": 326–327. He refers to children who attended school or played soccer in the streets in Pripyet the day of the accident; to soldiers working

without protection and living in tents throughout the summer; to the absence of information about those treated ("the majority") in hospitals in Kiev; and to the failure to provide any health warnings to the population in the first week ("contaminated products were eaten, and life proceeded normally").

11. Early Soviet estimates of the financial cost ranged from (official) 2 billion to (unofficial) 4 billion or more rubles. More recently, the Politburo placed a price tag of 4 billion rubles on the cleanup and another 4 billion rubles lost to reduced production (*Pravda*, January 15, 1988). In addition, future nuclear power plant construction costs, incorporating safety measures, will increase by 40 percent (CSM, April 27, 1987: 18). Marple describes a "crisis situation" that developed after Soviet RBMKs, producing 55 percent of the country's nuclear energy, were shut down for modifications and the very early and harsh winter set in late in 1986. Tight restrictions were imposed upon domestic electricity usage, and workers in industries using much electricity (especially machine building, which Gorbachev sees as the key to Soviet economic progress) had to work at nonpeak hours and weekends. See also his discussion of the impact on the East European power grid system, and of the ecological consequences to the north Ukraine (Marple: 342–343).

12. RL 27/88 (January 21): 2.

13. ZumBrunnen, "Gorbachev, Economics and the Environment," Joint Economic Committee, *Gorbachev's Economic Plans*, Washington, D.C., 1987. Vol 2: 403–404.

14. V. Belkin, P. Medvedev, I. Nit, "Reforma: Model' perekhoda—shag pervyi, vtoroi, tretii," *Znanie—Sila*, No. 12, 1987: 5.

15. NYT, December 27, 1987: E14.

16. Cited in Tucker, *Political Culture and Leadership in Soviet Russia*: 167. Tucker provides a brief summary of environmental debates at the Congress.

17. The rivers to be diverted were the Ob-Irtysh and the Vychegda-Pechora. Aganbegyan claims that public opinion was significant in stopping this project, especially in discussion over the guidelines for the Twelfth Five-Year Plan, which still included funding for the river diversion. He says that at a meeting of the Presidium of the Council of Ministers that he attended, opinion remained divided over whether to continue digging, but the opposition of Premier Ryzhkov and others was enough to kill the plans (and to write off more than 100 million rubles already spent): *The Economic Challenge of Perestroika*: 200–201. For a more cautious assessment, which sees Gorbachev "soliciting public opinion" to bolster his case with the Politburo, see Tucker, *Political Culture and Leadership in Soviet Russia*: 168–169.

18. Shmelev, "Novye trevogi": 171–172; Belkin et al., "Reforma: Model' perekhoda,": 5.

19. This movement is often connected with the village prose movement in literature, with a rejection of crude notions of progress and of urbanization, and an implicit emphasis upon absolute and eternal, i.e., non-Marxist, values.

20. This information is from RL 27/88 (January 21): 3.

21. *Komsomolskaia pravda*, April 26, 1988; RL 368/87; RL 396/87.

22. Ann Sheehy and Sergei Voronitsyn, "Ecological Protest in the USSR, 1986–1988: RL 191/88 (May 11): 1–3.

23. CSM, February 4, 1988.

24. See the articles on public resistance to setting up oil rigs in the Baltic region (CDSP, Vol. 39, No. 24, July 15; NYT, September 27, 1987); Georgian opposition to a mountain railway construction project (RL 368/87 [August 25]:1–7); a decision in Armenia not to construct a second nuclear plant in that republic, apparently bowing to pressure from an environmental group (RL 130/87 [March 30]); the decision to abandon one in which 40 million rubles had already been invested (NYT, January 31, 1988); discussion, following the collapse on March 16 of a dam in Sargazan, Tadjikistan (resulting in heavy loss of life), of the danger of building large dams in the Pamirs, an area of major seismic activity. The danger is not only that earthquakes could prompt the collapse of such dams, but also that the weight of water stored behind the dams could itself prompt earthquakes. The massive Nurek dam, east of Dushambe, is of particular concern (RL 155/87 [March 26]). *Pravda* (April 18, 1988) reported that "tens of thousands of people" had joined a letter campaign to complain against pollution by the city's chemical industries, and that demonstrations had occurred. On April 6, according to *Komsomolskaia pravda*, demonstrations took place in Nizhnii Tagil over a similar issue, and in Kazan residents voiced opposition to plans to build a biochemical plant (CDSP, Vol. 40, No. 4: 21). In Iakutsk citizens petitioned against city development plans (*Izvestiia*, January 8); in Achinsk, sixty-five individuals sent a letter protesting that they were "suffocating from dust" generated by a city aluminum plant (*Pravda*, January 29). See also, for other controversies, CDSP, Vol. 39, No. 47 (December 23, 1987).

25. *Pravda*, January 21, 1988.

26. *Komsomolskaia pravda*, January 27, 1988; in CDSP, Vol. 40, No. 3: 9.

27. NYT, December 27, 1987.

28. ZumBrunnen, "Gorbachev, Economics and the Environment": 398.

29. Ibid.: 411–413.

30. Ibid.: 397.

31. Ibid.: 415.

32. Ibid.: 402–403.

33. Ibid.: 398, 407.

34. RL 27/88 (January 21): 2 (my comments on the new Committee are drawn largely from this report).

35. Cited in Ibid.

36. CDSP, Vol. 39, No. 39 (October 7): 6. In the same talk, Izrael pointed to progress in stabilizing air pollution and improvements in the conditions of the Volga River and Caspian Sea. The river diversion project, envisioning rechanneling Siberian rivers into Central Asia for irrigation purposes, was canceled last year, but proponents continue to argue their case (*Novyi mir*, No. 7, 1987; and CDSP, Vol. 39, No. 31 [September 2]: 6–7).

37. Judith Thornton, "Soviet Electric Power in the Wake of the Chernobyl Accident," *Gorbachev's Economic Plans*, Vol. 1: 514.

38. *Gorbachev's Economic Plans*, Vol. 1: 492, 496. According to this expert survey on the key elements of the Soviet energy policy puzzle: the Soviet petroleum base should now be viewed as a "physically constrained energy resource opportunity." After a century of exploitation it can no longer be relied upon to

expand very much in the intermediate-term (though heroic efforts can provide short-term gains); natural gas, though also facing depletion problems, is the best energy opportunity for the next few decades; hydropower, though renewable, has a ceiling on annual flow and seasonal variations; coal remains a vast resource but is plagued by problems of technology and cost, low-grade energy content, inferior quality, lack of ready accessibility, transport expenses, and troubles of usage; nuclear energy is capital intensive to develop at a time when energy is already corralling the lion's share of investment resources of the country, and is limited to generating electric power. Much of future Soviet energy supplies will be located ever farther from current consuming centers, and high-voltage transmission over great distances will introduce technical problems not now within the Soviet grasp to solve. Finally, the Soviet Union is still dependent upon revenues from exporting energy to obtain hard currency. In sum, this source concludes that the problems are remarkably similar in kind to those being faced, and sometimes ignored, by the United States. The most attractive combination for the Soviet Union is nuclear plants coupled with coal and hydropower to provide greater overall capacity and system diversity in the electric power sector, with oil and gas transported over long distances as well as exported.

39. On April 20, 1988, five more nuclear reactors of the Chernobyl type were commissioned (two at Kursk, two in Smolensk, and one in Lithuania). Scientists reported that it was too expensive to stop work at this late stage but that no more of this type would be built (Tass, April 20, reported in RL 177/88 [April 18]).

40. CSM, April 27, 1987: 19.

41. *Gorbachev's Economic Plans*, Vol. 1: 571.

42. A marvelous description of how the rise of a bourgeoisie changed society's view of nature in Sweden at the turn of the century is in Jonas Frykman and Orvar Lofgren, *Culture Builders: A Historical Anthropology of Middle-Class Life* (translated by Alan Crozier [Rutgers, N.J., 1987]: 42–87).

43. ZumBrunnen, "Gorbachev, Economics and the Environment": 398. On the earlier emergence of a conservationist movement during NEP, and its crushing defeat under Stalin, see Douglas R. Wiener, *Models of Nature: Ecology, Conservation, and Cultural Revolution in Soviet Russia* (Bloomington, In., 1988).

44. Ibid.: 424.

45. "Moscow at the Crossroads," NYT, December 11, 1987.

46. ZumBrunnen, "Gorbachev, Economics and the Environment": 415.

47. CSM, November 18, 1987: 8.

8
Ethnicity

Just Conduct Arguments Without Losing Dignity

Glasnost has allowed problems long simmering among the nationalities to come to the surface—at writers' conferences, in the newspapers, and on the streets. As with other uncomfortable social issues, discussion of ill will, pent-up grievances, and persisting ethnic stereotypes has prompted a familiar response—blaming the West. KGB chief Chebrikov, speaking in Cheboksary on April 13, 1988, warned: "It is no secret that the imperialist states' special services and foreign anti-Soviet centers are actively building on extremist escapades involving a nationalist basis, and furthermore that they themselves are beginning to act as direct instigators of hostile actions aimed at fanning hatred and discord among the nationalities."[1] But others have contested the conspiracy theory and pleaded for tolerance. In an interview printed in *Izvestiia*, historian Iuri Poliakov argued that:

> National feelings are being manifested very actively now. Some people are afraid of this. They even believe that democracy should not be developed any further. But in the new conditions, it is especially important to become accustomed to a diversity of opinions and to the manifestation of national feelings. All that has to be done is to conduct arguments without losing human dignity, and with respect for one another's national feelings.[2]

And Lithuanian Communist party official Lionginas Sepetis asserted that "not every demonstration or rally is a manifestation of extremism." If there were extremists and nihilists at recent Baltic protests, "we created them, by not speaking the truth and by hiding [the truth about the past]."[3]

Everyone Wants to Know Who Is Feeding Whom

Until perhaps a decade ago, most people believed that ethnic concerns would die a slow death in the Soviet Union. Soviet Marxists talked about the eradication of differences (*sblizhenie*) or even full assimilation (*slianie*) as a "New Soviet Man" emerged (suspiciously resembling, many thought, an offspring of Russian culture). In the West, modernization theory posited that with urbanization, the spread of mass communications, and a determined Soviet policy of linguistic and cultural assimilation, a homogeneous culture would gradually emerge. *Homo Sovieticus*, socialist or not, would partake of the blessings of modern dress, speech, values, and behavior.[4]

However, since then, studies have shown that, as elsewhere in the world, ethnic identity remains stubbornly intact. Intermarriage among the peoples of the Soviet Union remains a rarity: In no republic does the level of endogamy fall below 81.7 percent—that is, at least four in five marriages brings together a couple of identical national origin. The overwhelming majority of individuals from ethnic groups remain rooted to their homelands, refusing to migrate even when job prospects are better elsewhere. Although the 1979 census showed that knowledge of Russian as a second language had substantially increased in recent years, very few non-Slavic people claimed Russian as their first language, and inability to communicate in Russian continues to be a serious problem in the armed forces. The proportion of Russians who know another language of the Soviet Union also remains insultingly low (4.6 percent) and is a major grievance of the minorities.

The federal political structure of the Soviet Union, earlier regarded by Western specialists as a fig leaf covering unsightly Slavic dominance of other cultures, is now seen as an important mechanism by which regional interests can be mobilized and articulated within the political process and a means by which ethnic identity is reinforced: "What many once thought to be a fraud may actually be a vehicle for legitimizing ethnic group political and economic interests and protecting these interests vis-à-vis the state." What many outsiders overlook is that the historical development of the Russian Empire and Soviet state, by incorporating minorities within their homelands and providing them with a federal structure, has resulted in a welding of the spatial and the ethnic: "By linking ethnic groups and their homelands to the very structure of the state, issues that might otherwise have become regional become ethnic instead."[5] Hence, the "ethnoterritorial basis" has permitted minorities to articulate displeasure with the social consequences of economic policies that take on ethnic dimensions. Thus, once again, we have the intricate interlocking of issues.

In Central Asia, the spread of secondary education and the emergence of a professional elite has been a vital part of Soviet strategy, "drawing non-Russians selectively into political and economic administration."[6] But it has also heightened the national consciousness by establishing a cadre of cultural bearers (much like the Ukrainian culture elite in the second half of the nineteenth century). Thus, the most ardent nationalists are among prose writers and native historians. The national consciousness has been sharpened by the economic decline since the mid-1970s, which has resulted in a measurable slowdown in access to positions in higher education and white-collar jobs (following a period of marked gains and heightened expectations in the 1960s). This sense of closure has been reinforced by new restrictions on party membership imposed since the early 1980s, which have partially reversed gains made by minorities in finding places in the power structure.[7] As elsewhere, here we see the implications of the decline in a belief in progress and open opportunity for all. At the level of the republic or minority group, life has become a zero-sum game. As one Soviet commentator put it: "Now everyone wants to know who is feeding and clothing whom."[8]

It is no surprise, then, that Western specialists studying the views of recent Soviet emigrés have detected a belief that relations among nationalities are getting worse. Resentment of pressure against minority languages has grown, especially in the Baltic republics where "identity revolves around language." In Central Asia, "socio-economic competition has emerged at the forefront of ethnic policies," as has been the case in the Ukraine since the 1960s.[9]

The stakes are high. The peripheral, border location of the largest ethnic groups make national identity a military and security issue, while uncomfortable dilemmas are posed by questions of indigenous recruitment into the power structure; of socioeconomic equality among the diverse ethnic groups, and of a common language of scientific, administrative, and economic communication. Many observers now believe that the ethnic issue is so explosive as to place in serious jeopardy Gorbachev's policy of glasnost and *demokratizatsiia*, threatening perhaps even his very survival as leader—should disorders get out of hand. Even before recent events, some scholars were predicting the ultimate dissolution of empire.[10] At the very least, nationalist unrest can put Gorbachev on the defensive and give the Politburo reason to move more slowly with liberalizing reforms.[11]

Baltic Spring

Riots in Alma Ata two years ago deeply disturbed the leadership. But of all the pressing minority concerns on the Politburo agenda, events in the Caucasus and the Baltic region are surely the most urgent. Events in the Caucasus in 1988 have posed a genuine crisis for the Politburo leadership, and five months of related strikes in Armenia have been very costly for the economy.

When Latvians or other Baltic peoples look at their neighbors in Scandinavia, or into their own past, they have reason to be unhappy, for they are worse off than their parents were and have less of everything, including freedom, than the Finns or Swedes. In Estonia, there has been unprecedented public discussion of the danger of local culture being submerged by the influx of Russians.[12] The Lithuanians also have a powerful national symbol in the Catholic Church (and an influential friend in Rome).

Thus, when a correspondent for the *Christian Science Monitor* reported that tourists returning from Riga saw considerable anti-Soviet graffiti on the walls and concluded that Latvia was in a state of simmering discontent,[13] it was easy to believe that major trouble was brewing. Concern over demonstrations in the Baltic region in 1987 fostered a siege mentality in the Politburo in late August and early September and contributed to the conservative resurgence. Since then, the political and economic demands in Estonia (and recently, Latvia and Lithuania), rather than diminishing, have escalated rapidly, to the point that calls for separate citizenship and full economic autonomy are being seriously discussed.

But the issues creating such turmoil in these areas have little in common. In the Caucasus, what began as yet another page in a long history of internal feuding between Christian and Moslem peoples is inexorably leading to embittered disillusionment with Moscow, with Russians, and even with Gorbachev. In the Baltic, Estonia's grievances have been manifestly against the Soviet system as such and against Russians: In August 1988, publication of the secret protocols of the Nazi-Soviet pact of 1939 (providing for the incorporation of the Baltic states into the USSR) led one caller on a radio program to inquire whether this now entitled the Estonians to ask the Soviets to leave. On the following pages, we look separately at each region, beginning with the Baltic, and especially Estonia.

The range of issues under discussion in Estonia—economic, political, and cultural autonomy; historical truth; religious freedom; the place of emigrés in the national tradition; the environment—is both extensive and familiar. Estonia has long been a place of economic experimentation; now, in establishing, with official authorization, the People's Front, it has become a showcase of political experimentation as well. It has advanced a radical program of economic change that, if implemented, would push perestroika far beyond current boundaries; likewise, the accompanying politial demands for separate citizenship are highly unorthodox. The full Estonian program is hardly likely to be realized, but what is remarkable at this stage is the level of political maturity and savvy with which it is being advanced, and the serious consideration it has received from the Politburo leadership. Most noteworthy, it offers concrete benefits to the Soviet system as a whole, and it provides precedents (Hungary and China) within the socialist world. The People's Front is explicitly not a political party and thus not a rival to the Communist party (one-third of its membership belongs to the reformist wing of the Estonian Communist Party [ECP]); rather, it has been set up to support and advance Gorbachev's platform. Finally, the political scene in Estonia has been remarkably free of violence (excepting ugly frays between youth gangs) and of reprisals (again, except for a handful of arrests).

Estonia's recent past has been marked by setbacks and disillusionment since the gains of the early post-Stalin period. According to Toivo Raun, "At the time of Stalin's death in 1953, Estonia's future looked extremely bleak."[14] The country's population had declined by almost one-third since incorporation into the USSR, and Russian immigration was substantial. Native Estonians had been removed from party leadership positions, and "Estonian culture appeared to be on the verge of extinction in the face of the heavy-handed application of the 'elder brother' concept of the superiority of all things Russian."

Under Khrushchev, life brightened considerably as mass repressions halted, Estonians were once again admitted into the party, the economy improved, a measure of experimentation was allowed in the rural section, and living standards began to climb. Contacts with the West increased, and Estonian culture revived. Even after Khrushchev was removed, these trends continued culminating in the centennial of the first all-Estonian song festival held in 1969. The song festival was, by all accounts, "a powerful national demonstration."

But beginning in the mid-1970s, things turned sour, and by the early 1980s many Estonians felt that the situation was truly desperate. The 1979 census showed that the ethnic population had dropped from 75 percent in 1959 to 65 percent and that Estonians made up only half of the population of Tallin. Ominously, Russians, who accounted for 4 percent of the population of Estonia in 1940, now made up 28 percent (not including the large numbers of Soviet troops stationed in Estonia). Large projects, such as the Muuga harbor enterprise, threatened to bring in even more Russians. The proportion of Estonians in the ECP began to drop once again, and leaders (such as Vaino Valjas, in charge of ideology) not sufficiently hard-line were dropped. The appointment of Karl Vaino to head the ECP in 1978 was especially insulting; born in Tomsk, he spoke no Estonian, adopted a centralist line on economic issues, and up to his dismissal resisted the ecological movement and demands for increased bilingualism as well as Estonian cultural strivings.

A combination of ethnic tensions, including curbs on publications in Estonian; inroads on the Estonian language in politics, the schools, and everyday life; and ongoing immigration of Russians led—beginning about 1980—to protests, letter-writing campaigns, and a combination of limited concessions and repression. According to Raun: "During the Vaino years . . . the social base of dissent has broadened and its major concern has shifted from political demands to the more fundamental issues of national and cultural survival."[15]

But at the same time, Estonians (and the Baltic area in general) have maintained the highest standard of living in the Soviet Union. In 1967, when the USSR first began experimenting with self-financing, 43 percent of the state farms included in the experiment were located in Estonia. Raun notes:

The success of the experiment [in Estonia] . . . led to the implementation of the self-management system on all Soviet sovkhozes by 1975. Even more than in industry, Estonia has emerged as an important experimental laboratory in Soviet agriculture in the post-Stalin era. The small size of the ESSR, an already developed agricultural base, and the skilled labor force make Estonia an attractive location for such experimentation, which could then provide models for the rest of the Soviet Union.[16]

Thus, in 1985, prosperity and limited economic experimentation combined with cultural, social, and political tensions to produce a situation unique both for the difficulties and for the opportunities it presented. Initially, after the April 1985 plenum, glasnost was applied cautiously in Estonia, focusing on safe topics such as corruption and alcoholism. Gradually, however, other taboos were lifted (the writers' congresses held in Tallin and Riga in the spring of 1986 were important turning points), and wide-ranging discussions now take place on history, religion, Baltic emigrés, the environment, language issues, and national rights. A public debate has long been under way on the status of indigenous languages. In addition, widespread opposition has been voiced (apparently successfully) to the mining of phosphorite in northeastern Estonia. The Soviet media, while still ascribing insidious designs to emigré political organizations and blaming emigrés for recent demonstrations, now openly recognize their contributions to the national culture. (Such recognition implicitly signals acceptance of the notion of a national culture reaching beyond the boundaries of the Soviet Union.) Throughout the Baltic area, works have been published providing candid descriptions as well as statistics on the deportations under Stalin in 1941 and 1949. In addition, extensive debate has taken place over secret protocols of the Molotov-Ribbentrop Pact of August 23, 1939 (consigning the Baltic states to Soviet control).

Discussion of these issues has varied in candor and extensiveness in the three Baltic republics. In the case of the Nazi-Soviet pact, the local press, backed by Moscow, has vigorously defended the official Soviet position (and either denied the existence of a secret protocol or, in the instance of one Latvian press representative, claimed it could not be published because "a copy could not be located").[17] On religious issues, too, the press continues to vilify religious activists (1987 marked the 600th anniversary of Lithuania's conversion to Christianity).

But reservations aside, the degree of openness in the Estonian press astounds analysts. In a conversation with me last fall, historian Toivo Raun stressed that the range of issues under discussion and the candor of opinions expressed was truly unprecedented. Since then, according to another source:

The pace has begun to accelerate. Topics that were handled with great delicacy and trepidation at the beginning of the year are now being discussed quite bluntly. Not only dissidents but an ever greater number of intellectuals and members of the cultural unions, making use of official channels, are stating their views on important questions and expanding the range of their criticism to include not only the security agencies and the bureaucracy but the communist parties themselves. . . . At the start of the year, the Estonians were the most outspoken critics and the boldest innovators, but in May and June (1988) Lithuanians and Latvians began to catch up.[18]

In 1988, the main forum for Baltic glasnost remains the press and public media. In an unprecedented move, the ECP decided in April to close down the republic's main Russian-language newspaper, *Sovetskaia Estoniia*, replacing it with a Russian edition of the Estonian newspaper *Rahva Haal*. In announcing the decision, the newspaper's editors voiced the opinion that a major reason for mounting ethnic tensions was the general unwillingness of immigrant Russians to learn local languages or to respect national traditions.[19]

But in addition to the press, other means of political expression have come to prominence: public commemorations, statements by cultural unions, and the establishment of informal political organizations. Perhaps the least promising, but most dramatic form of expression are the demonstrations, which began in Latvia in 1987 but have since spread throughout the other Baltic republics. The demonstrations in Riga on June 14[20] and on August 23, 1987, involved, by best estimates, 5,000 and 7,000 people, respectively. One observer called them "the largest known peaceful, non-communist political gathering(s) in the history of the Soviet Union."[21] Surprisingly large demonstrations followed in February 1988 in Estonia. By Soviet standards, too, press coverage of these events was reasonably objective. Sometimes, to be sure, this coverage left much to be desired; television cameras ranged over a demonstration numbering up to 10,000 participants in Riga as the announcer estimated the number of participants as a few dozen.[22] Remarkably, the police were restrained; the demonstrations were never forbidden, and in the aftermath of the June demonstration only one leader was arrested and another forced into exile.

But the official response to the rising tide of discontent in the Baltic region was, after initially tolerating demonstrations and permitting remarkably open discussion, to bear down by arresting leaders and forbidding further demonstrations.[23] First, in September 1987, street demonstrations by Tatars and Jews in Moscow were prohibited, and then, in November, plans for a demonstration commemorating Latvian Independence Day (November 18) were thwarted by a massive show of force in the streets.[24] Next, the authorities began sponsoring official meetings or alternative events timed to coincide with demonstrations, as in Riga, where street festivals and a two-day competition for disc jockeys were held to tempt people away from the August 23 demonstrations.[25] Ominously, in December 1987 the Central Committee passed a secret resolution condemning nationalism in Estonia.[26] In February 1988, in anticipation of Independence Day in Estonia, troops were brought out in force and the borders sealed to diplomats and reporters, but the demonstration was allowed to proceed. In May, officials themselves organized a gathering in Lithuania to commemorate the victims of Stalin but then dispersed a smaller unofficial gathering a few days later. In Latvia, the organizers of the demonstration commemorating deportation day, June 14, 1988, were put under house arrest.[27]

Nevertheless, this officially countenanced demonstration on June 14, which drew 100,000 demonstrators, soon became more than an anti-Stalinist rally, with calls for restoration of national sovereignty, radical economic reforms, and an end to censorship. Another rally of more than 10,000 demonstrators in favor of radical reform took place in Lithuania on the eve of the June Conference.[28] Finally, officials in Latvia, Lithuania, and Estonia authorized mass demonstrations to be held on August 23, 1988, the anniversary of the pact between Stalin and Hitler. Since these demonstrations are being tolerated, but not sponsored by the leadership, they may signal an end to Moscow's attempt to coopt or to repress the Baltic demonstrations.

The majority of demonstrations have been peaceful;[29] in February 1988, forty-eight prominent Estonian cultural figures called for patience and urged avoidance of confrontation, which in their view could only provide fuel for the Stalinists. But on a number of occasions in Estonia and elsewhere, youth have responded violently to aggressive police tactics, forcing the release of arrested demonstrators. In an uglier vein, gang wars between Estonian and Russian youth (from an organization called Molodaia Rossiia) have reportedly broken out on a number of occasions. In the fall of 1987, too, a group of Russian soccer fans painted red stars on their cheeks and traveled to Vilnius, where they chanted anti-Lithuanian slogans and beat up local residents.[30] In general, according to interviews carried out by a Finnish newspaper (*Helsingin Sanomat*, June 20) antireform sentiment is rising among the non-Estonian population of Estonia.[31] In August 1988, a Russian "internationalist movement" held its first conference in Tallin, where supporters discussed measures to oppose the Baltic autonomy movement.[32]

Throughout the Baltic region, the cultural unions (especially the writers' unions) have been in the forefront of events. In February 1988, the Lithuanian Writers' Union sponsored a meeting on ecological problems; on April 4 another meeting was held on nationality problems, and resentment against Russians, called a privileged nationality, was openly expressed.[33] In Latvia, on June 2, the Writers' Union passed a resolution demanding that Latvian be made the official language of the republic; that soldiers from Latvia serving in the Soviet armed forces be stationed at home; that the Molotov-Ribbentrop Pact be published in full and repudiated; that those who directed the deportations be stripped of honors; and that the ecological situation in Latvia be addressed. The resolution called for expanded opportunities to travel and study abroad and for local control of the economy. It urged that, because Latvians were becoming a minority in their own country, any further immigration be considered "an infringement of the rights of statehood."[34] The Latvian resolution echoed the platform adopted on April 1 and 2 by the Estonian Writers' Union.[35]

Perhaps the most remarkable document to emerge from the "Baltic Spring" is the set of economic proposals set forth by a group of mainstream Estonian social scientists in September 1988. The plan essentially called for turning Estonia into a "free economic zone" along the lines of the Chinese model, with an economy based on a convertible ruble, major cutbacks on restrictions on private enterprise, and full autonomy in trade relations abroad as well as in dealings with other republics of the USSR. Estonia would essentially have a market economy, and would gain full control over the use of local resources as well as over immigration from outside. In exchange for such concessions, the document argues, the USSR would see enhanced revenues from taxes and would also benefit from drastically increased trade and the transfer of technology to the USSR. In the months since this proposal first came to the surface, it has received much coverage in the press (where it was stridently attacked by party secretary Vaino), but no commitment from the Kremlin. Reportedly, Aganbegyan, whose authority is cited in the document, has attacked the concept of an economic free zone.[36] (In August 1988, Edgar Savasaar, a leader in the movement for economic autonomy, was named to a ministerial post and put in charge of implementing measures aimed to bring about limited economic autonomy which, the *Christian Science Monitor* reported, Gorbachev has decided to back.)[37]

Finally, public activism in Estonia has been capped by the establishment in April 1988 of the People's Front to Support Perestroika and subsequently, on June 3, of the Lithuanian Restructuring Movement. The People's Front to Support Perestroika is organizationally modeled after the Communist party, but avoids calling itself a political party. By June, it had 40,000 members in 800 local organizations, and it attracted 150,000 supporters to a rally in Tallin on June 17. The People's Front fielded a list of reformist candidates for the June Conference, but it succeeded in electing only a handful. Nevertheless, the organization's opposition to the platform and candidates advanced by Vaino reportedly led to his sudden removal on June 16. (He was succeeded as party secretary by a native Estonian, Vaino Valjas, then serving as ambassador to Nicaragua.)

According to some analysts, the People's Front sees itself as an alternative to the ECP, which is regarded as antiperestroika; it is headed by a group of nationally inclined Communists with close ties to the intellectuals who initiated the proposal to turn Estonia into a free economic zone.[38] Thus, the leadership constitutes "an active official opposition that uses high party standing to work within the system."[39] Since its founding, the People's Front has become a large grass-roots organization of unprecedented dimension in Soviet history. It has declared itself open to membership of all groups of like-minded people, but has stipulated that full-time Communist party, Komsomol, trade union, or state officials could not serve in leadership positions.

In its initial statements, the People's Front said it was proposing "citizen initiative" to "achieve soviet power"—that is, power by the parliamentary system of soviets rather than by the Communist party—and that its major principles included "socialist democracy and pluralism, the political and economic sovereignty of union republics, cultural autonomy for all nationalities," and defense of citizens' rights.[40] The People's Front produced a twelve-point platform for the June Conference; this document became the basis for the document adopted by the thirty-two-member Estonian delegation.[41] The delegation called for converting Estonian to full cost-accounting and self-financing beginning in 1991; for a law precisely regulating relations between the republics and the central government and among the republics themselves; and for a law placing all economic exchanges between republics on the basis of *khozraschet*; for transferral of all economic functions, including control over natural resources, prices, wages, credit, and tariffs to the republics; for the restoration of genuine "Leninist federalism," including the right to separate citizenship and official languages; for priority to the development of national cultures within the republics; for individualized educational programs; for revitalization of the soviets at all levels; for establishment of a constitutional court to adjudicate interrepublic and federal-republic disputes; for drawing firm boundaries between party, state, and soviets; and for referenda on major issues.[42]

The resolutions of the June Conference fell far short of the demands put forward by the Estonian delegation; this must surely have come as a disappointment. Yet the promised plenum on nationality relations is still forthcoming. Moreover, the very fact that the Estonians have managed to remove an odious party secretary (as well as the chief of ideology, replacing him with a reformist named Toomis), that the far-reaching proposal for an economic free zone has received polite discussion, and that the People's Front has received the endorsement of Zaslavskaia and others (and the equally polite silence of the rest of the leadership, including Chebrikov) represents a major advance.

The situation could easily and quickly deteriorate in the Baltic area; the far more moderate proposals of the "Berklavs Era" were crushed in 1959.[43] There are signs of a backlash among the Russian population (in 1979 there were 24 million Russians living outside the RSFSR—a sizeable constituency). At this point, however, what is most striking about these events is the simultaneous radicalization of demands and the political maturity with which they are being addressed. Rein Taagepera sees the emergence of a powerful third force of "autonomists" located between the centralized Stalinists and hard-line nationalists who, he argues, have no real political platform to offer (they want to return to the pre-1941 reality, but don't say how).[44] To be sure, there is, he continues, a real tension between advocates of perestroika who fear that nationalist demonstrations will play into the hands of Stalinists, and pro-independence activists, who fear that "autonomy might work out too well" and the population will lose interest in independence. The propagation of an economic platform in line with perestroika and offering concrete benefits for the USSR as a whole—and the care with which the grass-roots People's Front has avoided declaring itself an opposition party, the very language of fidelity to Leninist principle in which the recent platforms are stated—all bespeak a high level of sophistication, political realism, and determination to succeed. This is all the more remarkable in that Estonia and Latvia (not, in the short term, Lithuania) face a "real danger of national extinction,"[45] and in that the very survival of national culture and national identity is in doubt. What will need to be done, of course, is to convince Russian reformers that territorial autonomy (i.e., switching from the branch to the territorial principle of management) is not a prelude to secession. What will also need to be done is to convince human rights activists that economic autonomy is the first step toward cultural and political autonomy.

The Armenian-Azerbaijani Crisis[46]

Curiously, the Armenian-Azerbaijani conflict is not about anti-Russian feelings, or even about a minority's place within the Soviet system as such. Rather, it is the recrudesence of old economic, ethnic, and religious hostility in an area Richard Pipes once described as the most complicated in the world in terms of ethnic interweavings.

The Nagorno-Karabakh Autonomous Oblast (the NKAO) has become the site of a fierce ethnic and religious conflict that has preoccupied the Kremlim as well as the Soviet and Western press since October 18, 1987. On that date, more than 1,000 demonstrators in Erevan, the capital of Armenia, protested against clashes between Armenians and Azerbaijanis in the village of Chardakhly and called for restoring the NKAO (and the Nakhichevan ASSR) as Armenian territory.

The NKAO, which is approximately 75 percent Armenian, is a mountain enclave within Azerbaijan; the Nakhichevan ASSR, mainly Azerbaijani in population, is located between the southwest corner of Armenia and the Soviet-Armenian frontier. When Armenia initially came under Soviet power in 1920, these territories were assigned to Armenia, but less than a year later Nakhichevan was given to Azerbaijan and in 1923 Nagorno-Karabakh was made an autonomous region within the Azerbaijan SSR. For several decades the Armenians in the NKAO have complained of discrimination and have requested transferral to the Armenian republic, but the demonstration in October was notable in that it occurred in Armenia itself.

According to reports, an open letter calling for incorporation into Armenia was signed by 75,000 of the 125,000 Armenians living in the NKAO. On February 20, 1988, the Armenian deputies to the NKAO Soviet unanimously voted in favor of unification with the Armenian SSSR. When the Politburo gave notice on February 22 of a decision taken the previous day to refuse this demand, large-scale riots, strikes, and demonstrations ensued, continuing into the summer of 1988. On February 23, an estimated 100,000 protesters assembled in Erevan; on the next day crowds of equal size gathered and strikes and school closings were reported; and on February 25 demonstrations brought together more than half a million people in this republic of only 3 million.

On February 26, as perhaps a million people gathered in Erevan, Gorbachev met with two prominent Armenian writers and complained that Armenians were "stabbing perestroika in the back." At the same time, he promised a "just solution would be found." That same day, Gorbachev went on television to appeal for calm. He admitted distress existed among the leadership about recent events, claimed that "he did not wish to evade a sincere discussion of various ideas and proposals," but insisted that such a discussion had to take place within the legal framework provided by the Soviet Constitution. After this speech, the "organizing committee" of the demonstrations announced the decision to call off protests and strikes and to give Gorbachev a month to make good on his word (demonstrations continued, however, in Stepanakert, the capital of Nagorno-Karabakh).

On February 27, bloody violence began as Radio Baku reported that two Azerbaijani youths had been killed by Armenians. In the city of Sumgait, Azerbaijani mobs attacked local Armenians, raping, torturing, and killing, as small children were reportedly thrown from five-story buildings. Later reports put the number of dead from the rioting at thirty-two or more (estimates ranged up to 300). Curfews were imposed by March 1, as troops and armored vehicles were brought into the city. By March 6, Radio Baku was claiming that "life was returning to normal."

On March 9, a special meeting of the CPSU Central Committee met with party and government officials of both Armenia and Azerbaijan, and Gorbachev promised to establish a "special commission" to examine the issues. Throughout March large gatherings continued in Erevan to commemorate those who had been killed in the rioting. Demonstrations began once again in Stepanakert on March 17, and the local soviet passed a resolution demanding a positive response from the Politburo on the request to be reunited with Armenia. But on March 21 *Pravda* criticized the leadership of Armenia for raising the issue of Nagorno-Karabakh in order to deflect public concern from long-neglected socioeconomic issues. Simultaneously, it criticized the Azerbaijani leadership for neglecting the region's economic development. Both parties were criticized for fanning nationalist sentiments and slighting the "international upbringing" of their citizens. This article, and a similar one in *Izvestiia* the following day, only further inflamed local sentiment, leading to a general strike in Stepanakert and to renewed demonstrations in Erevan.

On March 23 the USSR Supreme Soviet rejected the Armenian's attempt "to resolve complicated national-territorial issues through pressure on state authorities" but announced plans for a package of economic measures and cultural concessions designed to ease conditions in the area.[47] A massive display of armed force in Erevan forced the Karabakh Committee in charge of the Armenian movement to call off a demonstration scheduled for March 26. On March 24 more details about the aid package were announced; at the same time a ban was imposed upon demonstrations in Erevan, and four organizers were arrested.[48]

On May 17, 1988, the trials of the suspects involved in the Sumgait violence began, accompanied by demonstrations in both Baku and Erevan calling for leniency and retribution, respectively. The first to be sentenced was 20-year-old Talekh Ismailov, sentenced to fifteen years for murdering an elderly Armenian.

On May 18, the cycle of violence was renewed, with 100,000 Azeris in Baku protesting the burning of a compatriot's home in Armenia, and with the gang killing of an Armenian youth in Stepanakert. On June 10 Moscow announced that a strike had been going on for three weeks in Nagorno-Karabakh and referred to daily demonstrations by tens of thousands of people.[49] The strike had reportedly begun on May 23 in protest against a statement by Ligachev to protesters in Baku that the problem in NKAO had "been solved." Similarly, a sit-down strike had begun two days later in Erevan and was still going on. In response to rumors that Azerbaijanis with knives were attacking Armenians in the streets, hundreds of thousands of Armenians demonstrated on June 12 and a three-day strike was declared in Erevan. However, the strike was called off the following day as the new party chief for Armenia, Suren Arutiunan, promised more than 100,000 demonstrators that the Armenian Supreme Soviet would support their demands.[50] Then on June 17, Azerbaijani Party Chief Vezirov promised 100,000 other demonstrators that the Azerbaijani Supreme Soviet would stand by Azeri rights. Western reporters speculated that the fact that both party chiefs had met with the Kremlin leadership before making their public pronouncements indicated high-level approval and that the first steps were being taken toward a compromise solution; along with the ten-year developmental package might come a separation of the NKAO from both republics and incorporation within the RSFSR.[51] On June 18 renewed violence broke out, this time in Masis, outside Erevan. On June 21, the NKAO soviet called for the USSR Supreme Soviet to take over administration of its region until a compromise could be worked out. The soviet also demanded that the same body take over the trials of the eighty individuals under indictment for rioting and violence against Armenians; apparently except for the young man sentenced to fifteen years, no action had been taken. But Suleiman Tatliev, chair of the Azerbaijan Supreme Soviet and deputy to the USSR Supreme Soviet from Stepanakert, warned that any such move could only spark even worse violence.[52]

By June 23, troops were deployed throughout the Caucasus, with no resolution of the problem at hand. Aside from the aid package offered in March,

Moscow had dismissed the party chiefs in Nagorno-Karabakh (in February) as well as in Armenia and Azerbaijan (in May). But the new leaders had immediately sided with their own ethnic groups and all sides rejected the aid package.

On June 25 *Pravda* announced that the leadership of Nagorno-Karabakh had unilaterally voted to secede from Azerbaijan.[53] Shortly thereafter, at a public meeting the residents of Nagorno-Karabakh voted to end the general strike, now under way for more than a month. The decision was prompted by weariness with the economic hardships caused by the strike and by the desire to give Gorbachev a breathing spell on the eve of the forthcoming June Conference.[54]

Those who looked forward to the Party Conference for a resolution to the conflict were disappointed. In his keynote speech Gorbachev condemned what he termed "attempts to abuse glasnost with the aim of recarving state borders." Both Vezirov and Arutiunan were restrained in their comments. Both stressed the seriousness of the situation and blamed current difficulties on earlier neglect of socioeconomic conditions during the period of *zastoi*.[55]

On the eve of the Conference, USSR Deputy Minister of Justice Vyshinsky had ruled out any type of compromise, such as placing the NKAO under the administration of the RSFSR, declaring that such an action would violate Article 78 of the Constitution (which states that any territorial readjustment must have the agreement of all involved parties), and reiterating that the final decision on the status of the NKAO rested with the Azerbaijan Supreme Soviet.[56] At the Conference itself, Azerbaijan delegates rejected the notion of transferral to the RSFSR as well as suggestions to transfer the NKAO to the Stavropol region or to place it directly under the control of the USSR Supreme Soviet.

On July 4 and 5 strikes once again closed down the Armenian capital, shutting down the main airport. The demonstrators were finally dispersed by club-wielding soldiers, and one person was reportedly killed.[57] A few days later, on July 13, the NKAO legislature voted to secede (its previous statements had been couched as requests); the vote was immediately rejected by the Azerbaijan Supreme Soviet.[58]

As the USSR Supreme Soviet prepared to meet late in July to decide the fate of the NKAO, Armenian activists called for a two-day strike, fearing a harsh police crackdown. On July 15, a meeting of the Armenian Communist Party leadership noted that the strikes had been very costly to the republic, that security forces had been lax, and that "activists" were serving to "provoke" ill will and unrest. The public accounts of the meeting signaled a move by the party away from the Karabakh Committee, which it had hitherto supported. But demonstrations on July 17 reportedly brought 300,000 Armenians onto the streets in Erevan, and at last report the general strike was on again in Nagorno-Karabakh itself.[59]

Finally, a stormy session of the USSR Supreme Soviet on July 18 rejected outright Armenian claims to Nagorno-Karabakh. In what journalists called "an emotional and stormy debate," party leaders from both republics defended their positions. The Armenian chief declared that the rejection of a compromise would have "unpredictable consequences," and the Azerbaijani party chief warned that any compromise would lead to violence worse than had already occurred. The NKAO chief, Genrikh Pogosian, "drew a picture of a small region under siege, with rail and road links to Armenia virtually cut and airline service greatly reduced."[60] He complained that the troops stationed there were taking over the province and countermanding orders by local officials.

At last report (July 22), half a million people had once again assembled in Erevan and voted unanimously in favor of a strike. At the same time, Moscow newspapers were taking a strident line, accusing several of those active in the Karabakh Committee of being "provocateurs" and describing the response of the local Communist party to these events as lax.

Events in the Caucasus and the Baltic states bear a few similarities. Both crises have created highly sophisticated political organizations: the People's Front in Estonia and the Karabakh Committee in Armenia.[61] Both events have revealed the potential for substantial popular mobilization around ethnic causes. In Estonia as well as in Armenia, crowds have carried portraits of Gorbachev and chanted slogans in favor of perestroika. In each case Communist party leaders (or many of them) have placed loyalty to the region or ethnic group over fealty to Moscow. Both cases represent a substantial challenge to perestroika, a threat to continued glasnost, and prima facie evidence that reining in the KGB is fraught with consequences for the country's stability.

The only other common denominator in these events is that they are unfolding at the same time. The possibility is that events in one area might stir up emotions and hopes elsewhere. At the July 18 session of the Supreme Soviet, Ukrainian Party Chief Shcherbitsky succinctly expressed leadership fears: "We have no right to forget that everything going on in Transcaucasia has a tendency to spread across the country."[62] It will be doubly tragic if the dismal events in Nagorno-Karabakh are used to crush the Baltic Spring, while achieving no resolution in the Caucasus.

But beyond these obvious comparisons the situation in the two areas is quite different. In Estonia there is no territorial dispute. There the issues are over language, in-migration, history, and cultural autonomy. The tensions are directly between Russians and Estonians. In the Caucasus, socioeconomic concerns loom large, but the dispute is an age-old one between Christians and Moslems, between clearly distinguishable races. Wherever Moscow's sympathies lie, it would be extremely dangerous at this juncture to take sides with the Armenians (Christian) against the Azeris (Moslem) in the light of tensions in the other five Moslem republics. Moreover, any attempt to adjust boundaries would introduce a practice that Moscow greatly fears. As Gorbachev noted in his February 26 television address: "All the republics, many oblasts, and even some of our towns . . . are multinational," thus implying that the situation of Nagorno-Karabakh could not be considered unique or exceptional. The Politburo would face a nightmare if its complicated federal structure were to be adjusted at this time. And the leaders are surely thinking not only of internal adjustments, but of borders in Eastern Europe and the Far East (Japan and the Kurile island chain; China and the Ussuri River).

One other contrast merits attention. In the Baltic, with some reservation we can say that press coverage of events has been both timely and reasonably open. In the Caucasus, however, the media has alternated between dramatic descriptive coverage, black-outs, denials, and vilification of participants. By allowing room for rumor and distortion, many argue, the media itself has exacerbated the situation. In an interview with the *Los Angeles Times*, Roy Medvedev went so far as to declare the policy of glasnost a victim of events in the Transcaucasus, overruled by the instinct to maintain order and declare a state of "normalization" before unrest spread.[63]

In Search of Official Policy

Gorbachev has certainly unleashed a storm, but what changes has he wrought in nationality policy? This question is difficult to answer if only because there seems to be no agreement on just what official policy has been in the past. We can begin with the obvious statement that the right to secession has always been, and will most likely remain, a convenient fiction. Hence the insistence, in the resolutions of the June Conference, that whatever else it encompasses, Soviet nationality policy must recognize that "our present and future lie in the consolidation and unity of all Soviet peoples."

What is new under glasnost is the insistence that a full and accurate history be written of the conquest of minority peoples under the tsars, and even under the Soviets. Glasnost should extend to the way Central Asia was colonized, to the forcible reincorporation of the Baltic states before World War II, and to the repressions and deportations of entire peoples under Stalin. Mincing no words, Sergei Baruzdin (editor of *Druzhba narodov*) insisted: "We should abandon the sloganeering postulate that all the peoples and nationalities annexed themselves to Russia in a purely voluntary way."[64] As a historian lamented: "We're past masters at hushing up difficulties in national questions. . . . When historians have kept quiet [about the deportations of the peoples of the Northern Caucasus], what respect can there be for history? . . . Let people find out the truth, not just listen to old wives' tales."[65]

But beyond keeping the empire together and letting out the truth about how it was put together (on which not everyone agrees), what is Soviet nationality policy? It is impossible to derive from Soviet government pronouncements or scholarship. One constant theme in Soviet nationality policy is that "[it] is designed to remove the social and economic inequalities among the ethnic groups;

the principal mechanism of this policy is economic development (understood as industrial development); the key to this program is a centrally directed socialist economy, with control over investment, technology and manpower enabling the government to plan and implement equalization directives."[66]

But then the question arises: How do we make compatible the goals of democratization and autonomy with central planning? If we grant autonomy (in Estonia), then what tools are available to maintain equality? Given resource dispersion, how is the same goal to be achieved under *khozraschet*? Or if equity is to be the goal, how are the goals of scientific technological revolution and increases in productivity—in short, efficiency—to be achieved? How do we reconcile social justice and perestroika on the republican level?[67] Finally, there is the military dimension. Strategic considerations dictate that industry be located in interior regions.

A second goal, that of assimilation, has drawn the attention of scholars in the West. Using the instruments of the media and the schools, promotion of the Russian language is seen as a first stage in assimilation (under the cloak of rapprochement) into a greater Russian culture. Ralph Clem concedes that in recent years Soviet authorities have adopted a "relatively aggressive posture" in promoting assimilation, but he disputes the argument that "increasingly widespread use of the Russian language is necessarily a harbinger of assimilation." Although 49 percent of non-Russians now know Russian fluently (compared to 37 percent in 1970), only 13 percent declare it their native tongue (only a slight gain from 1970). Thus, about two-thirds of non-Russians know Russian as their native or second language. But the "view that bilingualism is simply a way station on the road to assimilation is probably outdated," according to Clem. The Soviet government is content, for the time being, to teach Russian for the sake of economic, military, and administrative efficiency.[68]

The June Conference did little to clarify Soviet policy on nationalities in the context of perestroika. The resolution on ethnic issues remains in the realm of generalities, carefully skirting the most contentious issues (language, for example), bowing politely to the notion of interrepublic cost-accounting as "an idea meriting attention," and supporting the notion aired in the press that the Soviet Council of Nationalities should be given a stronger identity and more active role. The resolution also supports the idea of setting up a special all-union center to study nationality problems (commissions have already been set up in some republican Communist party organizations since 1987, and since May 1988, a special subsection for interethnic relations has been functioning in the Organizational-Party Work Department of the CPSU Central Committee). It rejects demands (made in the Ukraine and elsewhere) that children of a given nationality be required to study in schools where the local language is the language of instruction, and it is silent on Baltic demands that each republic be granted an official language.

In short, anyone looking for an explicit nationality policy will have to wait until the Central Committee plenum on nationality issues, which Gorbachev called for in a meeting with media leaders on February 18, 1988, but which has not yet been given a specific date.

The Ethnic Factor

It is intriguing how ethnic and regional concerns are interwoven with the other major issues on the Soviet agenda. One example is the growing concern for the environment (see Chapter 7). Here, growing national sentiment for the "homeland" has combined with a fear shared by all groups that economic progress has gone awry; local feelings that Russians may be plundering the republic's backyards for resources have led to strong resistance to several economic projects. In other areas, the Kremlin has intervened to halt murderous practices encouraged by the local leadership to meet economic targets (the scandal over major health problems in children stemming from the application of banned pesticides on the cotton crop in Uzbekistan is one such case).

The ethnic element is a factor in current debates about economic reform and especially about the introduction of market forces. As Archie Brown notes: "There is keen awareness that a market economy would widen existing regional differences and might very well exacerbate national tensions among the Soviet Union's more than 100 different ethnic groups."[69] The Joint Economic Report to the U.S. Congress concluded that, in general, Gorbachev's "investment policies favor the Slavic over the non-Slavic regions," but that "changing price policies will have a diverse impact." More specifically, the Western regions will benefit more than Central Asia, Eastern Siberia, and the Far East.[70]

Heightened ethnic tensions and regional conflicts do not necessarily involve directly anti-Russian sentiments, at least initially. But because political power is centralized, and because the upper reaches of the party, the military, and the security organs are dominated by Slavs, the resolution of all disputes will make Russians the focus of resentment. Even more important, as regional economic issues of equity and efficiency come to the fore, the state will "be the direct arbiter of well-being." In allocating scarce resources, it will inevitably step on toes, and, once again, as "Moscow" (i.e., the Kremlin leadership) is seen as Russian, the blame for decisions unfavorable to a particular region will be placed upon Russians (even when Russians, or the RSFSR, do not directly benefit). All of this is a powerful argument for a measure of *samostoiatel'nost* (independence) and *khozraschet* in the macroeconomic sphere. No information is made public about income distribution among the republics or about each republic's contribution to the "all-Union pot"; the result of this secrecy, according to the Soviet press, is that each republic tends to have an exaggerated notion of its contribution to the general well-being and to understate the benefits it receives in return. Glasnost, it is argued, would clear the air and reduce tension by providing a more objective perspective on the economy. It would also diminish the tendency to blame Moscow for all inequities or shortcomings.

Another dimension to the ethnic problem is the growing tide of resentment among Russians of "privileges" granted minorities in a time of growing scarcities and competition for resources (including access to universities). As ethnic demands escalated in 1988, the constituency of "aggrieved Russians" came to include many of the 24 million Russians who live in minority republics, who felt extremely threatened by demands to close down factories, establish separate citizenship, change admission procedures to schools—all to the detriment of outsiders. In *Pravda* in February 1987, Iuri Bromley, director of the Institute of Ethnology in Moscow, presented a list of "grievances" against minorities: the low proportion of industrial workers, high unemployment (one Soviet study this year put the number of unemployed in Uzbekistan at more than 1 million), low productivity, Muslim unwillingness to work in Siberia, poor knowledge of the Russian language (leading, among other things, to a breakdown of communications in the armed forces),[71] a preoccupation with cultural traditions, and too high a standard of living (often illegally obtained, to boot). A month later, another *Pravda* article argued that Russians are being pushed around. The author (Oleg Trubachev) extended his criticism to White Russia and the Ukraine (i.e., Slavic brethren).[72] Assaults on minorities, such as scoffing at claims for equality of languages, are defended as part of glasnost. But until early in 1988 minorities were not given equal time to air their grievances against Russians. Recent articles also make it clear that Soviet leaders are stopping preferential treatment of non-Russians; for example, they are ending special quotas for students, ending privileges for minority writers, and the like.[73]

Gorbachev, at the January plenum, appealed for "special delicacy and sensitiveness," and for rejection of all manifestations of nationalism, chauvinism, and anti-Semitism.[74] His key aide, Iakovlev, was demoted in the 1970s for openly opposing manifestations of Russian nationalism—thus, his sentiments are clear. Although groups such as Pamiat have espoused virulent nationalism and anti-Semitism (and may have up to 30 million supporters), anti-Semitism has also become the target of the press. Notably, the infamous forgery, Protocols of the Elders of Zion, purportedly revealing a conspiracy of Jews and freemasons to take over the world, has been ridiculed in the popular press for the first time. In 1986 Andrei Vosnesensky publicly decried the desecration of mass graves of Jews (from World War II) in the Crimea. Renowned scholar Dmitri Ligachev has spoken out against virulent Russian nationalism, as has historian Afanasiev.[75]

However, concern about the appearance of virulent strains of nationalism does not necessarily translate into support for all minority demands. Historically, liberalism in Russia has been concerned with the spread of civil rights within the empire. In other words, most Moscow-based reformers probably believe in the extension of civil rights and promotion of economic welfare within the framework of the existing multi-national state. It is doubtful that even among reform-minded leaders there are many who envision a real diminution of central control over the peripheries, and certainly few who would acknowledge the right of any nationality to secede.

The Western press has discussed the "population explosion" in Central Asia as a "looming crisis" for the Kremlin. But many scholars dispute the propriety of labeling the situation a crisis and challenge estimates that by 2000 every third Soviet will be a Muslim (instead, the figure will be closer to 20 percent).[76] Even if the demographic transition takes an unusual course (and the fertility rate in Central Asia does not decline, as it has in other nations, with urbanization and modernization), the Russians, although a minority, will still, as Slavs, make up nearly two-thirds of the country's population. Moreover, though opinion is divided, most area specialists feel that the Central Asians, by far the largest non-Slavic minority, have generally benefited by Soviet rule and are far better off than they were in the past. Just as important, the stability and incremental gains in living standards they enjoy are the more enviable when Central Asians look over their borders into Iran, Afghanistan, Iraq, and elsewhere. The Soviet leadership seems to have reached a tolerable modus vivendi with the Muslim hierarchy, and except for the disturbing spread of fundamentalist Sufism in rural areas, matters look rather good in Central Asia for the Kremlin. All the more disturbing, then, were the riots in Alma Ata in Kazakhstan in December 1986 after the replacement of local party chief and Brezhnev holdover Dinmukhamed Kunaev by Gennady Kolbin, a Russian.[77]

What impact will the drive against corruption have upon relations between Moscow and the Moslem republics? To this date, the anticorruption wave has concentrated on Uzbekistan.[78] A recent study of illegal income in European Russia and the Caucasus showed that "private sources" add 39 percent to the income of Leningraders and nearly triple the earnings of Armenians.[79] No comparable data are available for Central Asia, but it is a well-known fact that private trading and other semi-legal or illegal sources of income are pervasive in the area.

Several specialists have pointed to an informal "contract" in existence between Central Asia and the Kremlin, according to which Moscow tolerates traditional kinship patronage systems and illegal trade or even illegal production in exchange for loyalty, or at least lip service to communism and allegiance to Moscow ("Nationalist in Content, Socialist in Form"—reversing the old Stalinist dictum).[80] But what happens when this contract is broken, when a vigorous anticorruption drive disrupts age-old ways of getting along? This question applies to the impact of Gorbachev's reforms on Soviet life as a whole, where corruption has been tolerated as the only way to fill the interstices created by the inefficiencies of a service-oriented, goods-poor, and overcentralized economy.[81] But it takes on another dimension in Central Asia and the Caucasus, where such barter and haggle is the way of life (the socialist economy filling the interstices!).

There can be no question that in combination with other issues, ethnicity will be a major concern in the years to come. If, as conventional wisdom has it, the politics of the Brezhnev era were "brokerage" politics—in which the leadership mediated between interest groups and which required an ever-growing pie so that individuals, regions, and national groupings could all hope for something better as the years passed—then what is going to substitute for this pie in the near future? How will Gorbachev's planners decide the issues of equity against efficiency when it comes to allocating jobs, resources, and benefits among regions? If, as seems to be the case in the immediate future, planning will benefit the RSFSR at the expense of other areas, what trade-off can Gorbachev offer the Central Asians? If a decline in living standards will ensue with the assault on corruption, how will Moscow compensate? How, finally, will glasnost and perestroika be combined on the borderlands?

Notes

1. *Pravda*, April 14, 1988: 2, translated in CDSP, Vol. 40, No. 15 (May 11, 1988): 13. See also comments by Vladimir Karpov, head of the Writers' Union, in *Literaturnaia gazeta*, No. 10 (March 9, 1988): 2–3.

2. *Izvestiia*, March 22, 1988: 2.

3. *Moscow News*, April 17, 1988: 12.

4. For brief introductions to nationalities issues in the USSR, see David Lane, *Soviet Economy and Society* (New York, 1985): 202–240; Ralph Clem, "Ethnicity," in *The Soviet Union Today: An Interpretive Guide* (Chicago, 1983): 281–292.

5. Ralph Clem, "The Ethnic Factor," in *Understanding Soviet Society*, ed. by Michael Paul Sacks and Jerry G. Pankhurst (Boston, 1988): 18.

6. Rasma Karklins, "Nationality policy and ethnic relations," in *Politics, Work and Daily Life in the USSR*, ed. by James Millar (New York, 1987): 302.

7. Ellen Jones and Fred W. Grup, "Modernization and Ethnic Equalization in the USSR," *Soviet Studies*, Vol. 32, No. 2: 159–184. On the retreat from policies of preferential recruitment of minorities into the power structure, see the concise treatment by Clem, "The Ethnic Factor": 20.

8. *Moscow News*, April 3, 1988: 10.

9. Karklins, "Nationality policy and ethnic relations": 314.

10. See, for example, Helene Carrere d'Encausse, *Decline of an Empire: The Soviet Socialist Republics in Revolt*, translated by Martin Sokolinsky and Henry A. La Farge (New York, 1979).

11. See Philip Taubman's discussion in NYT, March 6, 1988: E3.

12. For reports of these events see WP, June 22, 1987, and November 17 and 18, 1987; CSM, June 16 and August 21, 1987, November 11, 1987 (for Latvia), May 5, 1987 (for Estonia), and August 10 and 27, 1987, for an overview; also

see NYT, August 30, 1987. National discontent has erupted most violently precisely in those areas where local cultures are most in danger of being entirely submerged (Latvia in the Baltic and Kazakhstan in Central Asia).

13. CSM, June 16, 1987.

14. Raun, *Estonia and the Estonians* (Stanford, 1987): 219. The following summary of recent Estonian history before 1985 is from this work: 219–220.

15. Ibid.: 196–197.

16. Ibid.: 201.

17. On this, see Radio Free Europe: *Baltic Area Situation Report*, No. 7 (October 28, 1987): 3–7; No. 8 (November 12, 1987): 3–6; No. 1 (January 21, 1988): 3–6; No. 6 (June 3, 1988): 27. In August 1987, the protocols were finally openly discussed in the Russian-language press in Estonia.

18. Saulius Girnius, "An Overview of Developments in the Baltic Republics in 1988": RAD Background Report/112 [Baltic Area], June 22, 1988.

19. BS, April 10, 1988.

20. Fifteen thousand Latvians were deported by boxcar to Siberia on that date in 1941.

21. Cited in CSM, June 16, 1987. Another small, "spontaneous march" is said to have taken place on April 19.

22. The demonstrations of 1987 receive careful coverage in Baltic Area SR, No. 7 (October 28, 1987): 15–20; and No. 8 (November 12, 1987): 7–10.

23. CSM, August 27, 1987. Since then, however, arrests have been made in all three Baltic republics, and some organizers have been exiled to the West.

24. CSM, November 19, 1987 and NYT, November 18, 1987 (on that day Janis Barkans, head of the Riga-based Helsinki 86 human rights group, was placed under house arrest).

25. Baltic Area SR, No. 7 (October 28, 1987): 17.

26. This, according to Baltic Area SR, No. 1 (January 21, 1988): 11–13.

27. NYT, May 23, 1988; Baltic Area SR, No. 3 (1988): 7–12 (Estonia) and 31–37 (Lithuania); No. 6 (June 3, 1988): 27 (Lithuania).

28. The so-called "Riga Spring" reportedly provoked a tense debate at a June 18 meeting of the Latvian Central Committee, with the head of the local KGB calling for a clamp-down, and with subsequent troop movements in the area of Riga (CSM, June 27, 1988).

29. In addition to the June 17 demonstration in Tallin, which brought out 15,000 people in support of the People's Front, there was a gathering of 70,000 Estonians on June 10 to celebrate the national song festival (and sing the long-suppressed national anthem as well as fly the national colors); and gatherings of 10,000 in Tartu, as well as 2,000 to 3,000 in Tallin, on June 14 to commemorate the Stalinist deportations.

30. Baltic Area SR, No. 7 (November 12, 1987): 7–11.

31. The *Washington Post*, reprinting a Reuters dispatch, also refers to disturbances in Tadjikistan and Kirghizia, as well as to fights between students of "different nationalities" in Moldavia (WP, June 22, 1987).

32. CSM, August 23, 1988.

33. Girnius, "Overview": 2.

34. The resolution and accompanying material, including a report on the

subsequent Central Committee Plenum, is in CDSP, Vol. 40, No. 25 (July 20, 1988): 1–4.

35. See Baltic Area SR, No. 6 (June 3, 1988): 3–19.

36. The proposal was first published in *Edasi* (Tartu) on September 26, 1987. A translation and discussion can be found in Baltic Area SR, No. 7 (October 28, 1987): 7–10.

37. CSM, August 23, 1988.

38. This, according to Baltic Area SR, No. 5 (May 20, 1988): 7.

39. Ibid.

40. Ibid., citing *Edasi*, April 30, 1988. See also *Sovetskaia Estoniia*, June 7, 1988: 2.

41. *Sovetskaia Estoniia*, June 18, 1988. The People's Front platform was published on June 7 in the same newspaper (and translated in CDSP, Vol. 40, No. 25: 5–6).

42. *Sovetskaia Estoniia*, June 18, 1988: 1–2.

43. Berklavs was first secretary for Riga (1953–1960); he and others called for more extensive use of the Latvian language and promotion of indigenous cadres, for industries based only on local raw materials and benefiting directly the republic (Baltic Area SR, No. 7 [October 28, 1987]: 11–12).

44. Rein Taagepera, "Estonia Under Gorbachev: Stalinists, Autonomists, and Nationalists," paper prepared for the Conference on Soviet Cultural Politics: Gorbachev and the Non-Russian Nationalities, USIA Office of Research and IREX, Washington, D.C., April 29, 1988: 1–7.

45. Girnius, "Overview": 5.

46. This section was drawn up with materials collected by Kate Sly, working primarily with Radio Liberty Research reports written by Elizabeth Fuller: especially RL 101/88 (March 15): 1–7. I have edited, updated (from March 1988), and rearranged this material, as well as added my own perspective. The reader should note that the original sources are all Russian-language and Moscow-based. Only a thorough study using sources in the local languages will provide a full and reliable account.

47. RL 149/88.

48. Ibid.

49. WP, June 12, 1988.

50. WP, June 16 and 17, 1988.

51. WP, June 15, 1988.

52. *Radio Liberty Daily Report*, June 22, 1988.

53. WP, June 26, 1988. There is some confusion over exactly what was stated in the various resolutions; a discussion can be found in *Radio Liberty Daily Report*, June 27, 1988.

54. WP, June 27, 1988.

55. See *Radio Liberty Daily Report*, July 1, 1988, for detail.

56. Ibid.

57. NYT, July 19, 1988.

58. CSM, July 18, 1988.

59. CSM, July 18, 1988.

60. NYT, July 19, 1988.

61. On this, see the CSM, July 22, 1988.

62. NYT, July 18, 1988.

63. *Los Angeles Times*, June 19, 1988.

64. *Literaturnaia gazeta*, No. 10 (March 9, 1988): 4; translated in CDSP, Vol. 40, No. 11: 6.

65. Iuri Poliakov, in *Izvestiia*, March 22, 1988.

66. Ralph S. Clem, "The Ethnic Factor": 11.

67. Ibid.

68. Ibid.

69. He continues: "The Russians themselves would probably lose ground to the more developed Baltic republics and to the Caucasus. Thus, on its own a market might leave Central Russia even poorer than before and would not necessarily solve the problem of tapping the rich but remote and intractable resources of Siberia." "Soviet Political Developments and Prospects," *World Policy Journal*, Vol. 4, No. 1 (Winter 1986/7): 55–87.

70. John Hardt and Richard F. Kaufman, "Economics: Prospects and Risks," *Gorbachev's Economic Plans*, Vol. 1: xvi. As contributing factors the authors point to the decisions: (1) to defer new construction, renovating existing plants instead; (2) to shift investments in agriculture from bringing new land under the plow to improving storage and transportation; (3) cancellation of the Siberian river diversion project and rejection of new grand schemes on the scale of BAM. The infamous river diversion project is a classic case of economic issues becoming intertwined with nationalism. Russians opposed the "plundering" of their native resources (i.e., diverting the rivers of Siberia) to supply another region (a parallel comes to mind in the conflict between southern and northern California, but there, of course, there is no ethnic component). The diversion project, thought dead, has prompted new debate this year: see RL 205/87 (May 27): 1–5.

71. This problem is frequently noted, particularly as it involves relations between officers (predominately Slavic) and soldiers (disproportionately Central Asian). See, for example, CSM, April 13, 1987. On the recruitment of non-Slavs into the officer corps, see RL 383/87 (September 28).

72. This criticism perhaps was in response to sentiments expressed at writers' conferences in February and March 1987 in the Ukraine and White Russia that the local languages were in danger of being submerged and that the tongues of the Slavic minorities were treated with condescension, if not outright contempt, by Russians (BS, May 5, 1987).

73. Much of the above is from an editorial by Vladimir Shlapentokh, CSM, May 22, 1987.

74. RL 211/87 (June 5): 5–6.

75. See his criticism of writers Vasily Belov and others for anti–Semitic views, of Pamiat, and of the Protocols, in *Ogonek*, *Sovetskaia kultura*, *Moskovskie novosti*, *Izvestiia*, and *Komsomolskaia pravda*, all cited in RL 211/87 (June 5): 2, 6–7. But for evidence of persistent and nonofficially inspired anti-Semitism, see the descriptions of the virulent response by passers-by to a demonstration on the Arbat in February on behalf of Joseph Begun. Witnesses testified to cries of "Beat the Jews and save Russia" (the slogan of Tsarist pogromists): RL 239/87 (June 26).

76. Ralph S. Clem, "Ethnicity," in *Soviet Society Today* (1988 edition): 312.

77. Details on the disturbances of December 17 and 18, 1986, are still sketchy, but the best estimates put the number of demonstrators at about 10,000 (an official Soviet comment argued that no more than 3,000 were on hand "at one time"); the number wounded at perhaps 200, and the number killed at two (one "public order volunteer" and one demonstrator). As of May 1987, three people were known to have been convicted and sentenced for taking part in the rioting. For a survey of evidence, see RL 3/87 (December 23, 1986) and RL 203/87 (May 25).

78. See WP, April 29, 1987. On June 4 the Baltimore Sun reported that Abduvakhid Karimov, former party first secretary for the Bukhara region, was sentenced to death in Moscow for corruption. Last year, former Uzbek Minister of Cotton Production Vakhbbozhan Usmanov was also given the death penalty. It is possible that the former party chief for all Uzbekistan was spared a similar fate only by his timely natural death a few years ago. For the anticorruption campaign in Turkmenistan, see a report in RL 49/87 (January 30): 1–5.

79. Gregory Grossman, "Roots of Gorbachev's Problems: Private Income and Outlay in the Late 1970s," *Gorbachev's Economic Plans*, Vol. 1: 213–229.

80. On this, see the stimulating book by Michael Rywkin, *Moscow's Muslim Challenge: Soviet Central Asia* (New York, 1982).

81. On this, see the fine article by James Millar, "The Little Deal: Brezhnev's Contribution to Acquisitive Socialism," *Slavic Review*, Vol. 44, No. 4 (Winter 1985): 694–706.

9
Conclusion

Russians Have Been Floored and Flattered . . .

The events of the past two years have fundamentally shaken the popular image of Soviet politics and culture. According to this view, the USSR was unchanging, frozen in a Stalinist mode, and dominated by rigid leaders with narrow, dogmatic views and a concern only for personal advancement or, alternatively, for implementation of a Grand Design set forth by Lenin some time ago now, but modified only to meet the circumstances of the day. Many who recognized that the Grand Design had been filed away believed, nevertheless, that the Soviet system had produced a new bureaucratic class which ruthlessly suppressed all initiative and talent. The writer Joyce Carol Oates, after meeting with Gorbachev in Washington, put the issue succinctly: "What just astonishes me is I can't understand how this man, saying the things he's saying, came up by way of the Soviet system."[1]

Even those scholars who recognized that, within channels, far-ranging debates take place among Soviet leaders failed to predict the scope or pace of events that have been described in this book. Stephen Cohen asserts that, given the restructuring of domestic and foreign policy, events present "an unparalleled historical opportunity for change."[2]

In this book, we have looked at the emancipation of the media, at the establishment of informal political groups, and the emergence of a powerful in-system movement for reform in Estonia. We have considered the complexities of the popular mood, investigated the growth of the idea that economic reform is impossible without unfettering public initiative, and pondered the meaning of social justice. We have also touched upon ugly phenomena such as corruption, social degradation, mutual recrimination, and the unmistakable rumblings of a nativistic backlash against glasnost and perestroika. In these events the personality of Mikhail Gorbachev looms large, but it is against a backdrop of forces and developments that have long been building up.

A much-neglected aspect of the changes taking place today is that, whatever reformists say about the infamous period of stagnation under Brezhnev, the present leadership is building upon trends that were evident well before 1985. A case has been made that despite the conservatism, circumspection, even backpedaling of the Brezhnev years, the period was not entirely stagnant, even in official circles:

> Whereas ideology at the highest level stagnated after 1964, the elbowroom of the professional or adviser interested in middle-level questions was expanded in nearly every field of policy . . . (even with political taboos and the ultimate power of the party) . . . the richer coverage and discussion of policy questions should impress anyone delving into Soviet publications of the day.

In the economic arena, contested issues included decentralization, investment strategy, the energy problem, the USSR and the world economy, the slow progress of Soviet technology, wages and incomes, and the role of private plots in Soviet agriculture. In legal affairs, debates occurred over the relative roles of prosecutors and defense attorneys, handling citizens' complaints, multicandidate elections, the role of trade unions, the increase in corruption, and the powers of central and local organs. Social controversies aired in the press included pollution, income equality, affirmative action programs for minorities, the sad state of village life, women's rights, alcoholism, juvenile delinquency, and the failures of the educational system. "In short, the same regime that locked dissidents in psychiatric clinics and outlawed proposals for radical change also countenanced the most candid debate seen in Soviet Russia since the 1920s on all manner of within-system issues."[3]

Former *Washington Post* correspondent Dusko Doder observed the same "incremental change," "relaxation," and diminution of "regimentation" in the lives of his acquaintances,[4] or "ginger reforms in the area of individual liberties."[5] Under Brezhnev, controls over religion were loosened, as was pressure for conformity in numerous areas of life, from dress to hairstyle. In culture, in particular, despite the hard line taken against those who crossed the lines of the permissible, those boundaries themselves have been gradually, but inexorably, expanded ever since Stalin died. Despite oppressive censorship, the regime was "compelled to deal with the public's actual cultural preferences, rather than considering them putty from which a new Soviet Man would be formed."[6] Even more marked was the privatization of Soviet life, the withdrawal of the state from attempts to control and shape all aspects of Soviet citizens' lives. Timothy Colton rightly points to the introduction of the five-day work week in the late 1960s as a turning point. Recreation is an excellent example of privatization. Despite feeble attempts to convince the population to devote its time to self-improvement and to participate in civic happenings and organized outings, the state has tacitly now accepted the right of one to be alone, to seek frivolous entertainment, and to waste one's time. In literature, a preoccupation with the rights of those who have violated the canon of acceptable writing, and the punishment they have suffered for such trespass, has resulted in neglect of the real evolution of the socialist canon and the emergence of middle-class as well as village prose, "concerned with the psyches and moral problems of ordinary people without much reference to their work, or even to the party." This is not to deny that many have suffered or that avenues have been closed off. Critics have noted the suppression of new writers by the "fathers" of the Khrushchev generation—at the Writers' Congress of 1981 only 3 percent of the participants were under age 40.[7] The point is simply that the decline of the notion of the positive hero has led to very fruitful ambivalences in all areas of Soviet culture.

Thus, even under Brezhnev, "a good deal of pragmatic adaptation" took place, involving "creeping innovations . . . not abrupt divergence from precedent . . . [whose] cumulative significance cannot be denied."[8] Before Gorbachev, the Soviet Union may have been acquiring "the rudiments of a civil society" by default, "one that operated stealthily and in the interstices of the state." This civil society operated in semi-clandestine fashion, largely through the workings of the pervasive second economy and through the growing choice of the "exit option," or essentially individual withdrawal from meaningful participation in official culture and society.[9]

The American media, which tends to entirely dismiss "within-system reform" in the Soviet Union, is not particularly sensitive to such change. As British scholar Archie Brown comments: "Large sections of the American mass media ignore or discount Soviet policy innovation or internal criticism that is not obviously rejective of the Soviet system."[10] Scholars, too, have been mildly myopic on this topic.

Robert C. Tucker eloquently summarizes the changes under way when Gorbachev came to power and the impetus he added to these changes:

> Something of historical import is involved here: the appearance of a no-longer-wholly-regimented society in Soviet Russia, one still closely connected with the state, but no longer its mere tool. A shift of this sort took place in tsarist Russia starting in the late eighteenth century. . . . A civil society started to emerge, albeit against obstacles—at the end of the nineteenth century it was still in the process of formation. Today a society has again begun to emerge from under the shroud of what has been an all-encompassing state. This phenomenon's beginnings may be discerned in Khrushchev's time and its quiet continuation under Brezhnev. . . . What we see now is no longer the Stalin period's "monologue of the state with itself" [from Kliuchevsky] but the birth of a dialogue between state and society.[11]

Timothy Colton, writing early in 1986, argued that "post-Brezhnev initiatives have been more tepid in foreign than in domestic policy," because the Gorbachev coalition has been built around domestic issues and objective opportunities for initiatives are poorer in foreign affairs: "The system of states . . . by its very nature, is less malleable than civil society."[12] These incisive comments, revealing the inherent difficulties of achieving progress in foreign policy, must, however, be modified in light of the striking success Gorbachev has achieved in the international arena.

As in domestic affairs, "foreign policy ambitions have outstripped achievements," but "under Gorbachev the initiative in East-West relations seems to have shifted to Moscow."[13] Whatever the concrete results to this date, Gorbachev has enormously increased both his own prestige as well as respect for the Soviet Union abroad; for the first time since 1917, a Soviet leader is more popular throughout the world than the American president.[14] According to Gary Lee, "This is the overwhelming view expressed . . . by a score of senior Moscow-based diplomats from Western Europe, Asia, Latin America and the Middle East." In Britain, people were asked in a Harris poll whom they trusted most, Gorbachev or Reagan, and Gorbachev came out ahead, 34 percent to 24 percent. In an Italian television poll, Gorbachev came out far ahead. In West Germany, when queried about who was "really concerned about peace," Gorbachev outpolled Reagan 49 to 46 percent. Gorbachev rather than Reagan has generally been given credit in West Germany, France, and Britain for recent progress in arms negotiations.[15] My own queries of journalists, largely from Third World countries and sojourning in the United States under the auspices of the Alfred J. Friendly Foundation, produced a similar response, only weighted even more heavily in favor of the Soviet leader.

Aside from the relative status of the two leaders, Gorbachev has improved how others view his country. In West Germany between May and September 1987, the proportion of people who believed that the Soviet Union posed no threat jumped from one-third to two-thirds. In Finland, where an even higher proportion now dismiss the Soviet threat, although young people uniformly believed that daily life in the USSR was unenviable, they appraised Soviet foreign policy favorably, and Gorbachev even more so.[16]

Even in the United States, the perception of a Soviet threat has diminished; 60 percent of Americans believe relations between the United States and Soviet Union are improving, and 59 percent now believe that economic competitors pose a greater threat than do military adversaries. Twenty-seven percent of Americans expressed "grave concern" about a military conflict; 50 percent expressed similar concern about foreign investment in the United States. According to a Gallup pollster, "There has been a momentous change in attitudes toward the Soviet Union." Today 45 percent of Americans have a "positive attitude towards the Soviet Union, compared to only 11 percent eleven years ago."[17]

Gorbachev has enhanced the image of the USSR in ways that can only help him, not only with the intelligentsia, but also with the "new breed" of diplomat and party politician so much in evidence in the past decade. The population at large is also proud of the new look in foreign policy. Perhaps with a touch of hyperbole, *New York Times* correspondent Bill Keller notes:

> Russians have been floored and flattered by polls showing that Mr. Gorbachev is widely admired in Western Europe and the United States. They have watched with pride the pilgrimages of Western leaders to the Kremlin to meet the first Soviet leader with Western charisma.[18]

He's Stepping on So Many Toes . . .

But even if Gorbachev has initiated, or stepped up, a dialogue between state and society, many Western observers who strongly admire him believe that, all in all, Gorbachev is "a strong leader in a weak position." Marshall Goldman of Harvard's Russian Research Center argues that "he's stepping on so many toes . . . he won't last four years." And Peter Reddaway of the Kennan Institute believes that if "he continues with his present policies, he will be removed within the next two or three years."[19] Reddaway argues that given the "enormous . . . perhaps insurmountable obstacles" Gorbachev faces, he appears "almost a tragic figure."[20] Even George Kennan concedes that Gorbachev faces formidable forces of resistance and that his present position is difficult. He writes: "The point at which he has arrived—where his program has advanced just far enough to create discomfort in many quarters, and to bar any retreat, but not far enoughh to produce conspicuous positive results—is obviously the point of greatest strain and danger."[21]

Dire predictions may well prove true. Few would deny that an overhaul as thorough as that called for by Gorbachev must encounter setbacks and meet growing resistance as the program itself becomes explicit and implementation undertaken. After all, vital interests are at stake. Moreover, the "socialist pluralism" Gorbachev now seems determined to create conflicts with traditional Russian political culture, which has generally been characterized by a strict political hierarchy, deference to authority, strong police rule, emphasis upon order, a reluctance to engage in autonomous activity,[22] and a strong proclivity to reduce the possible options to "order." But to assume that resistance spells defeat is to consign all meaningful reform to the dustbin of history.

It may well be that Gorbachev has precious few diehard supporters in the Politburo (by all agreement he does not have a majority in the Central Committee). We don't know where key figures such as Zaikov and Ryzhkov, or even Yazov, stand. Gorbachev confronts multiple interlocking hierarchies of power and privilege. Philip Taubman concisely articulates the widespread opinion that "the veiled message Ligachev seems to be sending is, if the party finds Gorbachev too radical but does not want to abandon the general effort to modernize the economy—if, that is, the party finds itself in the market for a more moderate reformer—he, Ligachev, might fit the bill."[23] Noted CIA analyst Marc Zlotnik also argues that Ligachev is "positioning himself to become Gorbachev's successor."[24] Even George Kennan concedes "that Gorbachev's personal position, at this juncture, has elements of precariousness [that] cannot be denied."[25]

To me, however, the more plausible interpretation is that Ligachev's views intersect with Gorbachev's and that he is committed to reform but that he disagrees over the role of the market and the limits to glasnost. He wants to influence Gorbachev and to help shape the agenda, but he has little interest in removing him. The view that in the Soviet Union one must either wholeheartedly endorse or entirely oppose a leader and his policies is an archaic remnant of Stalinist times. Ligachev is, in all probability, pursuing an agenda encompassing a variety of contingencies, of which the most unlikely is the replacement of Gorbachev.

As I noted earlier, there seems to be agreement that a "precrisis" state exists in the Soviet economy and that reforms are essential. Although Ligachev has defended certain aspects of Stalinism and of Brezhnev's rule, he has not rejected the label *zastoi* (stagnation) as applied to the 1970s. And it is often said that both the KGB and the military recognize the urgent need for modernization as well as an end to corruption, which, along with the black markets, seemed to be growing exponentially and threatening to throttle all legitimate economic activity before Gorbachev's rise to power.[26] Ligachev and others may feel that technocratic modernization without decentralization, along with a heavy dose of discipline, would address the issues, but they also seem to acknowledge the importance of the "human factor," the need to rebuild morale and a sense of fairness.

They must also address the claim, made by Gorbachev in February 1988 that "if reconstruction peters out, the consequences will be extremely serious for society as a whole, and for every Soviet person in particular."[27] Or, as he said in Riga after the tense January 1987 plenum, "I have posed the issue in many places, even in the Central Committee, `If there is any alternative to perestroika and acceleration, then propose it."[28] Kennan puts the issue more bluntly: What if Gorbachev himself were removed?

A removal of Gorbachev, in the present situation, would also have incalculable ulterior consequences. It would come as a serious and unsettling shock to the Soviet intellectuals—his sole wholehearted supporters. Could they again be tamed and cowed as they were under Stalin? It seems unlikely. This is another epoch. Glasnost is a genie which, once released from the bottle, will not be easily put back in again. And how about the non-Russian nationalities within the Soviet Union? These, if the private letters published in the book [Gorbachev's *Perestroika*] are any indication, have a much better understanding of what Gorbachev is trying to do than does the

Russian center. And how about the reactions in the Eastern European "satellite" countries, where Moscow's political hold is already tenuous, and where . . . a new generation, much more attuned to Gorbachev's music, is waiting in the wings?

And how about world opinion? Hundreds of millions of people the world over, electrified by Gorbachev's striking appearance at the Washington summit, have been moved to a new level of hope for real progress, at long last, in the overcoming of the nuclear nightmare. Are these hopes to be dashed and compelled to yield to a proportionate level of consternation and despair, with Moscow appearing as the party guilting of this spectacular setback?[29]

But, if Gorbachev's hold on power seemed tenuous in the winter of 1987-1988, he has since gained ground. His perspective evidently has found support, as numerous signs indicate that after a temporary retreat in November, the pro-Gorbachev, radical reform faction was once again on the attack in the Spring of 1988.

Khrushchev Revisited?

William Faulkner once quipped that the past is not only not dead, it's not past. History, as we have seen, is the battlefield on which the basic issues of glasnost are being fought out. But in the West as well, history is also on the minds of many scholars groping for an understanding of events in the USSR. Historical analogies usually obscure more than they illuminate, but they are useful exercises, even in refutation. As one determined to reform the system in order to save it, Gorbachev has been aptly compared with Tsarist minister Peter Stolypin (particularly Stolypin's "wager on the strong," or attempt to create a class of prosperous property-owning entrepreneurs). Far less convincingly, Dimitri Simes and others have compared Gorbachev to Ivan the Terrible, Peter the Great, or even Catherine (and apparently such comparisons are current in the Soviet Union as well).[30]

The Soviet period, too, has seen its reforms and reform debates.[31] Peter Reddaway suggests we consider a historical analogy between Gorbachev and Khrushchev. Khrushchev also tried to "get the country moving again"—by offering a new domestic and foreign policy program, providing a variety of material incentives, attempting "moral" suasion (releasing political prisoners, etc.), and promoting democratization and worker self-management, glasnost, and personnel replacement. Reddaway argues that "the general pattern of Gorbachev's strategy and actions in his first two years reveals a strong similarity to what Khrushchev attempted three decades ago in an environment that was not very different."[32] But, he continues, Khrushchev was undone by his combination of "naive radicalism" and "ineptness." And he concludes:

The Soviet system is not, in my view, more susceptible of transformation today than it was thirty years ago. I suspect that the only remedies for this situation may be the ones that have been required in Russian history for nearly two centuries—either a serious breakdown in public order, or defeat in a war.

But, as Thane Gustafson argued last year, Gorbachev has been supremely skillful in unfolding his program;[33] neither naiveté nor ineptness apply to his approach. Moreover, despite the undoubted similarities in programs, the historical conjuncture is most decidedly not the same as in 1956 or 1964.[34] As Reddaway himself notes, Gorbachev puts forth his agenda "in a less optimistic setting." Just as important, the sense of emergency is much more widespread. If, for example, it can be argued that Ligachev is something more than a mere opportunist, that he accepts the definition of the situation as "precrisis" and calls for both technocratic modernization and a crackdown on corruption, then the potential alliance between the so-called Leningrad group and the vast phalanx of middle-level bureaucrats (both party and government) concerned only with their perks and power can at best be a tenuous hand-holding. Although Gorbachev has railed repeatedly against an obstreperous bureaucracy, and although Tatiana Zaslavskaia, in the now classic *Novosibirsk Paper*, identified the middle level of the bureaucracy as the main impediment to reform, we should not see either party or government as entirely uniform. For one thing, the boundaries between officialdom and the intelligentsia are far more porous than the common view would have it. Moreover, as former *Washington Post* correspondent, Dusko Doder said in his account of the rise of Gorbachev, a "coalition for change" that emerged in Brezhnev's waning years brought together all those unhappy with policy drift, "the lack of determined leadership and cohesion, and the alarming economic indicators." This group included technocrats and scientific researchers, "new and younger elites in the provinces," even the KGB and armed forces.[35]

The personalities and public images of the two leaders are also vastly different: Khrushchev embarrassed the new middle class and scientific community with his hayseed antics on the world stage, while Gorbachev, as we have seen, has gained much political capital within the leadership, and especially among the middle classes, with his foreign policy and his style in the international arena.

In addition, although Khrushchev was undoubtedly shrewd and experienced at survival, he was impetuous, seemingly indifferent to coalition building, and prone to push schemes with little thought to design or implementation. Gorbachev is "a formidable politician," with "striking courage, a forceful personality, skills of persuasion, a flexible mind, inexhaustible energy, lack of vanity, mastery of maneuver," and the ability to "keep his opponents off balance."[36]

The international environment is also markedly different from the 1960s. Even more important, "the greater porousness of Soviet frontiers to information from the global environment" renders it virtually impossible to "suppress inconvenient truths about Soviet society, or to sustain some of the more facile myths once swallowed whole."[37] Some years ago John Bushnell wrote that the "New Soviet Man" had turned "pessimist." The decline in the belief in inexorable progress, in the ultimate breakthrough to universal prosperity and abundance, has come not only through slowing growth rates and emptying meat counters but also through ever-growing contact with the outside world. The result of this contact, and of a strikingly successful educational system (despite its problems today)[38] has been the emergence of a far more differentiated, skeptical, and discriminating population today than in the 1960s, not to mention under Stalin.

Finally, perhaps the most important difference between Gorbachev and Khrushchev is that Gorbachev has had the opportunity to learn from Khrushchev's mistakes. To give but one example, consider Shmelev's comments concerning the interrelationship between economic and political change:

> It is impossible to ignore that profoundly economic changes are in reality but part, and perhaps not the most important part at that, of the whole problem of perestroika. As authoritative voices have often let us know, the economic reforms of the fifties and sixties came to naught because the political structure of society remained immobile. Today we are fully aware of the vital need for democratization, glasnost and fostering public initiative.[39]

A Gravely Ill Person Who Has Forgotten How to Walk?

So, learning from the failures of the past, Gorbachev and his advisers have come to see reform as an integrated process. Many analysts now argue that Gorbachev puts political change first and believes that the "human factor" is primary. Without changes in popular attitudes, without restoration of trust, enthusiasm, and genuine popular initiative, all attempts at economic reform will be doomed from the outset. These goals will not be easy; as Shmelev writes, "We are much like the gravely ill person who, after a lengthy interval confined to bed, only with great exertion makes his first step, and, to his horror discovers that during this long confinement he has virtually forgotten how to walk."[40] But the point remains that however ramshackle the structure Gorbachev has put together, it is consciously viewed as a whole and it is informed by the lessons of the first "thaw." We have noted that many of Gorbachev's advisers came of age during the Khrushchev period and suffered bitter disillusionment from its failures and the subsequent retreat.

Reddaway certainly has a point in arguing that only serious breakdown or defeat in a war can ensure major change (he might have added large-scale ecological crisis). But, after all, the same could be said of most societies (especially large ones) and most reforms. Russia, too, has had its share of successful reforms; the Great Reforms of 1861-1874 are a remarkable example, and the Stolypin reforms of 1906-1911 are another. To be sure, the country has also had more than its share of accompanying crises and defeats in war. But if the precipitant of reforms was a foreign policy setback or fear of loss of Great Power status, in virtually each case reform had been in the making within the bureaucracy long before the "crisis" setting it off. And it can further be argued that the trigger was not in fact a "crisis" but a "precrisis"; that is, a recognition by far-sighted leaders that if changes were not made then, the situation would deteriorate radically in the future. We are not mere quibbling over terminology; in a state of genuine crisis, leaders must deal with imminent revolution, internal collapse, or invasion and conquest from without. Reforms carried out in a time of precrisis are done without such pressing exigencies, which radically constrict one's choices and reduce the time allotted for carrying out drastic change. A crisis situation, for example, excludes the opportunity to implement gradual, staged measures.

The most striking comparison that can be drawn between events today and the past is with the Great Reforms of 1861-1874.[41] There a reluctant tsar confronted a precrisis; a situation of relative decline (both militarily and industrially) after a period of internal repression and stagnation, which, because of international successes, was only seen as such after the fact. A failure in armed conflict (but by no means a total defeat—the Russian heartland was not invaded, and Russian arms triumphed in the Caucasus) as well as a sense of "moral crisis" (the mounting conviction that serfdom was evil) led the Tsar to lift censorship, enlisting intellectuals in his support during a tumultuous "thaw." It was, coincidentally, in the period that the terms "thaw" and "glasnost" were first widely used in the way we understand them today.

Initially unsure of his goals, the Tsar undertook reform and, in the process, devised a program that became increasingly sweeping and radical in its implications. A policy of withdrawal and retrenchment in international affairs accompanied the domestic reforms. The result was not only the emancipation of the serfs and state peasants but also a complete overhaul of the military, the educational system, censorship policies, and state finances. The reform led, too, to the establishment of local elected organs of self-government (*zemstvos* and *dumas*), remarkable anomalies within an autocratic structure, and to the creation, virtually ex nihilo, of a court system that, for the first and only time in Russian history, separated the judicial from executive branches and provided an unprecedented degree of political freedom for political opponents of the system.

Flaws there were, and some backsliding took place in the next half-century. But, if we keep in mind that it took the United States a bloody civil war to free only 10 percent of its population, and then without fully erasing the legacy of slavery, we must admit that Alexander II accomplished a remarkable feat in liberating, against the will of the vast majority of the noble serf-owners, 80 percent of his subjects from what was in all but name slavery, and providing them with land (admittedly at a steep cost).

How did he accomplish this? First, he had the support of a segment of the bureaucracy deeply imbued with a reformist ethos and convinced that change had to come through the autocratic system, in a *Rechstaadt* tradition, rather than by democratic processes, which these reformers believed catered only to narrow, privileged interests. He encountered a ruling elite (the nobility) with no means of organized opposition to the tsar and with no moral or economic alternative to the path he selected—a ruling elite deeply divided in its interests and objectives. He mobilized the educated public by establishing institutions that allowed them to participate, within channels, in the implementation of goals set by the center. He never had in mind the creation of a parliamentary type of democracy or a genuinely representative government.

Thus, a lively tradition of reform, adjustment, and melioration[42] has been obscured, partly by reading history backwards (if the autocracy collapsed in revolution in 1917, how can the Great Reforms be labeled a success?) as well as by the lack of a comparative perspective. Such a perspective makes the historian more appreciative even of modest reform and aware of the nearly universal tendency for grand design to be reduced, in the end, to ramshackle compromise and a tepid rate of change. Considering the reform tradition within the Russian historical context allows us, too, to understand under what conditions reforms take place, what shape they may take, and how they are likely to be pursued. It allows us, most of all, to escape the deep-rooted prejudice that to be successful, reforms must take on a Western (and notably a parliamentary) form.

Dress a Monkey in Silk . . . ?

What, then, are the prospects for reform? This book has emphasized the boldness of initiatives taken since the April 1985 plenum, as well as the evolutionary changes preceding Gorbachev that prepared the ground for such initiatives. We have considered the resistance to perestroika and glasnost among the leadership and in the provinces and the ambiguities of the popular mood. I have expressed agreement with the argument that the biggest obstacles to radical reform are not in bureaucratic or political opposition, but "in the immense inherent difficulties of achieving the goals of the reform itself."[43] Among these obstacles are the difficulties of integrating short-term needs and long-term goals, balancing graduated reform with sufficiently large-scale changes, finding the proper combination of planning and market forces, devising incentives for workers and managers, describing reforms in a way that is ideologically palatable, pushing radical measures from the center without crushing local initiative, and keeping that local initiative from getting out of control, particularly in the border regions. Finally, the leader is confronted with the task of prying open the truth about the past without entirely discrediting the ruling party, without whose support reform would ultimately founder. Paradoxically, glasnost may be vital to perestroika; but it may also be its undoing.

Again, the perspective of the historian seems most appropriate. Abbott Gleason poses the question:

> Can he succeed? Or, it might be better to ask, to what extent can he succeed? Considering how long and hard the struggle has been over issues of authority and autonomy in Russia, how many pyrrhic victories there have been, and how many relapses, it is hard to believe than any kind of final victory can be won. . . . Opponents of reform have always abounded in Russian history. There are always powerful figures who remain committed to secrecy and coercion as the keys to getting things done in Russia. The historian, rooting for Russia, would be satisfied with more modest triumphs: an acceptable framework for the introduction of some market forces into Soviet economic life; a diminution of cultural and political authoritarianism; a less exclusive and narrow sense of "Russianness"; and a more general and public acceptance of the idea that the creation of wealth for oneself and one's own is not the worst thing in the world and that it is better to level up than to level down.[44]

There is a distinct tendency in the West to vacillate between two views. The first is the increasingly implausible view (pushed by many in the emigré community, understandably suspicious of claims of change) that everything Gorbachev has done to this date has been merely "cosmetic" ("dress a monkey in silk and he'll still be a monkey").[45] The second view is expressed by those who voice impatient demands that he change everything overnight.[46] Even those who believe Gorbachev is sincere are confident in the expectation that his great experiment is bound to fail. A variant of this view, "strongly held among . . . emigrés, scholars and news correspondents," is that, even if they desired change, the leaders were a powerless superstructure unable to challenge the bureaucracy, which, in vulgar Marxist terms, representeds the "dominant economic class." Hough argues that this view represents the application, by dissidents and emigrés, of the "Marxism the system had taught them" to their own experience; that is, of a rigid determinism in inverted form. The upshot has been to reinforce the notion of an unchanging political order.[47]

That Gorbachev is a determined reformer is becoming harder and harder to deny. But it is entirely possible that Gorbachev will be removed or kicked upstairs; it is also plausible that a compromise solution will emerge, or that Gorbachev will remain while his program is gutted.

However, we must also acknowledge that Gorbachev may well be a good enough politician to make tactical steps backward, only to advance again when the moment is right. He had to give up Yeltsin, and his programs have come under attack, but we must keep in mind the breathtaking distance that has been covered since March 1985. As Reddaway notes, "We are light years away from the ponderous ideas of Brezhnev and Chernenko." Stephen Cohen argues, "It may be that even if he doesn't succeed in the end, the reforms are going to start a turnabout in that system."[48] And Robert Tucker asserts: "Gradual change with circumscribed goals can be more enduring, and more likely to pave the way for further change in the same direction, than rapid and radical change."

In fact, the turnabout has already begun. The diminution of political and cultural authoritarianism, though not yet irreversible, is far advanced. Something momentous is in the making in the Soviet Union: "Its larger importance is as instruction in how humans are tested, how they survive, and how they may transcend what they have been."[49]

Notes

1. NYT, December 13, 1987: 22.

2. WP, December 2, 1987.

3. Timothy Colton, *The Dilemma of Reform in the Soviet Union* (New York, 1986): 18–19.

4. Dusker Doder, *Shadows and Whispers* (New York: Random House, 1986): 31–37. But see also his reservations on page 37.

5. Colton, *Dilemma of Reform*: 23. Doder also discusses at length the role of Andropov, head of the KGB, in the gains in legality in Soviet life. He concludes that despite the abuse of psychiatry and other, more subtle forms of harassment, Andropov's time (1967–1982) marked a real improvement in the lives of the Soviet people.

6. S. Frederick Starr, *Red and Hot: The Fate of Jazz in the Soviet Union, 1917–1980* (New York, 1983): 318.

7. Katerina Clark, "New Trends in Literature," in *The Soviet Union Today*, ed. by James Cracraft (Chicago, 1983): 261–265. On this, see also Doder, *Shadows and Whispers*: 35–37.

8. *Dilemma of Reform*: 19. Colton, however, does understate the backsliding and regression, particularly in the area of economic reform, that took place in the late Brezhnev period. On this, see Gertrude Schroeder's numerous discussions of the Soviet economy in the past few years; notably in reports submitted to the Joint Economic Committee, arguing that the "reforms" of 1973 and 1979 were backward moves. See also the comments by Anders Aslund in *Nordic Journal of Soviet and East European Studies*, Vol. 4, No. 4 (1987).

9. This is Colton's argument in "Gorbachev and the Politics of System Renewal," paper prepared for the East-West Forum, New York (April 24, 1987): 6.

10. Archie Brown, "Soviet Political Developments and Prospects," *World Policy Journal*, Vol. 4, No. 1 (Winter 1986/1987): 87.

11. Robert Tucker, *Political Culture and Leadership in Soviet Russia* (New York, 1987): 169–170.

12. Colton, *Dilemma of Reform*: 186–187.

13. These are the comments of an unnamed Western diplomat to Paul Quinn-Judge in CSM, March 11, 1987: 7.

14. *Pravda*, July 2, 1987; cited in WP, May 29, 1987.

15. According to a USIA survey in May; cited in NYT, July 26, 1987.

16. BS, November 1, 1987.

17. The Gallup poll was conducted in May 1988 and reported in the CSM, July 27, 1988.

18. NYT, December 6, 1987.

19. NYT, November 1, 1987.

20. "Gorbachev the Bold, " *New York Review of Books*, May 28, 1987: 21.

21. George Kennan, "The Gorbachev Prospect," *New York Review of Books*, January 21, 1988.

22. Archie Brown, in a talk at the Conference on Gorbachev Initiatives, Meridian House, Washington, D.C., November 1, 1987.

23. Philip Taubman, "Gorbachev's Gamble," *New York Times Magazine*, July 19, 1987: 42.

24. "Meeting Report," Kennan Institute for Advanced Russian Studies, April 29, 1987.

25. "The Gorbachev Prospect": 6.

26. On military support for economic reform, see the brief comments in Joint Economic Committee, *Gorbachev's Economic Plans*, Vol. 1: xv.

27. Speech to the Soviet trade union congress, *Pravda*, February 26, 1987; cited in Reddaway, "Gorbachev the Bold": 22.

28. *Pravda*, February 20, 1987; cited in Gustafson and Mann, "Gorbachev's Next Gamble": 3. See also the comments by George Kennan, cited earlier, that the party leadership is now committed extensively in formal documents to perestroika and that even if Gorbachev were to be removed, there could be no retreat from the basic guidelines.

29. "The Gorbachev Prospect": 7.

30. See, for comparisons, Alexander Yanov, *The Russian Challenge* (New York, 1987). Of course parallels can be found between, say, Peter and Gorbachev, but the differences in personality, strategies, conceptions of the world, and most important, surrounding circumstances, are so overwhelming that analogies of this kind are meaningless.

31. Cohen makes this point in *The Nation*, June 13, 1987: 789.

32. "Gorbachev the Bold."

33. "Gorbachev's First Year: Building Power and Authority," *Problems of Communism*, May–June, 1986. See also Jerry Hough, *Opening Up The Soviet Economy*: 27–53.

34. See Brown, "Soviet Political Developments": 65–67, on the fallacies of comparisons with the Khrushchev period: Objective trends are much more unfavorable now; Soviet leaders now perceive these trends as negative and dangerous; and the impetus for reform comes now not from the ministerial network (i.e., Kosygin in the 1960s) but from the general secretary, who possesses greater political resources; the international context differs today.

35. *Shadows and Whispers*: 83–84. See also similar comments, with a slightly different slant, by Dmitri Simes, after returning to the Soviet Union for

the first time in fifteen years (WP, November 21, 1987). Simes sees the emergence of Soviet yuppies who stand to benefit by Soviet reforms and like the notion of inegalitarian distribution of rewards as well as increased travel to the West (but do not support reductions in the power of the party).

36. Reddaway, "Gorbachev the Bold": 23.

37. Colton, "Gorbachev and the Politics of System Renewal": 9.

38. The total number of Soviet citizens with a secondary school degree increased from 31 million in 1965 to 101 million in 1982; in the same period the number with a college degree rose from 6 million to 17 million (Jerry Hough, "Gorbachev Consolidating Power," *Problems of Communism*, Vol. 36, No. 4 [July–August, 1987]: 22).

39. Shmelev, "Novye trevogi," *Novyi mir*, No. 4 (April, 1988): 175.

40. Ibid.: 167.

41. A. J. Rieber, in a now classic article, ("Alexander II: A Revisionist View," *Journal of Modern History*, Vol. 43, No. 1, 1971: 42–58) makes this argument about Alexander II's goals. A key Soviet reform magazine, *Eko*, ran a remarkable piece by Gavril Popov, the Moscow University economist, detailing, in popular fashion, the reform process that underlay the Emancipation, and leaving to the reader the obvious analogies to be drawn ("Fasad i kukhnia 'velikoi reformy'." *Eko*, No. 1, 1987: 144–175). In the West, Vladimir Shlapentokh also drew an explicit comparison between the Gorbachev period and the Great Reforms: "Aleksandr I i Mikhail Gorbachev," *Vremia i my* (No. 97, 1987). Unfortunately, his knowledge of history is weak, and his conclusions and evidence simply wrong.

42. For a forceful statement of the importance of the reformist theme in Russian history, see Marc Raeff, *Understanding Imperial Russia: State and Society In the Old Regime*, trans. by Arthur Goldhammer (New York, 1984).

43. Hough, *Opening Up The Soviet Economy*: 45–46.

44. BS, December 6, 1987 (I have altered the sequence of clauses in the original without, I believe, any change in meaning).

45. Miami Herald editorial, cited by Stephen Cohen, *The Nation*, June 13, 1987: 789.

46. See, for example, the preposterous "Letter of the 10" sent by prominent emigrés to Gorbachev ("Is Glasnost a Game of Mirrors?" NYT, Op. Ed., March 22, 1987), and the excellent response to it by Stephen Shabad (NYT, April 9, 1987): "Mr. Aksyonov and his fellow emigrés may feel understandably bitter about their own experiences with Soviet repression. But bitterness makes it hard to be fair-minded . . . . If the Soviet Union has been 'gravely sick' for 70 years, as the writers contend, one can hardly expect such an enormous country to get well in two or three years [as they demand]. It seems that for some in the West, the Soviet leadership is damned if it doesn't, damned if it does. For years we have rightly criticized its rigid refusal to budge from its authoritarian ways. Now that it has started to change in desirable directions, some are complaining that it is not moving fast enough. Yes, let's call for more change, criticize Moscow when we feel it is still misbehaving and keep a watchful eye on he process of reform. But let's also give praise for what has been done so far and look forward to more improvements in the years to come." Since the letter was printed, several who

signed it have expressed reservations about its content. In particular, Iuri Liubimov, returning to the Soviet Union in 1988, essentially repudiated the argument that nothing has or can change in the USSR under Communist party rule.

47. Hough, "Gorbachev Consolidating Power": 22.

48. WP, December 3, 1987.

49. BS, December 6, 1987: 7K.

Index